Longman Archaeology Series

The social foundations of prehistoric
Britain

Longman Archaeology Series

Advisory editor: Barry Cunliffe

Richard Bradley

The social foundations of prehistoric Britain

themes and variations in the
archaeology of power

LONGMAN
London and New York

Longman Group Limited
Longman House, Burnt Mill, Harlow,
Essex CM20 2JE, England
Associated companies throughout the world

*Published in the United States of America
by Longman Inc., New York*

First published 1984

British Library Cataloguing in Publication Data
Bradley, Richard, *1946 –*
   The social foundations of prehistoric Britain
   1. Man, Prehistoric—Great Britain
   I. Title
   936.1'01   GN805

   ISBN 0-582-49164-9

Library of Congress Cataloging in Publication Data
Bradley, Richard.
   The social foundations of prehistoric Britain.

   (Longman archaeology series)
   Bibliography: p.
   Includes index.
   1. Man, Prehistoric–Great Britain.   2. Social
archaeology–Great Britain.   3. Great Britain–
Antiquities.   I. Title.   II. Series.
GN805.B696   1984   936.1   83-26761

   ISBN 0-582-49164-9

Set in 10/12pt Linotron 202 Bembo
**Printed in Singapore by
Selector Printing Co (Pte) Ltd**

Contents

List of Tables

List of Figures

Preface

When my book *The Prehistoric Settlement of Britain* was published in 1978, one of my colleagues remarked: 'Now that's out of the way, you can write about what really interests you.' At the time I was puzzled by this comment, but in a way it did lead me to consider a change of direction. It was then that the present book was planned. As the text has grown and changed, been rewritten and rewritten again, I have come to look back ruefully on the simple optimism with which I embarked. As I worked, the full complexity of this new subject became painfully obvious. So too did the need for *someone* to trawl these troubled waters. Having completed the manuscript, I can no longer tell the size of my catch.

It is easier to recognise the help of others than it is to assess one's own contribution. Many friends have allowed me to refer to their work in progress, and Bob Chapman, Barry Cunliffe, Mike Fulford, Henry Gent, Ronald Naled, Brendan O'Connor, Nick Thorpe and Sandel van del Leeuw have all commented in detail on sections of the manuscript. I owe a similar debt to my colleagues and students in Reading.

Jo Say and Jeany Poulsen carried out running repairs on the English and Lorraine Mepham twice reduced a dreadful manuscript to order. Katherine allowed me to become increasingly impossible. I hope that the final version is some compensation for their patience. This book is dedicated to my parents, who supported and encouraged my metamorphosis from lawyer to prehistorian fourteen years ago, and to Francis Pryor and Maisie Taylor for being so good at archaeology.

December 1982

Acknowledgement

We are grateful to Martin Secker & Warburg Limited and Harcourt Brace Jovanovich Inc for permission to reproduce the text 'Trading in Cities 4' from *Invisible Cities* by Italo Calvino, 1st Ed. 1974, p. 61.

For my parents
and for Francis and Maisie

'In Ersilia, to establish the relationships that sustain the city's life, the inhabitants stretch strings from the corners of the houses, white or black or grey or black-and-white according to whether they mark a relationship of blood, of trade, authority, agency. When the strings become so numerous that you can no longer pass among them, the inhabitants leave: the houses are dismantled; only the strings and their supports remain.

From a mountainside, camping with their household goods, Ersilia's refugees look at the labyrinth of taut strings and poles that rise in the plain. That is the city of Ersilia still, and they are nothing.

They rebuild Ersilia elsewhere. They weave a similar pattern of strings which they would like to be more complex and at the same time more regular than the other. Then they abandon it and take themselves and their houses still farther away.

Thus, when travelling in the territory of Ersilia, you come upon the ruins of the abandoned cities without the walls which do not last, without the bones of the dead which the wind rolls away: spiderwebs of intricate relationships seeking a form.'

Italo Calvino, *Invisible Cities*

1 Oaths of Service
– *The possibility of a social archaeology*

'We are not born for freedom. But determinism is a mistake as well.'

Albert Camus, *Carnets* vol. 2, 72.

'They were offered the choice between becoming kings or the couriers of kings. The way children would, they all wanted to be couriers. Therefore there are only couriers who hurry about the world, shouting to each other – since there are no kings – messages that have become meaningless. They would like to put an end to this miserable life of theirs but they dare not because of their oaths of service.'

Franz Kafka, *Couriers*

In 1954 Christopher Hawkes offered some suggestions on method and theory to an audience in the New World. More recently, we have become accustomed to advice travelling in the opposite direction. Paradoxically, Hawkes's advice has had more influence in British archaeology than it has in America, for it was on this occasion that he put forward his famous 'hierarchy of inference'. It is worth quoting from his original account (1954: 161–2):

To infer from the archaeological phenomena to the *techniques* producing them I take to be relatively easy . . . To infer to the *subsistence-economics* of the human groups concerned is fairly easy. Operationally, of course, it is laborious . . . But its logic is simple and need never be anything but straightforward . . . To infer to the *social/political institutions* of the groups, however, is considerably harder . . . To infer to the *religious institutions and spiritual life* may seem superficially, perhaps, to be easier . . . (But) in general, I believe, unaided inference from material remains to spiritual life is the hardest inference of all.

A year later, M. A. Smith was still more pessimistic. In a paper entitled 'The limits of inference in archaeology', she wrote the following (1955: 7):

. . . Since historical events and the essential social divisions of prehistoric people didn't find an adequate expression in material remains, it cannot be right to try to arrive at a knowledge of them in archaeological interpretation. A recognition that archaeological evidence, when it is confined to material remains, demonstrably supports only a limited range of conclusions about human activity is incompatible with too ambitious a programme for archaeology. It is incompatible . . . with a claim to recognise prehistoric societies from their surviving relics, so that the subject could be compared either to history or to social anthropology.

Until recently, this view of archaeology has inhibited the study of prehistoric society. If such arguments were more convincing, this book would not have been written.

Such pessimism characterised British archaeology between the death of Gordon Childe in 1956 and the reassessment of our prehistory which began in the 1970's. One effect of such comments was to emphasise the importance of economic archaeology, which had already received a stimulus from the publication of Grahame Clark's classic work in 1952. Throughout the 1960s, greater attention was paid to prehistoric subsistence economies. Unfortunately, too many archaeologists now treated Hawkes's hierarchy of inference as an explanatory model in itself; because subsistence was relatively accessible to study, it must also be the prime mover. This was a tendency that Hawkes (1954: 162–3) himself had been concerned to avoid:

. . . The critical factor, standing between fair intelligibility and stark unintelligibility is surely ecology, the study of the physical environment. So long as you can depend on that, . . . your exercise of this sort of archaeology is rewarding . . . But now transcend that, and your returns diminish sharply. There is nothing in North American ecology, by itself, to compel either Iroquois institutions . . . or the Constitution of the United States.

Economic patterns were amenable to archaeological analysis, and in time they came to dominate the research of a whole generation, but the fact that this evidence seemed increasingly easy to analyse did not mean that it was sufficient to *explain* the character of the prehistoric sequence. The emphasis on 'man-land relations' reveals a basic environmental determinism. Sometimes this was made explicit, but more often ecological explanations were employed as a last resort because the field of study had been too restricted from the outset.

It is precisely at the level of *explanation* that Smith's criticisms are weak. This can be seen from her comparison between archaeology and social anthropology. She equates anthropology with ethnography, which is like defining archaeology as excavation. She argues that an archaeologist would be unable to create as full a picture of the Trobriand islanders as Malinowski achieved through ethnographic fieldwork. Indeed, the archaeologist would probably misinterpret certain aspects of Malinowski's evidence. Interestingly, these 'misinterpretations' would result from an undue emphasis on human ecology, supposedly the easier level of archaeological inference. Smith does not appreciate the different objectives of the subjects which she compares. Archaeology is concerned with the study of the *past*, and with changes in human societies *through time*. This is the *historical* approach that Malinowski rejected. Even if archaeologists were able to duplicate his ethnography, they would contribute little to their broader objectives. In any case, Smith treats Malinowski's interpretations as self-evident, and uses them to belabour the archaeologist. The fact that functionalist anthropology is so unfashionable suggests that this is not the case. The ethnographic record does not explain itself.

Such comments also encouraged the idea that ethnography set a standard against which archaeological interpretation was to be measured. In fact, it is doubtful whether it is as useful as some writers have thought, since the impact of colonial societies has been so powerful that these sources betray the effects of acculturation (cf Trigger 1981). For this reason some anthropologists are taking more interest in history. On both sides of the Atlantic there is increasing emphasis on the problems of social change. This can be seen from the titles of two of the most influential publications: in America, *The Evolution of Political Society* (Fried 1967) and, in Britain, *The Evolution of Social Systems* (Friedman and Rowlands 1977).

The contrast drawn by Smith works the other way. Anthropologists do not possess a long time scale and are unlikely to acquire one now that the isolation of traditional societies is breaking down. They may propose sophisticated theories of social change, but they cannot test them in the field. This can be achieved only by historical methods, and since so few societies have written documents, this places a greater emphasis on the techniques of archaeology. Social anthropologists have already published excellent studies which use archaeological data (e.g. Ingold 1980). If prehistorians are afraid of the limits of inference, their colleagues may be more enterprising.

In any case the anthropological literature should have shown that the steps of Hawkes's hierarchy of inference are a product of our own division of experience, and need not apply to other societies, in which it may be impossible to separate food production or technology from the field of social relations. Even religion, the most elusive of Hawkes's four categories, can structure 'economic' production (Godelier 1977). These distinctions are unhelpful because they lead archaeologists to conduct their work in terms of quite arbitrary classes of information. 'Theory cannot be built successfully by reifying categories of archaeological data' (Gledhill and Rowlands 1982: 148). As they point out (*ibid.*: 145)

economic and socio-political conditions cannot . . . be separated . . .: we cannot understand economic processes in the narrowest sense in isolation, but neither can we argue that real development(s) . . . are determined by purely 'cultural' or

'political' processes . . . Theorising about long-term socio-economic change
in prehistory involves us in the construction of models of total social systems
in which ideological, political and economic processes are linked to one another
in a dialectical interplay.

The hierarchy of inference can be replaced by a more integrated approach.

At last the situation is changing; a number of studies (such as Burnham
and Johnson (eds) 1979; Barrett and Bradley (eds) 1980; and Renfrew and
Shennan (eds) 1982) have covered fresh ground during the last decade.
These more ambitious studies have tended to concentrate on limited
periods or regions. The aim of this book is to provide a still broader view
of prehistoric Britain. It tries to answer the complaint that 'by avoiding
the social meaning of their material, archaeologists are choosing a rather
narrow personal mythology' (Bradley 1978a: 3). Indeed, the particular
emphasis on the relationship between society and the subsistence economy
forms a bridge with earlier work.

Having set out the objectives of this book, let us consider its organisation. This is a work of interpretation, not of pure theory. For this reason,
there is no attempt to present an entirely uniform account of the prehistoric
sequence. Rather, the organisation of the chapters has been influenced by
the quality and accessibility of empirical data in each period, and each
chapter is a detailed analysis of one important aspect of social change. For
the most part these models are taken from the current literature. The most
prominent patterns in the existing data may well prove to be the most
relevant ones, but this remains to be considered in the light of future fieldwork. In the same way, the geographical areas considered in this book are
determined almost entirely by the availability of adequate information.
Although this does entail an emphasis on southern England, where there
is a particularly long history of fieldwork, it does not mean that the latter
area was more important than any other. These different studies are
designed to have a cumulative effect, and models introduced in the earlier
parts of this account may apply equally strongly to later periods of
prehistory. This point will be developed in the final chapter, which will
attempt to draw these different themes together and to suggest some of
the long-term patterns which are shared between the separate studies.

This book is about power and its expression, and these provide a
common theme running through the separate chapters. Five main subjects
are considered. These case studies are presented in chronological order,
with a chapter for each of the major periods in British prehistory. One
model is considered in each section (see Table 1.1). Thus Chapter 2 is concerned with the exploitation of ancestry and is a study of Earlier Neolithic
society between 3500 and 2500 bc. The following chapter lays more emphasis on the production and exchange of prestige objects and is concerned
with the Later Neolithic period, between about 2700 and 2000 bc. In Chapter 4 we consider the roles played by large monuments and by burial rites.
This study overlaps part of the period treated in Chapter 3, but also consid-

Table 1.1 Terminology and chronology in relation to the chapter divisions in the text. Calibration of radiocarbon dates after Clark (1975)

	Earlier Neolithic	Later Neolithic	Final Neolithic & Earlier Bronze Age	Later Bronze Age	Iron Age
	3500	2500	2000	1300	600 bc	43 AD
Chapter 2	————				
Chapter 3		————			
Chapter 4			————		
Chapter 5				————	
Chapter 6					————
Chapter 7	————————————————————————————
	4375	3245	2520	1595	800 BC

ers the Earlier Bronze Age. The division with the next chapter comes at about 1300 bc, although again there is a small area of overlap. Chapter 5 continues the discussion of prestige objects begun in Chapter 3, but this time the emphasis falls on the problems of their deposition, rather than those of production and circulation. Chapter 6 considers the Iron Age from yet another perspective, analysing the distinctive changes which took place during this period in terms of Britain's changing position within a larger regional system. This account begins at about 800 bc and runs through to the Roman Conquest. Unlike the other sections, Chapter 6 employs calendar dates rather than a radiocarbon chronology. Lastly, Chapter 7 draws out some of the long-term tendencies observed in these separate accounts, and sketches the relevance of these patterns to British prehistory as a whole.

Archaeologists are divided between optimists and pessimists. This chapter began with the pessimists, but what follows is an optimistic approach. We must not delude ourselves that many of the problems have been solved. If that were true, this book would have been written more easily, and probably by someone else. 'Social Archaeology' is not a single school of thought. A recent collection of essays with this title needed six separate editors, and covered virtually everything from symbolism to the role of National Parks (Redman *et al.* (eds) 1978). My title is equally general, but my approach is less ambitious and probably less dogmatic. It would be wrong to substitute a rigid 'social determinism' for the other brands on the market. There must always be room for intuition and imagination. So long as these remain, we can cope with a few wrong answers. Too many archeologists have lost their confidence, and they must win it back. This may be too much to ask, but it is why the book was written.

2 Constructions of the dead
– The ancestors and their descendants
(3500–2500 bc)

'. . . Who
Is not perpetually afraid
That he's unworthy of his trade
As round his tiny homestead spread
The grand constructions of the dead?'

W. H. Auden, *New Year Letter*

'Small talk comes from small bones'.

Ezra Pound, *Homage to Sextus Propertius*

INTRODUCTION

The previous chapter considered some of the limitations of the prevailing approach to prehistory and the potential of a more broadly based 'social' archaeology. The contrasts between the two now form the main theme of this chapter. The Earlier Neolithic period, which runs from about 3500 to 2500 bc provides an opportunity to compare the two approaches, and highlights some of the major difficulties of the traditional method. The whole scope of this debate is summed up by the paradox that in a period which is defined by its subsistence economy, the most common field monuments should refer to the dead rather than the living. Too many discussions of Neolithic society are forced to run backwards through time, starting with these great corporate monuments and looking for their origins where the trail of evidence runs out. This chapter suggests that our observations can be explained more naturally if the role of the dead is allowed to retain its central position. For this reason my title carries a double meaning. At an empirical level it refers to the various mounds and cairns which commemorate the dead, and on the theoretical plane it refers to the importance of ancestry.

Before this discussion can begin, we must summarise the data which have allowed such different reconstructions. The term 'Neolithic' refers to both an immigrant population and to its agricultural economy. Similarly, 'Mesolithic' describes a type of economy – hunting, gathering and fishing – and also the native people who practised it. The main reason for making this division is that the wild ancestors of the domestic crops and animals of Neolithic Britain were not native to the country (Whittle 1977: 14–29). The strongest argument for colonisation from overseas is the development of a material culture of European inspiration, combined with a range of elaborate monuments whose prototypes are found on the Continent (*ibid.*). There seems no reason to dispute this conclusion, and it is the basic premise of the following argument.

The precise chronology of settlement is as controversial as the processes by which it took place. These problems may be no nearer to resolution. There seems to be some agreement that the main source was in the Rhineland, where clearance of the loess soils was reaching its limits (Whittle 1977: 242–4). The earliest indications of farming in Britain probably appear in the first half of the fourth millenium bc, although much of this evidence comes from pollen analysis rather than artefacts or monuments (Bradley 1978a: 6–10). The first monuments belong to a later phase and, generally speaking, different types appear in sequence (Table 2.1). Mounds of cairns associated with the dead are found from about 3300 bc, and these are joined by large earthwork enclosures, mainly between 3000 and 2500 bc. By the latter date, settlement covered most regions of Britain and Ireland, extending well beyond the more fertile lowlands into the Northern and Western Isles (Fig. 2.1).

The meagre economic evidence suggests a regime of cereal and livestock farming, which accompanied the increasingly centralised production of

Table 2.1 Terminology and chronology used in Chapter 2 in relation to major types of monument. Calibration of radiocarbon dates after Clark (1975)

	3500	3250	3000	2750	2500 bc
Terminology		*Early Neolithic*		*Middle Neolithic*	
Plain ware	——————————				
Decorated ware		– – – – —————————			
Long barrows/cairns		—————————————			
Enclosures		– – – – – ———————			
Regeneration phase?				————————	
Expanded axe 'trade'?				– – —————	
Cursus monuments and bank barrows?				————————	
Oval barrows				————————	
	4375	*4040*	*3785*	*3530*	*3245* BC

1. Tulloch of Assery
2. Tulach an T–Sionach
3. Camster
4. Dalladies
5. Mid Gleniron
6. Hastings Hill
7. Hanging Grimston
8. Dyffryn Ardudwy
9. Skendleby
10. Maxey
11. Roughton
12. Aldwincle
13. Hurst Fen
14. Fornham All Saints
15. Broome Heath
16. Swale's Tumulus
17. Pen Yr Wirlod
18. Crickley Hill
19. Lanhill
20. Abingdon
21. North Stoke
22. Whiteleaf
23. Windmill Hill
24. Avebury
25. West Kennett
26. Knap Hill
27. Wayland's Smithy
28. Staines
29. Orsett
30. Robin Hood's Ball
31. Stonehenge Cursus
32. Woodford
33. Fussell's Lodge
34. Nutbane
35. Barton Stacey
36. Hambledon Hill
37. Wor Barrow
38. Dorset Cursus
39. Thickthorn Down
40. Hembury
41. High Peak
42. Maiden Castle
43. Portland
44. Trundle
45. Bury Hill
46. Offham
47. Alfriston
48. Carn Brea

1000 ft.

Fig. 2.1   The main sites and regions considered in Chapter 2.

various artefact types, notably axes and fine pottery. The settlement pattern consisted of dispersed farmsteads, with only limited evidence of larger groupings, apart from the enclosures.

The end of the Mesolithic period gives rise to more difficulties. The radiocarbon dates do not form a clear-cut pattern, although in many areas they go no later than 3500 bc (Switsur and Jacobi 1979). Such dates are fairly few in number and come mainly from two types of environment: isolated areas of marginal ground, for example the Yorkshire Pennines, and also parts of the coastline. There is some reason to suppose that coastal resources were becoming more important as the environment changed during the later Mesolithic (Jacobi 1973). At the same time, many of the latest dates from the shoreline come from areas of Highland Britain in which the land level has risen since the Neolithic, whereas most of the contemporary seacoast in the lowlands has now been lost (Fig. 2.2).

Only where a complete pattern survives this process can we speculate on relations between the native and immigrant peoples. The best evidence comes from Ulster, where it seems that early farmers avoided the regions with a stable Mesolithic economy, and that the native population assimilated agricultural practices only gradually (Woodman 1976). The Mesolithic subsistence economy may have been unusually productive, and change could have taken place much more rapidly in other parts of Britain. It seems likely that the speed with which farming was taken up depended largely on the circumstances of the native population. In some areas they may have practised land clearance on their own account, but the full extent of this activity is unknown (Mellars 1976). Otherwise it appears that the introduction of agriculture may have meant a dramatic change. There is little evidence of a 'stable frontier' between the two communities. With this outline in mind, we can proceed to compare the different explanations of how these processes worked.

THE TRADITIONAL MODEL

The traditional model places an absolute primacy on agriculture, and so it combines the two meanings of the term 'Neolithic'. It also depends on a series of assumptions concerning the process of colonisation and supposes that social relations were entirely subsidiary to the problems of food production. This reconstruction is based on a mixture of ethnographic analogy and empirical data from Neolithic research on both sides of the English Channel. Perhaps its most compelling expression was published by Case in 1969, and it is this approach which will be considered here.

His main intention was to shift the emphasis in Neolithic studies away from undisciplined comparisons with the Continental sequence and towards a closer study of the actual process of settlement. This entailed a detailed discussion of marine technology and pioneer farming, but these

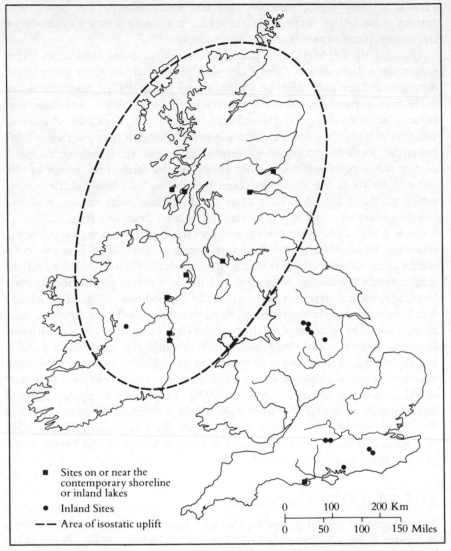

Fig. 2.2 Mesolithic sites with radiocarbon dates partly or wholly in the fourth millenium bc, plotted in relation to the area of isostatic uplift (area of uplift after Morrison 1980).

are not the immediate subject of this review. Rather, the broader assumptions of his study need to be reconsidered.

The argument appears to assume that Britain was colonised over a relatively limited period early in the fourth millenium bc, and that such settlement would probably have been undertaken along the shorter sea routes. Case suggests that the crossing would have been hazardous and, quite possibly, permanent. On arrival, the settlement of an unfamiliar area would have involved the large-scale destruction of woodland and could have been so demanding that the development of stable agriculture was extremely slow. As a result of the practical difficulties of settlement, extensive social networks could have lapsed, leaving a series of small isolated communities.

Their isolation would be reflected in two ways. There would be the gradual extinction of direct contacts with the homeland and a similar breakdown of existing relations among the immigrant groups. Little time could be spared for the maintenance of a traditional culture, with the result that there may be little archaeological material in Britain which can be compared directly with that in the homeland, and possibly a restricted range of artefacts of any kind. The same might apply if the number of immigrants had been very small. Case believes that the development of monuments which require a significant investment of labour could only have taken place when a mature farming system had evolved. They would act as a visible index of the ability to master the local environment, and because of the effort needed in order to create them would appear only when more complex social relations had been resumed.

The disruption of social contacts would also mean that the building of similar sites in different areas came about as a result of a rather uniform process of growth. For Case, the colonisation of Britain may have taken place at an earlier date than was once supposed. It involved so many practical problems that it resulted in a period in which communities were isolated from one another. The resemblances between later monuments in Britain and Europe must be explained as the result of *parallel developments* in both of these areas. Whittle, for example, sees both the British Neolithic and its European counterparts as alternative developments from an ancestral tradition in the Linear Pottery Culture (Whittle 1977: 238–44). Much the same sequence of monuments can be detected through north Germany, the eastern Netherlands and Denmark, but direct contacts between these regions and Britain are no longer discussed. A curious feature of Whittle's biological analogy is that these different lines seem to *converge* with time.

COMMENTARY

Little has been said of the contribution of the native community. This is because the Mesolithic is treated only as an economic phenomenon. Case and Whittle avoid taking this position, but in the literature as a whole, successful farmers have social relations with one another, while hunter–gatherers have ecological relations with hazelnuts. The Mesolithic population loses its only role when its subsistence pattern is changed, and thereafter it exists only as an 'influence' on Neolithic technology.

This approach is no longer acceptable. In the first place, the character of the native population has been underestimated, perhaps because burials and monuments are so often treated as the only measures of social complexity. There is evidence for the development of regional artefact styles during the Late Mesolithic period which have been interpreted as marking 'social territories' (Jacobi 1979: 63–8). This is a difficult point to test, but it has been claimed that such distinctive artefact styles will be more likely to symbolise group identity in periods of economic strain (Hodder 1979a). Considering all the problems mentioned earlier, this would be just the time when the native communities could have emphasised their social bonds. There is also evidence of long distance exchange among the native communities, although it is not clear whether this increased at the same time. Worked and unworked pebbles were being transported over considerable distances, and sometimes raw materials for implements were also moved. The Isle of Portland, for example, seems to have been a major quarry site, and certain areas of clay-with-flints in southern England may have been producing axes for wider distribution (Care 1979). Similarly, ground stone axes were being made and distributed in Ireland, an important point in view of the time and effort involved in their production (Woodman 1978: 108–14).

Both of these patterns continue into the Neolithic period and suggest that far from entering a featureless social landscape, the early farmers may have formed alliances along already existing lines. The major styles of Neolithic pottery in southern England are distributed over rather the same areas as the artefacts which define several of the 'social territories' of the Late Mesolithic (Whittle 1977; Fig. 1.1). It is quite possible that the avenues by which these styles were transmitted already existed by the beginning of the fourth millenium. The same point may be made by considering the basic patterns of lithic exchange. In southern England many of the same stone sources were employed in both periods and even the location of some of the larger monuments may have been influenced by this pattern (Care 1982). For example, the enclosure at Maiden Castle occupied an important flint source and was well placed to control the continued distribution of Portland chert. Similarly, one of the stone sources employed in the making of ground stone axes during the Neolithic period was already providing objects for exchange in the Late Mesolithic (Care 1979; 1982). In short, the isolation of the first farmers may have been exaggerated.

This point can also be made by retracing the stages of Case's argument. It seems likely that he has overemphasised the limitations of contemporary navigation and thus the difficulty of settling new areas and maintaining long distance contacts after doing so. Although he considers that Neolithic settlers would have been obliged to use the shortest sea routes, the earliest evidence for their arrival comes from the north and west of Ireland, and not from southern England as his argument implies (A. G. Smith 1975; Lynch 1981: 117–21). A more generous estimate of their abilities would allow us to accept at least some of the comparisons which have been made between elements of Neolithic culture in different parts of Britain and of Europe. These include the long barrows of Denmark, the pottery of the southern Netherlands, the flint mines of Belgium and the monumental tombs of Atlantic France. Instead of emphasising the isolation of Britain, we should consider whether its location might allow contacts with a range of mainland communities which were quite widely separated from one another. A recent study by Cherry (1981) suggests that larger islands may be settled more rapidly than others. The peculiar character of the British Neolithic could result from an eclectic mixture of outside contacts, rather than the traumatic effects of pioneer settlement. Unlike the River Lethe, the English Channel does not cause amnesia.

If the problems of marine contacts have been exaggerated, there no longer seems much reason to insist upon a period of isolation after the first settlement. Not only are there an appreciable number of continental arte-facts in Britain – jadeite and dolerite axes, and flint axes of Scandinavian type (Pitts 1980: Fig. 25) – but it is simpler to see the development of tombs and enclosures in different areas of northern Europe as a broadly homogeneous process, rather than an example of parallel development. This would account for the links in the *late* fourth millenium observed by Stuart Piggott (1954), while accepting the reality of some Neolithic settle-ment in Britain before that date. Indeed, this fairly close relationship could have continued until the mid-third millenium when apparently it *was* severed. Taking this perspective, it is logical to view the settlement of Britain by sea as the *extension* of a continental social and economic system, rather than its *fragmentation*. There seems to be no need to treat this process as being different from the spread of Neolithic culture between north Germany and Denmark, and no justification for suggesting a dramatic break at this stage in the sequence (cf. S. Piggott 1979: 13–15). The British evidence needs explaining in terms of general theory rather than special circumstances.

Lastly, ethnographic analogy can itself be a two-edged weapon, and it is just as easy to argue for the maintenance of social links among early colonists as it is to suggest their isolation. The settlement of Canada has often been quoted in discussion of pioneer agriculture (e.g. J. Coles 1976), and it is particularly interesting that so much should be known about the changes in material culture which took place at this time. Mannion, who has studied a series of Irish settlements in East Canada concludes that any changes (1974: 173–4; *my emphasis*)

'are explained not by *the social and economic conditions of the migration* . . . but by contrasting conditions in the New World. Among these conditions the pattern of group settlement was more important than the physical environment, but the differences in the rural economy were supreme in determining differences in the transfer and survival of homeland traits.'

The subsistence economy of Neolithic Britain is little understood, but again one is reminded of Ian Hodder's idea that communities are more likely to symbolise their distinctive identity during periods of economic stress (1979a). This is a very different view from that of Case, who considers that traditional material culture might have been relinquished because of the demands made by agricultural colonisation. Moreover, without the co-operation of other groups, very small areas of Britain could ever have been cleared, and the immigrant strain in the population would have died out fairly rapidly.

At this point it may appear that the traditional approach is poorly equipped to explain the characteristics of the British Neolithic, but despite its debatable premise, this model has one more element, for the burial monuments themselves have been related directly to subsistence. Some of the impressive tombs have been identified as shrines, into which a variety of settlement refuse was introduced (Case 1973). This 'symbolic manure' supposedly possessed magical properties, and its presence on these special sites has been interpreted as evidence of a concern with agricultural fertility. Similar deposits in the ditches of Neolithic enclosures might also possess a special character, although the original sources of such settlement debris have never been found (I. F. Smith 1971: 111). It seems ironic that in a period in which domestic sites are relatively rare, the discovery of what seems to be settlement refuse should be explained in such an unusual way. Ashbee, for instance, refers to these sites as 'soil fertility shrines' (1978: 77–80). A less extreme position is to rationalise the building of chambered cairns as a side effect of land clearance (Atkinson 1965: 127).

According to the traditional model, the building of burial monuments is linked to the celebration of economic success (Case 1969: 181; *my emphasis*):

Pottery and long barrows or megalithic tombs form the evidence most often adduced [for Neolithic origins]. But concentrating on household luxuries and large ritual works means disregarding the probably long, hazardous and absorbing struggles needed at first to maintain the farming cycle . . .
Demanding refinements are unlikely to have belonged to the period of early settlement but rather to *stable adjustments of mature and fully extended economies in favourable environments.*

Now consider a very different portrayal of the relationship between subsistence and mortuary rites (Huntingdon & Metcalf 1979: 95):

Funeral rituals are the most important cultural institutions in traditional Malagasy societies. The expenditure of time and resources for death rituals and the maintenance of tombs are considerable, especially in the light of the often meagre economic base. The conspicuous burial of the dead is the central activity in Malagasy systems of religion, economics and social prestige.

This passage is a reminder that our own perception of what was important in society may be extremely distorted, but this description cannot be taken as a ready-made analogy to the Neolithic situation. It is useful only when we know why the dead should assume such prominence.

THE IMPORTANCE OF ANCESTORS

It is widely agreed that ancestry was important for farmers, although authorities can differ in their explanations for this pattern. A particularly influential scheme was suggested by Meillassoux (1972) in a comparison of the social structure of hunter-gatherers and agriculturalists. He argues that the acquisition of food among hunter-gatherers is a relatively simple matter, involving the participation of an informal work group and direct consumption of the resulting provisions. There is no need to store food, and hunter-gatherers can lack the sense of territory found amongst farmers. Because hunter-gatherers carry out a series of relatively 'instantaneous' transactions, it is not necessary to depend on the work of earlier generations.

The position changes with the adoption of agriculture. The time-scale is very different. It is necessary to plan sowing and harvesting; food must be stored and made to last in between the harvests; and sufficient seeds must be retained for future sowing. Farmers make use of specific areas of land, which may have been cleared by their ancestors, and can be tied to a particular area from one generation to another. This means that they will work to a much longer time-scale than hunter-gatherers and may rely on the efforts of past generations for the system to keep going. These differences help to account for the importance of ancestry among agricultural communities. Food production now transcends the generations, and ancestry can be used to validate the use of particular areas of land or other resources.

There are problems with Meillassoux's approach. He contrasts two ideal types, both taken from African ethnography, and in some ways this approach shares the disadvantages of the archaeological scheme which proposes an equally simple equation between subsistence economy and social organisation. It does not account for those hunter-gatherers with more complicated social arrangements, and makes no allowance for the role of food storage and the development of sedentism. Both of these are likely to be found in the Late Mesolithic.

But his paper has raised some interesting questions for prehistorians, even if the argument is too schematic. Why do some communities commemorate the dead in an archaeologically visible manner, and why do others seem to disregard them? There is a growing literature concerned with the emergence of formal burial sites, and already some consensus that these are most likely to emerge in areas and at times when critical but restricted resources are coming under pressure (Chapman 1981). This approach interestingly cross-cuts the ideal types of Meillassoux's paper, since it applies as much to developed hunter-gatherers as it does to farmers. Thus cemeteries may be found among semi-sedentary groups in the Mesolithic of Brittany or of Denmark, but may not occur among shifting agriculturalists. Similarly, they are found among Neolithic farmers only as the land available for grazing and cultivation began to be in short supply. This explanation applies both to flat cemeteries and to monumental tombs. Renfrew has already suggested that megaliths may have acted as territorial markers (1976).

The important issue here is not only that ancestors strengthen the cohesion of the community and its economy; they also establish that community's claim to the resources which they are controlling. For this reason there can be a close geographical relationship between a cemetery and a living area. This pattern is frequently observed in Neolithic Europe, for example in the Rhineland (Milisauskas 1978: Fig. 5.16), and apparently is consistent with the British evidence, where it provides an alternative viewpoint to the model considered earlier. It remains to see how these two approaches apply to the field evidence.

TEST IMPLICATIONS

How far can we make a direct comparison between these two interpretations? Although agricultural land is just one of the resources employed in the second framework, it is the only element which both theories have in common. If the building of funerary monuments can really be treated as an index of economic success, three expectations should be fulfilled. Such burial monuments should be clustered in regions with particularly productive soils, and so they should be found at the heart of the settlement pattern. Where any range of variation is exhibited by the monuments themselves, there ought to be a direct relationship between their elaboration and the quality of the surrounding land. Also, the overall distribution of such sites ought to favour the larger tracts of productive soil, rather than more limited areas with the same characteristics. Conversely, if the second model applied, the burial monuments would not necessarily appear in the regions of primary colonisation and would tend to cluster towards the edges of the settled landscape, where land was in shorter supply. Similarly, where the monuments showed much variety there would be an inverse relationship between the scale on which they were built and the productivity of the soil. This would happen because the most elaborate tombs could have been constructed in regions with more restricted resources. Lastly, such monuments would probably cluster around more isolated areas of good land, rather than those in which expansion was still possible. These predictions are summarised in Table 2.2.

Table 2.2 The location of monumental burials

	Traditional model	*Alternative model*
Location of sites	Central to better soils	Peripheral to better soils
Scale of sites	More elaborate on better soils	Less elaborate on better soils
Density of sites	Greatest in larger areas of good land	Greatest in smaller areas of good land

Although the available evidence is rather limited, there is little support for the assumptions of the traditional model. There is often a time-lag between the beginning of agricultural settlement and the appearance of formal burial areas. Although this could be due to the special character of pioneer settlement in Britain, this pattern is actually found very widely in Neolithic Europe, and it seems likely that British sites were built only after some of the better land had been occupied. There is virtually no sign of elaborate long barrows in the lowlands of southern Britain, although mounds with large quarry ditches would have been recognised from the air if they had been levelled by later ploughing. Rather, they often occur in more peripheral areas of high ground where exactly the same range of artefacts is represented. It appears that the contrast is between areas of primary and secondary settlement, rather than the extremes of any trans-humance cycle (cf. Holgate, 1981). The second question concerns the scale of different monuments. Here there is a clear suggestion of a relationship between the sequence of settlement and the amount of effort invested in building funerary monuments. By about 2700 bc the low–lying areas include a series of mortuary enclosures or simple turf long barrows (Loveday 1980: 86), whilst the sites on the higher ground were built on a more impressive scale. Similarly, there is a direct relationship between the complexity of megalithic monuments on the coastline of west Scotland and their height above sea level (Scott 1969; 1970). These studies claim that settlement in these areas would have begun with the fertile land on the coast and have extended only gradually into the raised ground further inland, but whilst Scott views this relationship as evidence of a typological sequence, his observation also implies that the more elaborate tombs were built in less productive areas.

This introduces the last of our questions. Does the distribution of burial monuments reveal a special emphasis on the *more restricted* areas of produc-tive land, or were the tombs located evenly in all areas of settlement? A recent study of the megalithic tombs of County Leitrim has shown that they tend to cluster on a restricted range of soil types, none of which cover particularly extensive areas (Cooney, 1979). Analysis of the accompanying maps, however, shows certain irregularities in this pattern and it is clear that some of the larger areas of good soil are without tombs, whilst these mounuments can be over-represented where the same soils have a more restricted distribution Figure 2.3 reveals the extent of this divergence. Once again the collective tombs can hardly be a direct expression of economic surplus.

At the same time, it would be wrong to assume that land is the only resource worth considering. A particularly important alternative is provided by sources of high quality flint, and we have seen that on the downland of southern England there may be a relationship between areas with long barrows and causewayed enclosures and deposits of surface flint which had already been exploited in the Mesolithic period. This point will be taken up later, but it may be worth mentioning at this stage that both Thickthorn and Woodford long barrows were built over flint extraction pits (Barrett *et al.* 1981: 212; Ministry of Public Building and Works 1964: 10).

DEVELOPMENTS OF THE MODEL

So far this discussion has concentrated on the relationship between monuments and resources. Under the conditions in which such sites might

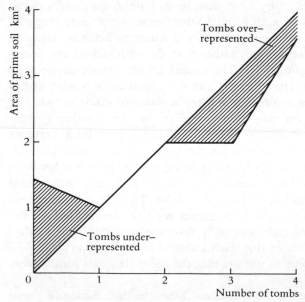

Fig. 2.3 The frequency of monumental tombs in County Leitrim in relation to the extent of areas of favourable soil apparently selected for their construction (data from Cooney 1979). The diagram suggests that whilst regions with one or two megaliths may show a fairly regular relationship between the extent of settled land and the frequency of burial monuments, the latter may be under-represented in the larger areas of favourable soil and over-represented where there was less room for expansion.

have developed, we would expect other changes to occur. Sahlins (1961) has suggested that in areas in which competition for resources is taking place, dispersed communities are likely to stress links with an ancestral lineage which might otherwise be permitted to lapse.

Andrew Fleming (1972: 62) has argued that this process is reflected in the layout of the collective tombs, many of which contain several distinct burial areas under the same mound. 'It is very tempting to speculate that Neolithic societies . . . were segmented in character, and that the form of the tombs (one mound, several compartments) is a fossilised record of the fission and fusion principle on which so many primitive societies are organised.' Communities which had spread across the landscape during the period of settlement might have maintained their links with the ancestral lineage and have symbolised both their incorporation and their independence through the use of separate parts of the same monument.

This idea may well make sense of some of the more puzzling aspects of megalithic tombs. Kinnes (1975) has observed that despite numerous local arrangements of the burial chambers, the number of individuals in these monuments was much the same. This implies that the reason for these differences was not to provide more space for the burials, but to allow a greater range of deposits. This is certainly suggested by the variety of patterns on these sites. In a few cases individual families may have been deposited in one chamber or one monument. This is perhaps shown by the skeletal evidence from Lanhill and Skendleby (Keiller and Piggott 1938: 131–50; Phillips 1935: 90–95), but elsewhere the bones brought to these sites were organised along very different lines. On a few well-preserved sites we find a broad grading by age or sex rather than family groups. For example, at West Kennett long barrow the skulls in the end chamber all came from male skeletons, whilst most of the bones in the south-east chamber belonged to children (S. Piggott 1962: 79). Similarly, two bone groups at Fussell's Lodge long barrow consisted of males and a third was made up entirely of infants (Ashbee 1966: 48–63).

Other sites saw stranger practices, including attempts to reconstitute individual skeletons from the disarticulated bones introduced to the tomb. At Lanhill, for example, the wrong jaw bones had been fitted to the skulls. Where individuals were not grouped in this manner, the bones had been arranged in other ways, for instance the grouping of skulls and long bones found in Severn-Cotswold and Clyde cairns (S. Piggott 1954: 139ff and 165ff). At West Kennett long barrow groups of vertebrae had been piled up together in parts of the north-west chamber, whilst the skulls in another chamber had been placed against its end wall (S. Piggott 1962: 21). Shanks and Tilley (1982) have examined such evidence in detail and suggested that the arrangement of bones shows four major patterns: contrasts between articulated and disarticulated skeletons; others between adult and immature individuals; different treatment of male and female burials and a distinction between the left- and right-hand sides of the body. There may be an analogy between the mixing and rearrangement of different skeletons and the way in which the dead of different communities may have been deposited on the same site. At one level the subdivision of the burial area could express the complexity of the social landscape, whilst the way in which different bodies were distributed amongst the chambers suggests that different classifications might have applied to the dead. Shanks and Tilley (*ibid*: 150) conclude that the arrangement of the burials constitutes 'an assertion of the collective, a denial of the individual and of differences between individuals'. It is also 'an expression of . . . the exclusiveness and solidarity of the local social group using the tomb'. The emphasis on the unity of the group could have meant that individuals living in a dispersed pattern of settlement were integrated into one community at their death:

World of the living:	*World of the dead:*
Dispersal of settlement; segmentary social structure	Common burial area; ideology of unity

Although Sahlins saw the development of this characteristic structure in terms of conflict between two populations, this scheme might be applied to groups undergoing *internal* competition. This would certainly be consistent with two observations made earlier in this chapter; that formal burial monuments seem to have been most common in areas of secondary settlement, and that those tombs located in more marginal areas could also have been the most elaborate. Just as we can show that the more complex tombs in western Scotland were located on the higher ground, we can also detect a relationship between the number of separate chambers on these sites and their distance from the best land on the coast (cf. Bradley 1978a: Table 11, p. 103).

COMPETITION AND RANKING

There is little point in suggesting competition, unless there is some evidence of change, and here we are faced by the very different problems of recognising ranking. On the theoretical plane there is good reason why the dead should form a medium for competition among the living, but only a few elements of the anthropological scheme have clear counterparts in the archaeological record. Friedman (1979) has argued that in some communities the ancestors will occupy a liminal position in relation to both the living and the dead. Due to their involvement in the supernatural, they are able to influence the success of food production. For this reason, agricultural surplus is regarded as the work of the gods and is attributed directly to the influence of the ancestors in the spirit world. Naturally, this provides a reason for treating the ancestors with respect, but at the same time any differences in economic fortune amongst living groups are represented as the result of influence achieved by their ancestors. This provides a means of ranking those ancestors in relation to one another, for the most influential ancestors must belong to the senior lineage. Similarly, the relative positions of the other ancestors will determine the status of their descendants. Those descendants are also able to convert economic success into prestige by the giving of feasts. Since the living owe their prestige not to their own efforts but to their ancestors, this will also demonstrate their special position in the community. They possess greater influence with the supernatural and that is why they can convert purely economic fortune into social rank. They are able to form alliances which give these differences of wealth and prestige an institutional form. These also allow them to increase their work force and to consolidate their earlier success. The sources of that success are concealed by a fictitious genealogy; the ancestors control the fortunes of the living and are their most important resource.

As archaeologists, we can make contact with two elements of this scheme, but can hardly test it in its entirety. At best we can show that Neolithic society was less egalitarian than is often supposed, and that the construction of ancestral tombs may have provided scope for competition. Until about 3000 bc here is little evidence for the large scale consumption of food or energy on any other type of site, but when this pattern changed, the importance of tombs declined. The question of ranking has not been treated systematically, because it is assumed this can be detected only from grave goods. Neolithic collective burials raise two difficulties for this approach: the rarity of many distinctive artefacts deposited directly with the dead, and the fact that such burials only occasionally isolate one body from the rest. It seems as if individual identities were deliberately merged. This is particularly striking since other Neolithic assemblages do show quite distinctive patterning. In any case analysis of grave goods is only one way of looking for ranking, and gives poor results on ethnographic material (Tainter 1978: 121). Two alternatives are to consider the complexity of different mortuary rites or to investigate the amount of energy expended in building the tombs.

It is obvious that only part of the Neolithic population received elaborate treatment in death. As in Denmark, the total number of deposits provides absurdly low population figures – so much so that Neolithic communities could hardly have dug their own graves – and in any case women and children are sometimes under-represented (Kinnes 1975). There is the further problem that different funerary monuments may have existed at the same time, but whereas ranked societies may bury different social groups in separate areas (Brown 1981), here several monuments may have been employed at different stages of the rites of passage. The importance of the dead may be reflected by the complexity of their treatment. At first sight the variety of these monuments is bewildering. They include long and round mounds or cairns, each with one or more chambers, individual flat graves, and also exposure areas. There is little evidence of chronology, but it may be possible to locate some of these monuments at different stages of the rites of passage.

This state of affairs is quite common in the ethnographic record, where funeral rites may be spread over several ceremonies, which happen at different times and places (Huntingdon and Metcalf 1979). Some groups distinguish between the passage of the deceased from the living to the dead, and their later transition into the spirit world. Different ceremonies mark different stages, but one basic element in this interpretation is that the dead cannot complete the cycle until the body is unfleshed. This explains the interval between the different rites. The simplest ways of inaugurating the process are the exposure or burial of the corpse. Each stage also rearranges the relationships among the survivors.

It may be possible to follow such a sequence in the archaeological record. It is certainly true that the dead were rarely placed in monumental tombs while there was flesh on the body. They had received preliminary treatment elsewhere, although it is harder to tell which practices were employed. It is known that flat graves did exist in the Earlier Neolithic period and might contain one or more individuals (Kinnes 1979: 126–7). This may have been a widespread practice before selected bodies were removed to other sites. There may also be evidence of exposure. At Hambledon Hill, the interior of a 'causewayed camp' included a number of pits with exotic artefacts and human bones (Mercer 1980: 22–5). The ditch of this enclosure contained a large number of skulls. The excavator has suggested that this area could have been used for exposing the dead and that the items in the pits might represent funeral offerings, which remained in the ground when the bodies were removed or destroyed.

Certain of the bodies were eventually taken to 'burial' monuments, where sometimes they were introduced in succession. If necessary, existing deposits were moved in order to accommodate them. Although the bones could now be arranged among the chambers, others had been lost by this stage. At Fussell's Lodge long barrow, where the burials showed no signs of later disturbance, some bones were under-represented. These included ribs, kneecaps, hands and feet, as well as larger parts like collar bones and shoulder blades (Ashbee 1966: 48–63). This basic pattern can be seen again at Wayland's Smithy, where the excavator suggested that these bones had been removed by predators (Atkinson 1965: 130). It might be worth exploring this question using our knowledge of taphonomy. Shanks and Tilley (1982) have noticed the same pattern but believe that the absence of some smaller bones is the result of intentional selection.

At this stage the individual identities of the dead may have been lost in the community of ancestors, and it is here that the more theoretical literature becomes so valuable. While the monuments could stand for the dead as an undifferentiated group, the bodies themselves were sometimes disturbed. At Dalladies long barrow all but one of the bones were removed (S. Piggott 1972: 43), whilst on other sites only certain parts of the body were taken. As this was such a formal procedure, we should not regard it as tomb-robbing. The ancestors could be celebrated at their tombs, even when their remains had been taken away.

One argument against tomb-robbing comes from the distribution of the 'missing' parts. At West Kennett long barrow, skulls and long bones were under-represented (S. Piggott 1962), whereas these are the commonest bones in the settlement sites of the period (Kinnes 1979: 125). Even when they remained in the tomb, they could be singled out for special treatment (Shanks and Tilley 1982). The fact that these particular bones are discovered might mean that such remains were selected from ossuaries and did not result from burial or exposure at the living site itself. If so, the last stage of the sequence could have been the return of the parts of the body to the settlement. At this stage ancestors were effectively transformed into artefacts.

In other cases a very different pattern is found. The burial chambers were set on fire and the bones within them were cremated. At one level this is a way of destroying the individual identity more completely than by mixing the remains. This practice, which is best represented on the Yorkshire Wolds, permits two quite different interpretations. It is known that only certain of the burial monuments in this area were set on fire, so the contrast between crematoria and other sites may reflect basic differences of status or identity. Manby has suggested that the two groups of monuments have different ceramic associations (1970: 21). Alternatively, the burning of the mortuary structure would have meant that relics could no longer circulate among the living, and to that extent it may imply a smaller concern with ancestry. This is important because the same region also provides the earliest evidence for single burials with grave goods (*ibid.*).

Several elements of these schemes are relevant to the question of ranking, for three significant changes can be seen between the stages of this process. Firstly, the number of individuals being celebrated diminished rapidly. At Hambledon Hill two long barrows are located near to the main enclosure. One mound may have held only one burial (Mercer 1980: 43), whilst the mean number of bodies in such monuments is about six (Kinnes 1975: 25–6). Another 350 people may be represented by skulls in the enclosure ditch (Mercer 1980: 63). There is another difference between the long barrow population and the bodies in this enclosure. Children are poorly represented in monumental tombs, but dominate the skeletal material at Hambledon Hill. They represent about 60 per cent of these deposits. Figures from other enclosures suggest that 40 per cent of the human remains there were of children or adolescents (Kinnes 1979: 122–3).

The third point is more difficult to assess. This is the suggestion that fine artefacts did play a role in certain stages of the funeral rites. The Hambledon excavation suggests that 'grave goods' were provided in an initial stage, but did not accompany the body into the tomb. The closest parallel to these deposits comes from the forecourts of certain mounds, or even from the land surface underneath them. These have been claimed as deposits of 'occupation earth' (Case 1973), but they are quite distinct from normal domestic debris. Whiteleaf long barrow and Swale's Tumulus have a high proportion of decorated pots, and the ratio of vessels to flint implements on these sites is roughly ten times that on excavated settlements (Childe and Smith 1954; Briscoe, 1956). Similarly, the 'settlement refuse' in Irish court cairns includes a high proportion of sherds and finished implements and a very small amount of knapping waste (*pace* Case 1973). The forecourts of some Scottish megaliths also contain decorated pottery, beads and stone axes, but their exact date is often uncertain (Henshall 1972: 100–10). The important point is that these deposits are associated with the dead as a group and not as individuals. Indeed, the only artefacts consistently found in the burials are the fine arrowheads associated with certain males (H.S. Green 1980: vol. 1 84–92).

Similar patterns are represented by the animal bones from these sites. Again, their deposition follows quite formal patterns. Cattle bones are normally found with the burials under earthen long barrows (Ashbee 1970: 158–60), and at Beckhampton Road, Avebury, an ox skull occupied the position normally taken by the burials (Ashbee, Smith and Evans, 1979, 247). The deposits outside these mounds are more explicitly connected with feasting and can contain a high proportion of pig bones. Pig is pre-eminently a meat animal, since it can be fattened rapidly and provides no secondary products. Hanging Grimston long barrow contained the remains of twenty of these animals (Mortimer 1905: 102–5).

The funeral rites were not the only opportunity for consumption or display. Surely the monuments themselves acted as *communal* status markers. Some useful ideas have come from Andrew Fleming (1973), who has assessed the likely impact of a number of sites by comparing the extent of the burial chambers with the overall area of the mounds. He points out that as a *circular mound* gets bigger, its visual impact becomes greater, but its effectiveness as a container decreases. The *long mounds* in his analysis divide into two groups. The smaller sites are quite efficient containers, whilst the larger are 'ostentatiously ceremonial in character'. If we consider the long mounds or cairns with several phases of building, it also appears that the ratio of chamber area to tomb area changes and that sites became more obviously monumental in character (Fig. 2.4). This trend is entirely obscured if only one dimension is studied, for example the lengths of the different mounds (Reed 1974; Hodder 1979b: 125, 142). It is also possible

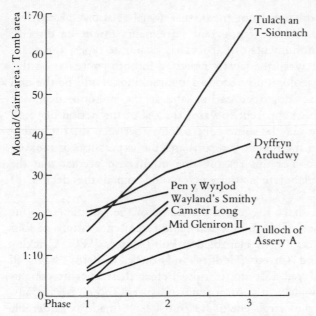

Fig. 2.4 The ratio of burial area to mound area on multi–period mortuary sites (selection of sites after Corcoran 1972, with additions).

that the forecourt became more important on the later sites, and activity clearly continued there after the tomb itself had been closed. Indeed, the northern British sites with elaborate forecourts may also produce the largest number of artefacts.

RANKING AND THE SETTLEMENT RECORD

If these patterns have been identified correctly, some of them should extend into the settlement record. Indeed, the basic model arouses certain expectations concerning the likely character of this evidence. These can be reduced to a few general propositions. The evidence for differentiation among Neolithic burials may mean that contemporary domestic sites will show a comparable variety. In view of the link between control over restricted resources and the exploitation of ancestry, the location of higher status settlements might have been influenced by similar considerations. The second expectation follows from the increasing scale of the monumental tombs. It seems likely that the construction of more elaborate settlements would involve at least as much manpower as the burial sites. Similarly, it is reasonable to suggest an overlap between the distinctive artefacts employed on some of these monuments and the finds from higher order settlements. One would also expect to find traces of lavish consumption, and in particular of feasting.

At the same time, this need not mean that social relations placed less emphasis on the dead. Rather, important settlements might be directly linked with funerary monuments of particularly elaborate types, and there could be an overlap between the rituals practised in both contexts. Lastly, the emergence of archaeologically recognisable ranking should be the end product of the processes described earlier, and so higher status domestic sites should become most apparent towards the *end* of the period of tomb building. Indeed, there may be some contradiction between the ostensibly 'egalitarian' patterns in the funerary record and the expression of ranking in the domestic sphere. For this reason, one might also predict that the emergence of more elaborate settlements would signal the decline of collective tombs.

A number of writers have suggested that some of the Middle Neolithic enclosures may have served these functions, and recent excavations of four sites, Carn Brea (Mercer 1974), Hambledon Hill (Mercer 1980), Crickley Hill (Dixon 1981) and Orsett (Hedges and Buckley 1978), have all suggested that they played a domestic role. Before these specific conclusions are applied too widely, it is important to express some reservations. Although the building of large enclosures must have made considerable demands on manpower, we should not assume that identity of form presupposes identity of function. The segmented ditch, the defining characteristic of the causewayed enclosures, is a constructional device which could be used on monuments of different types (Startin and Bradley 1981). A more detailed analysis is required if the argument is to proceed. If such elaborate enclosures were inhabited, their appearance would certainly suggest that some groups had assumed a prominent place in society, but this need not be true if these sites were used by a dispersed population for other reasons.

Much depends on deciding the character of the material in the enclosure ditches. The role of 'scrapers' is important here, since these are the most widespread artefact of this period. They were rapidly made and were discarded in great numbers. They are found on practically every sort of site, and whatever their precise functions, they can be treated as an index of everyday activities. The proportion of these artefacts on the enclosed sites matches that on open settlements with pits and houses (Holden and Bradley 1975: 101–2). Since internal features are poorly preserved on many enclosures, such comparisons are often the only basis for interpretation, but where less damaged sites have been investigated, houses or other structural features have been found. This applies to the sites at Carn Brea (Mercer 1974), Hembury (Liddell 1935), Crickley Hill (Dixon 1981), Hambledon Hill (Mercer 1980), Staines (Robertson-Mackay 1962) and Orsett (Hedges and Buckley 1978). Although we must be wary of treating all the enclosures as a single class, some of these earthworks contained quite extensive occupation areas and a large number of artefacts. At present, these sites constitute the only satisfactory evidence for nucleated settlement at this date. Enclosures with smaller amounts of associated material may well have played a more specialised role (cf. Drewett 1977: 222–6).

Our first expectation was that higher status settlements, like the first collective tombs, might be in areas with important but restricted resources, control over which may have been one factor in developing social status. This proposal has two aspects which can be examined by archaeological methods. Julie Carr has shown that causewayed enclosures are situated in areas which today include more productive land than the few open settlements for which dating evidence is available (pers. comm.). This certainly suggests that agricultural success may have played the role envisaged in Friedman's model, but this pattern needs further testing since open settlements are so much harder to identify.

There is an equally important relationship between some of the enclosed sites and lithic resources. These would have been of central importance since metal was not in use. The relationship takes two forms: a general coincidence of location between southern English enclosures and areas with accessible raw materials; and evidence that at least some artefacts were being made or finished on these sites. As mentioned earlier, Verna Care (1982) has shown that many of the enclosures in Wessex are close to important sources of surface flint which were probably in use in the Mesolithic and Neolithic periods, but not necessarily continuously. Among the enclosures located near to quarry sites are Maiden Castle, Hambledon Hill and Windmill Hill (*ibid.*). The rather curious enclosures at Bury Hill and Offham in Sussex are actually situated on flint sources, and there is evidence that raw material was being taken from these sites (*ibid.*). Outside Wessex, Carn Brea is located close to one of the main sources of ground stone axes. The second relationship is equally widespread. Axes were made of local flint inside the enclosure at Maiden Castle, whilst at Hembury arrowheads were produced from imported material. Axe roughouts may have been completed at Abingdon and the Trundle, both of which have produced polishing stones, and laurel leaves were made at the enclosures of High Peak and Orsett (*ibid.*).

Such enclosures not only command a number of important resources: they also reveal a substantial investment of manpower. Renfrew (1973) has postulated a tenfold increase in the labour requirements of causewayed enclosures, compared with those of earthen long barrows, but a more recent study by Startin and the writer (1981) has tended to play down these differences. It seems likely that the contrast between the requirements of these two types of monument has been drawn rather too sharply. Although a massive enclosure complex like Hambledon Hill would have made enormous demands (Mercer 1980: 59–60), the needs of smaller sites have more in common with those of elaborate tombs. Such calculations reduce the estimated work-load on the larger sites and in fact emphasise the similarities between different classes of monument.

This is particularly true of the organisation of the work force (Startin and Bradley 1981). The distinctive form of these enclosures probably arises because a group of small teams may have worked together on these sites, whilst maintaining their own identity. The ditches at Hambledon Hill were recut when they were almost obscured. but the existing causeways were carefully respected although it was inconvenient to do so. The excavator has commented that 'these causeways may well have represented gang divisions, and one is brought to wonder whether such divisions (perhaps they were family divisions or clan divisions) were an element of oral tradition' (Mercer 1980: 36). As with the burial monuments, the form of these earthworks may express the segmentary nature of contemporary society. There is evidence that barrows were built in a similar way. The quarry ditches were sometimes broken by causeways, whilst the mounds or cairns were constructed in a series of bays, marked by fences or low walls, which divided the working area into a series of clearly defined units (Startin and Bradley 1981). Again, the task of construction could have been shared between independent groups.

Our third expectation was that higher status settlements, like some of the funerary monuments, should be associated with evidence of feasting, consumption and special types of artefact. Here, much of the evidence from the enclosures is already well known. Indeed, the large amounts of animal bone have underpinned the specifically 'economic' interpretation of these sites. Windmill Hill, for example, included large amounts of meat, apparently consumed on the spot (I.F. Smith 1965: 9). Isobel Smith (1966) has argued that such deposits possessed a special character and had been carefully buried. Despite the evidence for large numbers of dogs on the site at Windmill Hill, the animal bones had not been gnawed (Megaw and Simpson 1979: 84). The Stepleton enclosure at Hambledon may also have seen 'periods of high meat consumption' and Legge (1981: 174, 179) suggests that the animals found there 'represent the surplus available from economies based at [other] Neolithic sites'. Similarly, the cereals at this site may be 'processed' grain introduced from outside (*ibid.*, 174–5). At Windmill Hill, even the pots differ from those on ordinary settlements, with fewer large storage vessels than Broome Heath and more bowls suitable for serving food and drink (Howard 1981: 13–20; Wainwright 1972: 22–46). Exactly the opposite pattern is suggested for sites engaged in redistribution (Toll 1981)

The artefact assemblage from some of the enclosures has characteristics which it shares with a few burial sites. Until radiocarbon dating was applied to the Neolithic, it seemed possible that the ceramic sequence in lowland Britain began with a series of plain wares and that decorated pottery developed much later. This no longer appears to be the case, and certain styles, including Abingdon, Mildenhall and Whitehawk wares, were current as early as most of the 'public' monuments. Plain and decorated wares were used in parallel throughout the late fourth and third millenia. Pottery is not a common find from burial monuments, but it is interesting that there should be some emphasis on decorated vessels at these sites. For example, Fussell's Lodge long barrow yielded an important collection of Mildenhall Ware dated to the late fourth millenium bc (Ashbee 1966: 18–21).

Although there is no firm evidence that the decorated wares were centrally produced, the artefacts on these sites might have possessed a special character and have been selected from among a broader range. The same could apply to the few lithic artefacts in Earlier Neolithic burial sites, which include arrowheads and axes.

Both groups of material can shed some light on the character of the enclosed sites, although there are few published figures available for this purpose. First, it can be shown that the incidence of flint and stone axes on the enclosures is higher than on open settlements of the same period (Bradley 1982a: 31–2). In Fig. 2.5 the number of axes on a series of published sites is compared with figures for scrapers, which are again taken as a virtually ubiquitous index of human activity. Despite the small sample, the resulting pattern recalls the presence of stone axes in megalithic tombs. A further analysis can be made incorporating decorated pottery, axes and arrowheads (*ibid.*, 32–3). Laurel leaves are also included since they are so closely related to arrowheads.

This shows a tendency for the percentage of these items in the lithic industry to vary with the percentage of decorated vessels among the pottery. It is worth highlighting the position of Whiteleaf long barrow, the one group from a burial site for which precise figures are provided. This lies on the same axis as a variety of 'richer' enclosures like Abingdon, Orsett and Windmill Hill. This is also true of an apparently unenclosed site like Hurst Fen. It is clear that this scheme shows continuous variation; it does not divide these assemblages into a series of mutually exclusive groups. This contrasts with the growing separation of different assemblages in the Later Neolithic.

It is not particularly original to recognise elaborate artefacts on some of these enclosures, but they have generally been interpreted in a different way. Instead of regarding such sites as settlements with a specialised assemblage, some writers have seen them as 'central places', supplying a wider hinterland. The most popular analogy has been with a medieval fair (Megaw and Simpson 1979: 84). No-one would deny the existence of contacts between the enclosures and a wider area – the evidence for introduced commodities shows this – but there is no reason to envisage a benevolent relationship. The exotic axes supposedly exchanged *through* such sites were often worked down completely, and other artefacts may

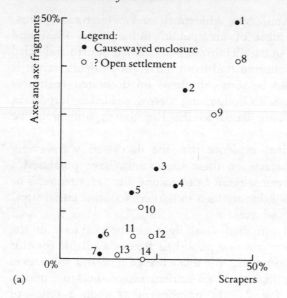

Legend:
● Causewayed enclosure
○ ? Open settlement

Enclosed sites:
1. Hembury
2. Windmill Hill
3. Maiden Castle
4. Abingdon
5. Whitehawk
6. High Peak
7. Orsett

Open sites:
8. Hurst Fen
9. Broome Heath
10. Hazard Hill
11. Putney
12. Bishopstone
13. Windmill Hill
(pre-enclosure deposits)
14. Haldon

(a)

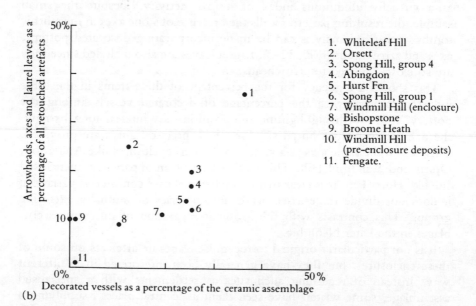

1. Whiteleaf Hill
2. Orsett
3. Spong Hill, group 4
4. Abingdon
5. Hurst Fen
6. Spong Hill, group 1
7. Windmill Hill (enclosure)
8. Bishopstone
9. Broome Heath
10. Windmill Hill
(pre-enclosure deposits)
11. Fengate.

(b)

Fig. 2.5 (a) The ratio of axes and axe fragments to scrapers on excavated Neolithic sites.
(b) The proportion of axes, arrowheads and laurel leaves in selected lithic assemblages in relation to the incidence of decorated pottery on the same sites. (After Bradley, 1982a with minor changes).

have an equally restricted distribution. Foreign items certainly reached the enclosures, but they apparently stayed there. Still less can one show the exchange of livestock through these sites, since the faunal remains belong to animals that had been consumed on the spot. The imported artefacts in Neolithic enclosures appear to have been fully used, and unless settlements in the surrounding area eventually produce similar material, these items are more likely to express the exclusiveness of certain sites.

Our fourth expectation was that important settlements might emphasise the role of the dead. The place of certain enclosure in the rites of passage has already been considered, and it is not necessary to repeat this material here. Suffice it to say that human bones are a common feature of sites with an ostensibly domestic role (Kinnes 1979: 125). Several enclosures also suggest an emphasis on whole cattle skulls which mirrors their representation in long barrows. The animal bones on such sites may show a marked emphasis on cranial fragments, for example the pig bones from Abingdon (L. Cram, pers. comm.).

At a more general level, the geographical relationship between Wessex enclosures and long barrows is sufficiently clear for Renfrew to suggest that each enclosure dominated a specific territory defined by a cluster of burial mounds (1973: 54–8). Other writers have commented on this pattern (e.g. Ashbee 1970: 104–5). Occasionally mounds are situated so near to enclosures that a direct association may have been intended. For example, Adam's Grave is a dominant feature on the skyline from Knap Hill, and a similar barrow is incorporated into the main enclosure at Hambledon Hill (Mercer 1980: 40–44). The distinctive deposits in its ditch match those in the causewayed enclosure. On a less monumental scale, there is a long mortuary enclosure next to the site at Abingdon (St. Joseph 1965), and a similar pairing of monuments at Roughton in Norfolk (Edwards 1978: 93–4, Fig. 47).

There is another, more striking, pattern. Two sites of domestic character are directly linked with funerary monuments of elaborate or aberrant forms. The enclosure at Maiden Castle was actually replaced, not by another settlement, but by an enormous long barrow which slighted the earlier earthworks on the hilltop (Wheeler 1943: 18–24). The enclosure at Crickley Hill contains a similar 'long mound' (Dixon 1981). These mounds are surely an extension of the long barrow tradition, but take the elaboration of such monuments towards its limits. The Maiden Castle bank barrow was associated with deposits which would be in place on a more orthodox funerary site.

A similar development took place with mortuary enclosures, which seem to have developed into cursus monuments. These enormously elongated enclosures are discussed in Chapter 3. Their function and even their dating remain rather enigmatic, but certainly three examples occur in close proximity to causewayed enclosures: those at Fornham All Saints, Hastings Hill and Robin Hood's Ball (Hedges and Buckley 1981). If cursus monuments are related to bank barrows, the link between mortuary rites and elaborate settlements would have operated in two ways. The building of some enclosures could have come about after a prolonged period of competition, expressed through the medium of funerary ritual. At the same time, elaborate settlements were replaced by equally elaborate monuments to the dead.

Lastly, there is the question of chronology. If funerary ritual was one sphere in which social antagonisms were worked out, it must have changed once more complex settlements came into being. Their existence surely means that differences of power and prestige were no longer hidden through the celebration of ancestors. The building of the more impressive enclosures surely marked a drastic change of strategy. If so, one would expect two possible developments to take place. One might see the gradual discontinuance of undifferentiated collective burial and the commemoration of specific individuals. Alternatively, we might find that newer funerary monuments, whilst taking the same outward form as their predecessors, no longer played quite the same role, but acted as a demonstration of an elite's power over human labour.

The chronological evidence agrees with these ideas. In some areas, for instance in Wessex, the burial monuments were first constructed earlier than the earthwork enclosures, and the latter were built towards the end of the main currency of long barrows. By that time the frequency of collective tombs may have been decreasing. Elsewhere, for example in Sussex, the two types of monument may have developed together, but here again the largest number of enclosures was in use in the second quarter of the third millenium bc. Although enclosures were first constructed at different times in different areas, the later phases of most sites coincide with changes in the use of burial monuments.

Apart from the anomalous site of Skendleby 1, whose dating evidence is contradictory (Phillips 1935), nearly all the long barrows thought to have been built after 2750 bc show certain departures from earlier practice. Whilst some of the mounds retain the traditional form, others are somewhat smaller and are oval rather than rectangular. Apart from the site at Alfriston (Drewett 1975), they tend to contain male burials, often only one per site. Examples include the oval barrows at Maxey (F. Pryor, pers. comm.), Barton Stacey (Grimes 1960: 248–9), Hambledon Hill (Mercer 1980: 40–4) and Whiteleaf (Childe and Smith 1954). Where a larger number of burials have been excavated, male skeletons predominate, for example at Wor Barrow (Pitt Rivers 1898: 78–9), Nutbane (Morgan 1959) and Aldwincle (Jackson 1976: 16–30). Usually, these burials retain their articulation and the bones of different individuals have not been mixed. Other oval long barrows contain both articulated and disarticulated skeletons, including Wor Barrow and Wayland's Smithy 1 (Atkinson 1965). In all these cases it seems as if important changes were taking place which to some extent were hidden through the adaptation of traditional forms of monument.

The opposite tendency is shown by the long mounds and cursus monuments, which may have developed during the same period. There is a radiocarbon date of 2722 ± 49 bc for the long mound at North Stoke in the Thames Valley (BM 1405), and the mound overlying the causewayed enclosure at Maiden Castle was associated with the same styles of artefact as the earlier settlement (Wheeler 1943: 144–62). The Dorset Cursus was constructed whilst long barrows were still being used, but most of the mounds closely associated with this monument are oval barrows of the type just considered. At one end of the cursus there is an oval mound without any burials, whilst a mound at its other terminal possesses a curious tail which turns it into a 'bank barrow' (fieldwork by the writer, 1982). Again there is an unusually lengthy barrow aligned on the eastern end of the Stonehenge Cursus. This contained only one possible primary burial (Cunnington 1914: 383–4). In such cases the link between these three types of monument is fairly direct.

CONFLICT AND CHANGE

Although so many of these features anticipate developments in the Later Neolithic, it is clear that a radical break did occur at this stage. Here again a purely ecological model has had a considerable influence.

In two papers published in 1978, Whittle and the writer both drew attention to a phase of possible forest regeneration towards the middle of the third millenium (Whittle 1978; Bradley 1978b). This could be traced in the pollen record in several areas, and even where it did not occur there seemed to be some relaxation in the intensity of land use. Indeed, there could have been a fall in the number of new clearings (Bradley 1978a: 106). As Whittle points out, this evidence is not compatible with the continuous growth suggested by earlier writers. However this phenomenon is explained, it could prefigure the less assertive economy of the Later Neolithic. Although the evidence is not at all strong (Fleming, 1982a), it is hard to find an alternative explanation.

In putting forward these arguments, the writer fell into one of the traps which this chapter is attempting to expose. Since the regeneration phase appeared to *follow* the main use of enclosures and tombs, it looked as if the expansion of settlement had been checked by ecological factors: soil erosion, crop failure or disease. There is little independent evidence of these processes. It also appeared that these changes had such a drastic impact that few public monuments were built during the next few centuries. There is a close resemblance between this argument and Case's view that Neolithic people would need to achieve a stable adjustment to their surroundings before they would be free to build formal tombs.

Such arguments can be countered on purely empirical grounds. Since the original idea was mooted, far more dates have become available, both for the supposed regeneration phase and for Neolithic enclosures. This produces a significant realignment, since many of these sites now seem to have been built *during* the period of 'recession'. It follows that the lapse in monument building need not be a consequence of these developments. Indeed, by the middle of the third millenium, the pollen record suggests signs of recovery.

The traditional approach has also emphasised the economic consequences of artefact production. The great increase in the making of axes has been related directly to an expansion of the subsistence economy after the Neolithic 'standstill'. The axes themselves are seen as agricultural tools, and their widening distribution is supposed to reflect the increasing pace of settlement (Bradley 1978a: 107–9). Again, this neat scheme breaks down for empirical reasons, since Isobel Smith has shown that axe production expanded during the period in which economic decline is proposed (1979).

For these reasons it is not sufficient to interpret the 'Neolithic standstill' as an 'economic' phenomenon. Does the approach followed in this chapter have any more to offer? At this point it will be useful to introduce two other elements to the argument, neither of which is predicted by the traditional model. Both concern evidence of competition and conflict, and in each case it is the evidence of the enclosed settlements which is all important. We have suggested that during periods of stress or competition, communities are more likely to symbolise their distinctive identity through coherent styles of artefacts or monuments. In applying this idea to British prehistory, however, Ian Hodder and the writer (1979) commented that 'there is no evidence for discrete spatial units among causewayed enclosures', basing this view on a detailed study by Palmer (1976). This no longer appears to be correct. Julie. Carr has suggested that Palmer's regional classification should be amended to transfer Orsett from his Thames group to his Midland group (pers. comm.; Fig. 2.6). This single change would mean that his classes of Neolithic enclosure would now correspond to major style zones of contemporary ceramics. His southwestern group of enclosures covers the distribution of Hembury Ware; his Sussex group coincides with the distribution of Whitehawk Ware; his Thames group now matches the main distribution of Abingdon Ware; and his Midland group probably corresponds to Whittle's Eastern Style of Neolithic pottery. It seems likely that this is more than a coincidence and Hodder's theory may be applicable in this case.

The second relevant point is the discovery that several Neolithic enclosures in southern England in fact assumed defensive proportions. Recent excavations have shown that some sites, far from being easily accessible

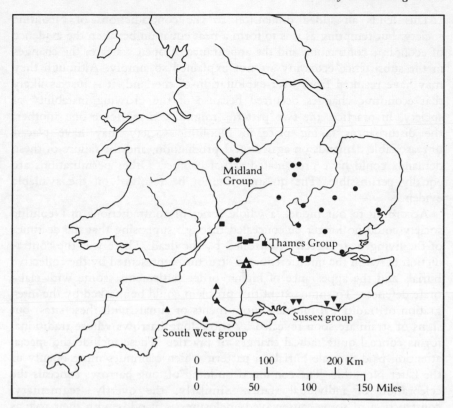

Fig. 2.6 The regional groups of causewayed enclosures (after Palmer, 1976, with minor modifications).

'central places', were defended on the same scale as Iron Age hill forts. Both Crickley Hill (Dixon 1981) and Hambledon Hill (Mercer 1980) had strongly defended gateways; the defences at Crickley incorporated stone walling and palisades, and Hambledon Hill had a timbered rampart of a type more at home in the first millenium. Similarly, Carn Brea was defended by a massive wall (Mercer 1974). Other enclosures occupy sites which were reused by later hill forts. It is clear that some Neolithic enclosures saw action. Ditches at Hambledon and Crickley Hills were recut without their causeways and four sites may have been attacked. At Carn Brea this is suggested by the vast number of arrowheads inside the enclosure; at Hambledon and Crickley Hills there was a concentration of arrowheads around the gateways, and the ditch at Hambledon contained a body with an arrowhead embedded within it. The ditch at Hembury contains quantities of burnt material, perhaps from the rampart (Liddell 1935). Given this evidence, it is hard to see these sites going out of use simply through economic recession; the Earlier Neolithic ended in actual conflict.

This lends an added dimension to the contradictions of Neolithic society, but tempting as it is to form a neat equation between the evidence of economic contraction and the appearance of open warfare, the changes in the subsistence economy are not explained so simply. Although they may have resulted from over-exploitation of the land, it is just as likely that economic changes occurred because of the growing instability of society. In practice, the two patterns might even reinforce one another; the disturbances taking place in Neolithic society may have placed unreasonable demands on agricultural production, and the failure of these demands could have precipitated actual conflict. Other permutations are equally permissible. The question cannot be resolved on the available evidence.

According to our model, a whole series of contradictions in Neolithic society could no longer be concealed through supposing that the destinies of the living were directly controlled by the dead. There was the contradiction between the undifferentiated structure represented by the collective burials and the appearance of higher order settlements, some with elaborate defences. To some extent this problem could be masked by the integration of traditional funerary monuments or rituals with these sites, but signs of strain are soon revealed by those long barrows whose traditional forms conceal quite radical changes of practice. These include the special attention paid to male burials, a pattern which continues more openly in the Later Neolithic. The continued building of long barrows conceals the celebration of individual status. Similarly, the overtly 'segmentary' construction of some causewayed enclosures is at odds with their role as defensive sites, and in two cases the original design was abandoned.

In the same way, the changing scale of axe production reveals another radical change. Rather than reflecting the demand for agricultural tools, their increasing production and exchange surely reflects the formation of social relationships over increasing distances, extending beyond the more limited horizons of the local lineage system. Again, this is inconsistent with the relations expressed in the traditional burial rite. Long distance alliances were another characteristic feature of the Later Neolithic, but in the long term they were incompatible with the more bounded structures revealed in the layout of public monuments. There is surely a direct relationship between attempts to widen the alliance network and the increasingly warlike character of Neolithic society. Control over the production of distinctive artefacts could have assumed more importance at this stage, and this is certainly evidenced on some of the defended sites.

This chapter began with one paradox, and it will end with another. One of the characteristics of Neolithic archaeology is the way in which major changes could take place without many significant developments in the forms of artefacts and monuments. It is this impression of an unchanging system which has made the traditional model so attractive, and has placed such an emphasis on the business of food production. It has made the Middle Neolithic recession seem very abrupt and the changes of the Late Neolithic appear almost inexplicable. In fact it seems likely that developments at this time led naturally to the patterns described in the next chapter: the role of the individual became more evident; the scale of exchange increased; and control over the supply of special objects assumed a central position in society. All these changes had their roots in the past; but by the time that we can see them clearly, the ancestors had been overthrown and the living had come into their inheritance.

3 Weapons of exclusion
– The role of complex artefacts (2700–2000 bc)

'Might you not even remember the old worship?
I could name ancestors, it is not done any more.
It remains true that, before you are king, you must win.'

C. H. Sisson after Horace, *Carmen Saeculare*

'I ask respectfully to be given the government of the world. The reasons for my application are that I am a better, wiser and more individual man than anyone else . . . It is quite likely that some will dispute this and claim that it is they who are better. Their arguments, however, are without validity because they are not me and so they cannot know how good I am . . . I declare that our district is poor . . . In my house, too, things are not plentiful, because my brother-in-law has eight other people to support, apart from myself, two of them intellectuals. My application, therefore, cannot be supported by money or by armed might.'

Slawomir Mrozek, *The Ugupu Bird*

INTRODUCTION

One of the most distinctive features of the Earlier Neolithic was the way in which important social changes seemed to happen against a static background. The Later Neolithic period presents the opposite problem. There is evidence for considerable fragmentation. Contact with Europe was lost, and in Britain different local sequences may have had little to do with one another. New burials and new types of monument appear in widely scattered regions where society developed on quite different lines. Paradoxically, most of these developments are associated with a range of rather similar artefacts, which owes little or nothing to local prototypes but helps to build a bridge between these different areas.

There are two ways in which these problems have been addressed. The most common response has been to undertake detailed studies of the sequence in individual regions. Among the better known examples of these analyses are Renfrew's two studies of social evolution in Wessex and in the Orkneys (1973; 1979), Darvill's account of social change in Ireland (1979) and Pierpoint's discussion of the evidence from the Yorkshire

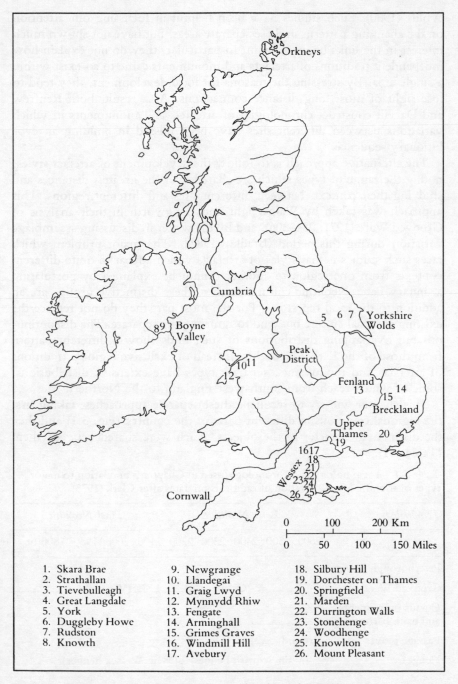

Fig. 3.1 The main sites and regions considered in Chapter 3.

1. Skara Brae
2. Strathallan
3. Tievebulleagh
4. Great Langdale
5. York
6. Duggleby Howe
7. Rudston
8. Knowth
9. Newgrange
10. Llandegai
11. Graig Lwyd
12. Mynnydd Rhiw
13. Fengate
14. Arminghall
15. Grimes Graves
16. Windmill Hill
17. Avebury
18. Silbury Hill
19. Dorchester on Thames
20. Springfield
21. Marden
22. Durrington Walls
23. Stonehenge
24. Woodhenge
25. Knowlton
26. Mount Pleasant

Wolds (1980). Such studies have been helpful in focussing our attention on the changing patterns in these separate areas, but have not shown much interest in the links between them. In particular, they do not explain how independent traditions of artefacts and monuments came to co-exist within a single area. By stressing the reasons for local development, they tend to lose sight of most long distance connections. As a result, both Renfrew and Darvill construct chronologies of artefacts and monuments in which variations between different sites have been missed in building an evolutionary sequence.

The alternative approach is to follow the development of artefact styles, noting the range of types which are shared over the greatest distances and studying their contexts between different sites and different regions. This approach was taken by Wainwright and Longworth in their analysis of Grooved Ware (1971: 234–306), and by the writer in discussing assemblage variation during this period (Bradley 1982a). The major problem which faces such studies is that styles of artefacts which appear in quite different contexts from one region to another cannot be explained by postulating a unitary Later Neolithic culture. Rather, these distinctive groups are an addition to the local repertoire. For the most part they do not replace the existing material culture but tend to remain quite separate. The discontinuous but overlapping distributions of such finds show a different pattern from those of the Earlier Neolithic. Instead of exclusive regional traditions of artefacts and monuments, separate types have extensive distributions, some of which reach from south-west England to the Northern Isles.

This chapter will try to reconcile these separate approaches, taking first the regional traditions in different parts of the country (Fig. 3.1) and then the distinctive character of the objects which were shared between them (Table 3.1).

Table 3.1   Terminology and chronology used in Chapter 3 in relation to major types of monument. Calibration of radiocarbon dates after Clark (1975)

Terminology	Later Neolithic						Final Neolithic		
	2600	2500	2400	2300	2200	2100	2000	1900	**1800** bc
Peterborough Wares									
Grooved Ware			——— (Orkneys & ——— (Wessex)———						
Cursus monuments and bank barrows		Scotland) ————————— – – – – –							
Passage graves	(Ireland) ——— (Orkneys)								
Henges	— (Main Scottish henges)— (Main Wessex henges)								
Beakers						———————————			
	3245	3095	2970	2850	2670	2520	2385	2230 BC	

At its point of departure it considers two patterns seen at the end of the previous chapter: the fragmentation of the social landscape towards the middle of the third millenium bc, and the signs that this was offset by greater production and exchange of fine objects. Some of the changes within local societies are suggested by the two quotations which head this discussion. The role of these objects is indicated by the title.

REGIONAL DEVELOPMENTS

An entire book might be written about the different regional sequences in Later Neolithic Britain; the evidence is so extensive that it is hard to contain. The simplest approach is to define a number of regions in which there is clear evidence of social change and to group these changes into three or four basic modes (Table 3.2). For simplicity the regions to be considered here will be described as 'core areas'. The most important of these are Wessex, the upper Thames valley, the fen edge, the Peak District, the Yorkshire Wolds, the lowlands of south-east Scotland, the Orkneys and the Boyne valley (Fig. 3.2).

Table 3.2   The main categories of archaeological evidence from the principal core areas

	Passage graves	Cursus monuments	Complex single burials	Henges	Complex artefacts	Grooved Ware
Wessex	—	X	x	X	X	X
Upper Thames	—	X	X	X	x	X
Fen edge and its periphery	—	x	—	x	x	X
Peak District	?	—	X	X	X	x
Yorkshire Wolds	—	X	X	x	X	X
East Scotland	x	?	—	X	X	X?
Orkneys	X	—	—	X	X	X
Boyne Valley	X	—	x	X?	X	—

X *important component*
x *minor component*
? *no clear evidence*

Some of these have been researched in more detail than others, but enough is known for some broad generalisations to be possible. With only three exceptions, the upper Thames, the fenland and the Peak District, all these regions are near the coast. As we shall see, these eight regions are also areas of outstanding natural fertility. There are valuable syntheses of the local evidence from several of the core areas. Apart from the inter-pretations already mentioned, there is Case's and Whittle's study of the upper Thames (1982), Hart's survey of the Derbyshire uplands (1981),

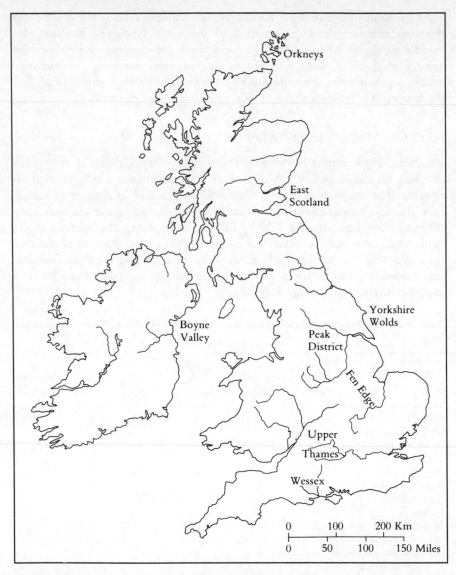

Fig. 3.2 The Later Neolithic 'core areas' discussed in the text.

Manby's two accounts of the Yorkshire Wolds (1974, 1975) and Herity's analysis of Irish Passage Graves (1974).

It is not easy to stand back from so much detail, but this is essential if we are to understand the distinctive character of the changes in each of these regions.

1. PASSAGE GRAVES
The celebration of ancestors remained important in two areas. In the

Orkneys excarnated bodies were treated in much the same way as they had been in earthen long barrows, although now the tombs were more elaborate and the number of bodies was far greater (Renfrew 1979: 150–72). A rather similar development occurred in the Boyne valley, and in other passage grave cemeteries in Ireland, but rather than mixing the unburnt bones, local communities practised cremation (Herity 1974: 117–23). The magnificence of the burial monuments in these two regions sets them apart from developments elsewhere; otherwise the arguments advanced in Chapter 2 apply in this case.

2. HENGES AND STONE CIRCLES

A second characteristic sequence concerns the development of large public monuments, the so-called henges and stone circles. For the most part, large henge monuments are not associated with burials, or at least burial does not seem to have been their principal function (Wainwright 1969; Burl 1969). As we shall see, the major group of single burials was in an area where henge monuments are poorly represented, and even where these two traditions coincide, the overlap is not particularly extensive. In some parts of the country the construction of enormous earthwork enclosures may be related to increased control over ritual and ceremonial as a means of building a power base. McKie (1977: 208–30) has referred to Neolithic 'theocracies' in Britain. This is an unfortunate term which carries some of the right connotations but rather more of the wrong ones. The role of these large public monuments will be considered at length in the following chapter.

The main areas in which henge monuments played an important part were in Wessex, south-east Scotland and the Orkneys, with other significant groups in the upper Thames, the Peak District and the Boyne valley. Some of these monuments contained settings of stones, whilst others included timber circles, a number of which were replaced in stone during a later phase. These monuments are also associated with very large mounds which have produced little or no evidence of burials. In Wessex these sites include Silbury Hill near Avebury (Atkinson 1970), the Hatfield Barrow inside the henge at Marden (Wainwright 1971) and the Great Barrow alongside the Centre Circle at Knowlton (Royal Commission on Historical Monuments 1975: 113–15). A similar mound of rather later date was built close to the henge at Strathallan in Scotland (Barclay 1981). The sequence of these sites is difficult to establish, although enough is known to suggest that they were not all built at the same time. The henges of the Orkneys and the Scottish mainland may be significantly earlier in date than the largest monuments in Wessex. On the other hand, most of these sites share certain distinctive types of artefact, in particular Grooved Ware.

3. CURSUS MONUMENTS

The third regional sequence is less well known. Cursus monuments have not played a prominent part in our discussion so far. This is because their date is so uncertain, although there are a few indications that this tradition was in existence by the middle of the third millenium bc (Hedges and Buckley 1981). The cursus may have developed at about the same time as the bank barrow, but it is not known how long it remained in use. Although some cursus monuments seem to be connected with causewayed enclosures, the locations of at least three other examples appear to have influenced the siting of henges (*ibid.*) Indeed, cursus monuments at Springfield and Dorchester on Thames contain pit and post circles just like those found on such sites (*ibid.*; Chambers and Bradley in prep.). Excavations at Llandegai in north Wales strengthen the link between these different types of monument (Houlder 1968). A pit circle like those at Dorchester has been found immediately outside the entrance of a large henge monument here and dates from the mid third millenium bc. Nearby is a linear feature which can be interpreted as a bank barrow.

In some of our core areas, the building of cursus monuments took place in a formative phase before other developments which are better known. Although these sites do not occur in three areas with large henge monuments, the Boyne valley, the Peak District and the Orkneys, these types do seem to be linked in both Wessex and the upper Thames. There is also some overlap with the distribution of early single burials. In each case special deposits were made in the vicinity of cursuses over a very long period.

In Chapter 2 we suggested that both cursus monuments and bank barrows were elaborations of the funerary sites of the Earlier Neolithic. If so, their distinctive layout can be seen as a reference to traditional practice, whatever the actual changes in society at this time. Indeed, their building may represent yet another variation on the exploitation of ancestry. As we have seen, the earliest single burials in southern England were effectively concealed through the use of traditional forms of monument. The building of cursuses and bank barrows may have had a similar basis.

4. SINGLE BURIALS

By contrast, in northern England a similar change to individual burial was emphasised by the form of the accompanying monument, which could be either a round barrow or a ring ditch (Kinnes 1979). Round barrows had already been used for collective burials, and it is more significant that the alternative of long barrow burial seems to have lapsed during the mid-third millenium. One of the largest round barrows, Duggleby Howe, was located at the centre of a causewayed enclosure (Riley 1980). The Yorkshire burials have been studied by both Kinnes (1979) and Pierpoint (1980). These burials contain a number of distinctive grave goods, including most of the types of artefact discussed in the second part of this chapter. The

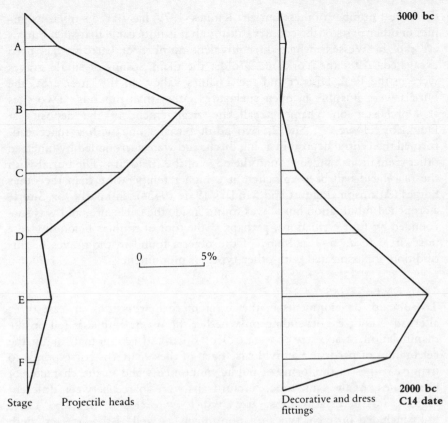

3000 bc

0   5%

Stage   Projectile heads

Decorative and dress
fittings

2000 bc
C14 date

Fig. 3.3 The changing representation of personal ornaments in Neolithic round barrows and ring ditches (after Kinnes, 1979, with minor changes).

majority of the graves were those of older males, although female inhumations with artefacts are also known. Often the male burials occupied particularly deep central graves. The inhumations of Duggleby Howe were followed by subsidiary burials which were discovered in the covering mound. These were cremations and were mostly without grave goods (Mortimer 1905: 23–42). Kinnes has shown that burials in round barrows and ring ditches can be divided into successive stages, during which the number of personal ornaments in the graves increased steadily (1979: Fig. 6.4; cf Fig. 3.3). Pierpoint has suggested that these changes in burial rite show the emergence of a distinctive elite. He favours a 'Big Man' social structure in which position depended on achievement rather than inheritance (1980: 212–42), but this interpretation may be unnecessarily specific.

It would be wrong to suggest that this emphasis on the individual was confined to the Yorkshire Wolds, although the latter area does account for

the largest number of these burials. Kinnes (1979) has traced similar examples in other parts of the country, although it is noticeable that such burials
are rare in Wessex, where an equivalent number of barrows has been
excavated. After the Yorkshire Wolds, the main groups of single graves
were in the Peak District and the Thames valley. In the latter area, the
burials were possibly in open enclosures rather than mounds. Two sites
at Dorchester on Thames recall the arrangement of the deposits at
Duggleby Howe. At Site 2, two adult burials, one with a macehead,
formed the central deposit in a ring ditch, and were surrounded by nineteen
other cremations ranged around the edge of the enclosure. The burial with
the macehead had been cremated at a higher temperature than the other
bodies (Atkinson, Piggott and Sandars 1951: 19–34). Similarly, on Site 1,
a crouched inhumation burial was found inside the enclosure, and was surrounded by four cremations, perhaps at the foot of timbers belonging to a
post circle (*ibid.*; 5–18). Many of the objects found in the graves of this
tradition are associated with other types of monument.

COMMON FACTORS

To sum up, developments in the different core areas took at least three
alternative courses, depending on whether the major emphasis fell on the
manipulation of ancestry, on control of ritual and ceremonial, or on the
celebration of particular individuals. Each of these patterns corresponds to
major changes in the forms of public monuments and in the character of
burial rites. At the same time, certain traits were shared between different
regions, not necessarily those areas which were closest together. These
links included different types of monument, as well as the artefacts with
which they were associated. In particular, *Grooved Ware* seems to be found
in all but one of the core areas. By implication these distinctive artefacts
may be connected with ritual and the expression of power. If the discussion so far has emphasised the differences between our separate core areas,
any account of these artefacts must consider their wider links. In order to
do so, we must review some of the characteristics of so-called prestige
objects.

PRESTIGE GOODS

A prestige goods economy is not simply an economy concerned with
making and distributing status symbols (Frankenstein and Rowlands
1978). Although certain objects may bestow prestige through their rarity
or their fine workmanship, they must not be freely accessible. They are
essential for the performance of particular types of transaction, for example
marriage payments, with the result that through limiting access to those
objects an elite is also able to control the transactions in which they are
used. The important element is that the supply of prestige items should

be restricted to one section in society. This can be achieved by a monopoly over the supply of special items, and also through sumptuary rules. These provide that certain types of artefact may be used only by certain individuals or groups, and perhaps only in certain circumstances. Consequently, the special character of such items has to be safeguarded.

One way of achieving this is by maintaining the exclusive character of certain objects. This can be done in two ways, either by restricting their exchange or by controlling their supply. The first method is best achieved through the separation of different spheres of exchange, with the result that special items can be exchanged only for other prestige objects, and normally only by equals (MacCormack: 1981). The purpose of this arrangement is to prevent certain items from gaining utilitarian value. They cannot be exchanged in the same sphere as subsistence goods, and it is impossible to convert items from one sphere of exchange to another. The effect is to maintain the restricted circulation of elite artefacts and therefore their special character. Hence my title for this chapter (cf. Douglas and Isherwood 1980). There is a second way of protecting their special character, since the main danger of such a system is that prestige items may become too common and may lose their value by this means. The supply of these objects must be regulated carefully, and in order to achieve this, prestige objects can be destroyed (Meillassoux 1968). Since they play a part in very specific transactions, there is a danger that they can be accumulated when those transactions are complete, and so they must be taken out of circulation when the relationships which they express are over. For example, marriage gifts must be destroyed when the marriage is at an end, for if they could be inherited, they could be treated as personal wealth and thus lose their distinctive character.

It is worth considering how far this scheme might help to explain the character of Neolithic society. Four areas may be worth investigating in order to decide whether the use of prestige goods might explain some of the long distance links between our core areas. This account will consider four main aspects of the question: the evidence that certain Later Neolithic artefacts did play a specialised role; the existence of parallel or ranked spheres of exchange; evidence for control over the production of special items; and corresponding evidence for control over their distribution and deposition.

In the previous chapter we noted that by the middle of the Neolithic some assemblages were taking on a specialised character. One aspect of this change was the increasing importance of decorated pottery and its association with more elaborate lithic artefacts, including certain objects which might have been made by specialists. We can start this discussion by considering how the pottery sequence developed.

Prehistorians have approached Neolithic ceramics with rather rigid expectations, assuming that different styles would group into distinctive regional patterns, or otherwise form a straightforward typological sequence. To some extent these expectations were fulfilled during the Earlier Neolithic period, but they are not met after that time. The successive styles of the later period – Peterborough Wares, Grooved Ware and Beakers – show increasingly diffuse and overlapping distributions, extending from early Peterborough Wares, which possess some regional integrity, to Grooved Ware, which is distributed discontinuously from Wessex to the Orkneys. There are two added complications. In the first place it seems fairly clear that although these styles developed in sequence, they remained in use together, alongside the plain pottery tradition which had evolved during the Earlier Neolithic. Each style also appears to have its own range of associations, whilst sharing those belonging to other assemblages. There are hints of this pattern with Peterborough Wares, but this becomes much more evident with the substyles of Grooved Ware and Beakers. Dr Isobel Smith interprets the emergence of Peterborough Ware as 'a gradual loss of cultural status' (1974: 113), and by referring to the Grooved Ware 'subculture', Wainwright and Longworth admit the difficulty without necessarily offering a solution (1971: 268). In fact, the framework used in Earlier Neolithic studies cannot cope with two new problems; the presence of parallel traditions and the lack of clear regional groups.

In the light of these difficulties, it seems a useful exercise to identify the special items deposited during the Later Neolithic and to consider how far they reflect these different ceramic traditions. One might suppose that the burial record would provide the decisive clues, for in other periods certain types of object occur almost exclusively in graves. To some extent this idea lay behind Stuart Piggott's concept of a Dorchester Culture, which was based almost exclusively on grave contents (1954: 351), but more recent work has suggested that some of its type fossils may be found in other contexts (Manby 1974; Bradley 1982a). We can use the funerary record to identify some of the more distinctive artefacts of this period and then trace their distribution into other spheres of activity. Further distinctive artefacts may be recognised from Later Neolithic hoards; like grave finds hoards are a class of deposit which lacks a mundane explanation.

It is possible to exclude from the account certain items which appear on most Neolithic sites: flakes, cores, blades and scrapers. By considering the time taken either to make or obtain different artefacts, we can propose a list of 24 'special items', only four of which, Seamer axes, antler hammers, antler maceheads and edge-polished adzes, appear to be limited to graves or hoards. The types which can be found in other contexts are leaf-shaped arrowheads, chisel arrowheads, oblique arrowheads, polished edge scrapers, polished flint knives, polished chisels, discoidal knives, planoconvex knives, laurel leaves, flint axes, stone axes, stone balls, stone maceheads, carved chalk objects, fragments of jet, jet beads, jet belt sliders, marine shells, bone pins and boar's tusk blades. This list does not include items which are absent from graves or hoards but occur in other types of context. Decorated antler is one example.

Once it is accepted that there is some overlap between grave goods and other finds, it is worth using those from burials and hoards as a yardstick against which to measure the apparent richness of the different ceramic assemblages mentioned earlier (cf Bradley 1982a). Five basic pottery styles can be considered: the undecorated Grimston/Lyles Hill Ware, Towthorpe Ware, Mildenhall Ware, the Peterborough Wares, and Grooved Ware. Peterborough and Grooved Wares have their own substyles which are combined in the following tables. Mildenhall and Towthorpe Wares are included together as broadly contemporary regional traditions. The first table sets out the number of different artefact associations shared between the individual burials and hoards and each of these ceramic styles (Table 3.3).

Table 3.3 The range of associations between complex artefacts and different Later Neolithic ceramic styles

Grimston/ Lyles Hill Ware	Towthorpe & Mildenhall Wares	Peterborough Wares	Grooved Ware
2	5	8	11

Grimston/Lyles Hill Ware carries on from the Earlier Neolithic, as to both Towthorpe and Mildenhall Wares. Like the Peterborough material, Mildenhall Ware is highly decorated. The second table sets out the number of these associations shared among these different groups (Table 3.4).

Table 3.4 The overlap between different Later Neolithic ceramic styles and their associations with complex artefacts.

	Grimston/ Lyles Hill	Towthorpe & Mildenhall	Peterborough	Grooved Ware
Grimston/ Lyles Hill	●	1	—	—
Towthorpe & Mildenhall	1	●	4	1
Peterborough	—	4	●	5
Grooved Ware	—	1	5	●

There are two ways of looking at these figures. They can be seen as evidence of a chronological sequence, or they may indicate a hierarchy of increasing complexity. The first approach is particularly tempting. It suggests that each successive style took on some of the associations of its predecessor, and developed further types of its own, but this will not explain all the chronological evidence. Although there is little doubt that these pottery styles did emerge in sequence, there is no reason to believe that they went out of fashion in the same order. Rather, the ceramic evidence suggests a more complex pattern, in which different assemblages were in use at the same time. This is not to deny that some of the associated artefacts might have taken the place of others. For example, antler maceheads were probably replaced in stone.

The broadening range of associations also reflects the different character of these distributions. Towthorpe and Mildenhall Wares are essentially regional styles; they may have been broadly contemporary with one another but are found in different areas of the country (Kinnes 1979: Fig. 6.3a). Peterborough Wares can be subdivided, not only in the classic area of south-east England where its substyles are well known, but in other regions also (I. F. Smith 1974: 112–17). They do not show a clear-cut regional pattern and, if anything, become more widely distributed with time. Grooved Ware is very widely distributed indeed, but it is possible that it originated in northern Britain and was adopted in the south only later.

The direct link with the burials suggests that once again decorated pottery styles and their associations may possess a special character. It is possible that these artefact assemblages were as restricted in life as they were in death, the major difference being the exclusion of Grooved Ware from some of the graves. It is likely that certain of the associated artefacts were exchanged over considerable distances. Some are made of non-local materials; others were apparently made at specific production centres, and others again are known from unfinished artefacts in hoards. The York Hoard, for example, included at least seven flint axes, a stone axe and nine laurel leaves (Radley 1967).

The Grooved Ware sites seem to be far richer than those associated with Peterborough Wares or other styles, and this may reflect a chronological development. The dominant position of Grooved Ware is apparent, if we consider axes, the most frequent of all the associated artefacts (Table 3.5). The sample used in this analysis consists of the Neolithic pits discussed by

Table 3.5 The distribution of flint and stone axes in relation to different ceramic styles

	Peterborough Ware associations (%)	Grooved Ware associations (%)
Flint axes	50	15
Stone axes	50	85

Field, Mathews and Smith (1964) and by Manby (1974; 1979). The great majority of these pits are in areas in which flint is easily available. It seems likely that these figures reflect the greater ability of Grooved Ware users to secure exotic materials. Similarly, in south-east Scotland, the types of arrowhead usually found with Grooved Ware are made from higher quality flint than those with different associations (H. S. Green 1980: 65).

Having considered the relationship of this material to the funerary evidence, it is worth exploring its relations to the public monuments. It is often supposed that there is a consistent relationship between the building of henge monuments and the use of Grooved Ware. This is not correct, although such an association can be seen in most of Wessex, in parts of Scotland and in the Northern Isles. Otherwise the clearest relationship is between the building of these centres and the use of decorated pottery, of all types from Abingdon Ware through Peterborough Wares to Beakers. For example, Grooved Ware is not very common at Avebury or on nearby sites (I. F. Smith 1965), but it does account for the entire assemblage at Marden only 12 km to the south (Wainwright 1971). It also dominates the finds from Durrington Walls (Wainwright and Longworth 1971).

The latter site is the most prolific of all the henges and has been excavated on a large enough scale for the distribution of finds within its area to be rather revealing. It appears that individual vessels of Grooved Ware had been deliberately broken and the pieces placed against the uprights of the Southern Circle. Deposits of arrowheads also occurred in this position. On other sites burnt bone may have been placed around the uprights, for example at Woodhenge (Cunnington 1929: 88–9). Dorchester on Thames (Chambers and Bradley in prep.) and Strathallan (Barclay 1981). The midden at Durrington Walls contains a large amount of material, including a mass of pig bones which could be the debris from feasting. Some confirmation of the special character of parts of the Grooved Ware assemblage can be found in their distribution at Durrington Walls (Table 3.6). Again, scrapers are treated as a baseline and the composition of the assemblage is compared between the platform and midden attached to the Southern Circle, the timber circles themselves and the enclosure ditch.

Table 3.6 The distribution of selected artefacts at Durrington Walls

	Platform and midden	Timber circles	Henge ditch
Scrapers	58	30	58
Arrowheads	27	17	3
Knives	5	4	—
Pins and awls	14	21	5
Beaker sherds or sherd groups	32	7	5

Beaker pottery is included in this table, and will be discussed on page 79. A comparable pattern can be seen at Mount Pleasant (Wainwright 1979a). In this case the ceramic assemblage on the site changed as soon as the site functioned as a henge. Here a prolific settlement is known from the land surface preserved under the west side of the monument. It seems likely that this settlement was in use immediately before the henge was built. There is a date of 2122 ± 73 bc (BM 644) for this occupation, which can be compared with dates from the primary filling of the ditch of 2098 ± 54 bc (BM 793) and 2108 ± 71 bc (BM 792). These three dates are indistinguishable and the only separation comes from the stratigraphy. The pottery, however, is completely different (Table 3.7).

Table 3.7 The stratigraphic sequence at Mount Pleasant in relation to different ceramic styles

	Plain bowls (%)	Grooved Ware (%)	Dates
Pre-enclosure activity	99.5	0.5	2122 ± 73 bc
Primary levels of north entrance	1.4	98.6	2098 ± 54 bc
			2108 ± 71 bc

Contrasts can even be seen between *different* sites associated with Grooved Ware. In this case the clearest separation is between artefacts made out of different raw materials. Since these are rarely of local origin, they evidence some form of *exchange*. Wainwright and Longworth have listed the contents of Grooved Ware sites according to the raw materials present (1971: 255), and their figures can be augmented by those published by Manby three years later. The 'domestic' sites with the largest range of materials are close to cursus or henge monuments, whereas the less varied assemblages are found very much more widely. Sites with between one and three raw materials are usually found in isolation, but virtually all those with more varied contents are within 3 km of a major ceremonial monument – a henge or a cursus. As early as 1948, Stone and Young had suggested that the number of separate items in Grooved Ware pits in England increased close to Stonehenge and Avebury. More recent publications do not support this view completely, but this pattern still emphasises the special character of such material.

Lastly, this point is reinforced by the recognition of Grooved Ware designs in other media (Simpson and Thawley 1973). Although this pottery is found over a very considerable area, some of the gaps in its distribution contain portable objects with similar designs, including the distinctive stone plaque from the Graig Lwyd axe quarry (Warren 1922: 29). Even on Grooved Ware sites, the same motifs may be shared between the pottery and other artefacts, for example the decorated bone bead from Mount Pleasant (Wainwright 1979a: 177), or the engraved stonework at Skara Brae (Shee Twohig 1981: 238–9). The most widely distributed Grooved Ware motifs are also found in Irish passage grave art (*ibid.*: 126–8). The fact that such widespread patterns should appear on tomb walls emphasises their special character. This connection will be discussed in more detail in the closing section of this chapter.

So far the discussion suggests that the assemblages of the Later Neolithic have one major characteristic. They reveal differences in access to rare or exotic items which play a special role in burials and public monuments. To this extent elements of the basic model seem to be fulfilled. It remains to see how much evidence there is concerning the production and distribution of these items.

Such a discussion faces many difficulties. Apart from the stone axes and maceheads, few of these objects have been characterised. The sourcing of flint axes is more advanced in some areas than in others, and virtually no work has been carried out on the composition of contemporary pottery. This restricts discussion to the so-called 'axe trade' (Clough and Cummins 1979). This is especially unfortunate since axe production sites have not been investigated fully. Of the flint mines, only Grimes Graves has been examined in detail (Mercer 1981), and the highland quarry sites have seen very little work.

Despite these limitations, flint mines and quarry sites had a great deal in common. Both were apparently outside the main areas of settlement and some of the axe quarries, notably Great Langdale, may have been inaccessible in winter. Work on these sites would have required outside support, ranging from a food supply to the provision of antler picks. In addition, the later stages of axe making were probably carried out at separate locations. Evidence from four different areas, the Lake District (Manby 1965), north-east Ulster (Jope 1952), north Wales (Royal Commission on Historical Monuments in Wales 1956: XLI–L) and the Norfolk Breckland (Healy 1981) suggests that the laborious task of grinding and polishing these axes took place at separate locations within a radius of roughly 30 km of the sources. During the Later Neolithic even more of the processing took place on such sites (Mercer 1981: 35). Each of the main quarries at Great Langdale is located for access from a different direction, and there may never have been a single 'axe factory' here. This could be tested further by sourcing the hammerstones introduced to these sites.

The same impression of fairly free access to the sources is provided by the distribution of finished products, which in most cases shows a regular fall off with increasing distance from the quarries (Cummins 1979). This is consistent with unrestricted hand to hand exchange (Elliott, Ellman and Hodder 1978). It is rather unlikely that stone axes were acquired through

long distance expeditions, and there is no clear evidence of close supervision of exchange.

There is little sign of a distinct class of 'axe trader'. Indeed, most of the
arguments in favour of such a group arise from a misunderstanding of the
lithic material on the production sites. For some writers, the discovery of
picks and other large artefacts recalls elements of the Mesolithic tool kit
(S. Piggott 1954: 282; H. S. Green 1980: vol. 1 186–91), and this has led
to the idea that axe production was in the hands of acculturated natives.
It is much more likely that such similarities arise from the specialised tasks
that these tools were fulfilling. There is little variety amongst the artefacts
used on quarry sites in different areas of Europe (Care 1979: 96–7).
Otherwise, the case for specialised 'traders' depends on the 'circumpolar'
affinities of the domestic artefacts from the Mynydd Rhiw quarries
(Houlder 1961: 1976). This interpretation is equally improbable, since the
excavation report indicates that such material was largely secondary to the
industrial activity on that site. It was associated with the radio-carbon dates
which overlap in the 12th century bc. Crude lithic industries of similar
type exist on ordinary settlements of that date (Ford, Hawkes and Bradley
1983).

Control could have been exercised at two levels: through monuments
situated within the regions where stone axes were being finished, or
through secondary distribution areas in other parts of the country. The
first point is difficult to document, although there is a fairly clear
geographical relationship between areas with axe production and the
distribution of 'public' monuments. In the highland zone there are groups
of henges near to the axe quarries in Cumbria, north Wales, south-west
Wales and Cornwall (Burl 1969). Other henges, including Arminghall
(Healy 1982: Fig. 2), Durrington Walls (Booth and Stone 1952) and the
Knowlton Circles (Barrett, Bradley, Green and Lewis 1981: Fig. 6) were
close to sources of flint. However, it is not easy to decide how direct this
link may have been. The henges of Llandegai, near Graig Lwyd, are
usually considered in this context (Houlder 1968: 1976), but despite the
careful deposition of two complete axes and a roughout on the site, the
finished artefacts came from Cumbria and south-west Wales. As with
causewayed enclosures, we lack satisfactory methods of distinguishing
between evidence of exchange and evidence of consumption.

Most Later Neolithic axe groups exhibit a relatively even fall off with
distance from their sources, although there is no published evidence for
those made of flint. Examples of this pattern include the Group IV axes
from Cornwall and others from south-west Wales and north-east England
(Cummins 1979). Even the more extensive distribution of the north Welsh
axes conforms to this basic pattern (*ibid.*). The axes of petrological groups
I and VI, those from west Cornwall and Cumbria, show very different
patterns, since their products are over-represented towards the limits of

their distributions. There is an unusually high proportion of Langdale axes in the Yorkshire core area and of Cornish axes in Essex. In each case Cummins has suggested the existence of a 'secondary distribution centre' (1979: 9–12). Axes from these source areas are best represented on Grooved Ware sites. The same basic pattern can be seen with maceheads. Although few of these have been characterised so far, it seems that they were generally made in western Britain, but occur most frequently in the east (Roe 1979). Both types may have been obtained direct from the source areas and then redistributed. Alternatively, access to these objects may have been restricted only when they entered certain parts of the country. Cummins (1979) argues that some of the axes were transported by sea. If so, the movement of these artefacts into inland areas could have been monitored from the henge monuments, which are often found beside major rivers. Indeed, this could help to account for their characteristic siting.

One way of considering how far the distribution of these axes departed from normal economic considerations is by calculating the distances travelled by the products of the three main centres: west Cornwall, Graig Lwyd and Great Langdale. If stone axes were being obtained in the most rational manner, each area would be dominated by products from the nearest source, assuming, as we must, that flint axes were not acceptable substitutes. A number of areas do not exhibit this pattern and axes from more distant sources occur in significant numbers. The areas which show the greatest divergence from the expected pattern are the Essex coast, the mouth of the Severn, the middle and upper Thames, Wessex and the fen edge (Fig. 3.4). These areas divide between regions which might have played a significant part in the movement of these axes, much as Cummins suggests, and three of our core areas.

To sum up: there seems to be little evidence for strong political direction of axe production at the quarries, although this need not apply to the making of other types of artefact. Whilst henge monuments can be sited close to major lithic sources, it has not been possible to show whether they played a significant role in the 'axe trade'. Still less is there a satisfactory case for the existence of specialist 'axe traders'. The best evidence is for the accumulation of 'foreign' axes at the opposite end of the exchange system. Although the distribution of most axe groups fits the model of hand to hand exchange, some of the products of the north Welsh and Cumbrian centres cluster towards the limits of their distribution. This could result from a form of 'directional trade' in which the movement of these axes may have come under political control (cf. Renfrew 1977: 86). Axes from these two sources are most often found with Grooved Ware.

This leaves one more question. We still need to ask why this material entered the archaeological record. The last stage of distribution is deposition. The studies summarised above all make the tacit assumption that

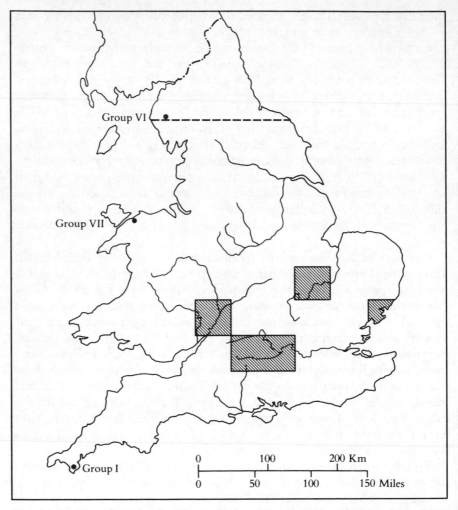

Fig. 3.4 Areas of England with particular concentrations of exotic axes. For details of the analysis see p. 55. Map compiled by Ros Cleal.

they are examining the distribution of chance losses. This need not be the case, but deliberate deposition is never easy to prove. It is worth starting this account with two anomalies in the archaeological record. In northern Europe many Neolithic deposits were placed in bogs or lakes, but in Britain we tend to take similar deposits more literally. In fact, the finds from British rivers have a puzzling character of their own, for example the large number of flint and stone axes found in the Thames (Adkins and Jackson 1978). So many of these are of high quality that the sample may be rather biased, but even so the proportion of stone axes (32 per cent) is higher than could be expected in a region in which flint is the main raw material. It is almost the same as that found in the upper levels of Windmill Hill (33 per cent) (I. F. Smith 1965: 110). Even if these finds resulted from mishaps when axes were being transported, this view cannot apply to finds of intact Peterborough Ware. A significant proportion of these pots have been recovered from riverbeds (Megaw and Simpson 1979: 167), but this does not apply to plain Neolithic vessels which are equally durable. Again, we must investigate the possibility of deliberate deposition.

A similar problem arises with the varied deposits from sites near to ceremonial monuments. Normally pits are all that survive below the surface and the only argument for a 'domestic' function is that these features could have stored food. Since a number of the items in these pits may still be serviceable, we must ask if these deposits could have been of special character, whether or not they took place inside a settlement. The same problem applies to hoards of stone artefacts, two of which were found in barrows. We also need to explain the many 'chance losses' of axes in the vicinity of ceremonial centres, especially those axes which show no signs of use. This problem has been highlighted by Pierpoint in his study of the Yorkshire Wolds (1980: 271–5). Here the Rudston monolith acts as the focus of four cursus monuments, but also lies at the centre of the distribution of numerous elaborate artefacts. Eighty per cent of the Grooved Ware on the Wolds is within 5 km of the monolith and all the sites containing between four and eight different materials are within 3 km of this point. Statistical analysis has shown that the monolith occupies the central point in the distributions of polished flint knives, stone maceheads and two forms of flint adze. A similar pattern can be found if contemporary arrowheads are scored for 'quality', admittedly a subjective procedure. Rudston dominates these artefact distributions so completely that all these types show a gradual fall off in numbers with distance from the monolith. There is no suggestion that these objects were distributed *from* this location, and so it seems possible that they were intentional deposits.

For the most part, then, the empirical evidence is consistent with the idea of a prestige goods economy: certain items are associated with special classes of sites and entire assemblages show very little overlap. The deposition of these objects may have been a rather formal procedure. Less is known about the production and distribution of these artefacts, although the basic model can account for some of the patterns that have been recognised. But even if this scheme comes a little nearer to answering the questions considered at the beginning of this chapter, the precise origins and character of such a system still require some discussion. We must begin with the question of chronology.

THE DEVELOPMENT OF INTERACTION

It is a valid objection that the analysis has included 'links' between regions whose monuments were not contemporary with one another and whose distinctive local sequences moved at quite different paces. To take only the most obvious examples, the last Boyne tombs need not be much later in date than the mid-third millenium (Herity 1974: 151–3), whilst the great henges of Wessex were built about 2000 bc (Wainwright 1979a: 224–37). Again, the tradition of individual burial in Yorkshire may have a fairly early beginning (Kinnes 1979: Fig. 8.1; H. S. Green 1980: vol. 1, 85–6), and in this area elaborate artefacts were being used in graves some time before the adoption of Grooved Ware. Similarly, the pit or post circles at Dorchester on Thames have produced sherds of Middle Neolithic pottery (Atkinson, Piggott and Sandars 1951: 108–18), but the timber circles on the Wessex chalk are of considerably later date (Wainwright 1979a: 229).

What appears to be an objection is really a vital clue. It emphasises the independence of these different sequences and makes it even less likely that they came about as a result of one clear stimulus, whether this be provided by astronomer priests (McKie 1977), a widespread Dorchester Culture (Piggott 1954), or even residual hunter-gatherers (H. S. Green 1980: 186–91). The available radiocarbon dates help to break down the problems created by an unresponsive ceramic chronology. They would seem to show that Grooved Ware originated in northern Britain and was adopted in other areas at a later date (cf Clarke 1976a). At the same time they stress the long lifespan of some of the prestige objects considered in this chapter.

At present it seems likely that the first of the core areas to develop a distinctive material culture was the Boyne Valley, where the great passage graves of Newgrange and Knowth may represent the culmination of a long sequence of local development (Bradley and Chapman, in press). The evidence from the Boyne Valley shows quite strong links with the Orkneys, although it must be remembered that passage graves as a whole represent an international phenomenon, itself linking up separate developments along the Atlantic seaboard (*ibid*). For present purposes, the connection with the Orkneys is significant, because the latter region is the other core area with a tradition of large passage graves. The Orkneys are also important because they seem to show the earliest evidence of Grooved Ware and some of its associations. This tradition is present throughout the stratified sequence at Skara Brae and must have developed around the middle of the third millenium (Clarke 1976a). This dating is reinforced by the presence on this pottery of motifs which are shared with Irish passage grave art (Shee Twohig 1981: 126–8). There are henge monuments in both the Boyne Valley and the Orkney mainland, but these present problems. The date of the Irish monuments is not very clear (Sweetman 1976), whilst those in Orkney are rather different from early sites in England and Wales (J. N. G. Ritchie 1976). Henges in east Scotland, however, have more in common with those further south and include timber circles like those in

Wessex. Although these sites seem to be significantly earlier than English examples, Grooved Ware is found with henge monuments from the Orkneys as far south as Dorset.

It is harder to establish a chronology for developments in England. The Yorkshire burials are very poorly dated, but significantly the pottery associated with early single graves is usually Towthorpe or Peterborough Ware (Kinnes 1979: Figs. 6.2 and 6.3). The same chronology may apply to the Peak District (*ibid*). In Wessex and the upper Thames, the Grooved Ware assemblage seems to appear around 2000 bc after a number of developments had taken place, including the construction of Stonehenge 1. The very different developments in Wessex, the upper Thames and Yorkshire all took place in regions where elaborate cursus monuments may have been built already, although these sites formed a focus for distinctive deposits into the second millenium.

If this sequence has been understood correctly, we can draw two conclusions. First, there can be no question of social changes proceeding at an even pace in different regions. Even if distinctive types of monument were shared between core areas, their adoption may not have been simultaneous. For example, the Wessex henges echo the structural sequence of the east Scottish sites, but apparently some time later. Secondly, there is reason to suspect that a complete range of prestige objects developed only when the Grooved Ware network reached its full extent.

The earliest developments may belong to a separate social network represented by the distribution of passage graves and their contents. There is some overlap between the grave goods from the Boyne tombs and parts of the Grooved Ware assemblage, just as the decoration of the Irish sites seems to have provided the inspiration for the designs on this type of pottery (Bradley and Chapman in press). The Orkneys occupy a pivotal position in relation to both Grooved Ware and passage graves. They are towards the northern limit of these tombs, and at the same time occupy the outer edge of the Grooved Ware distribution (Fig. 3.5).

Their isolated position off the northern coast of Scotland makes them the one area in which both patterns are represented strongly. From the Orkneys, passage graves extend through Ireland down the Atlantic seaboard, whilst Grooved Ware and its associations are distributed mainly through areas connected by the North Sea. It seems clear that the Grooved Ware assemblage originated in the Orkneys and spread southwards during the second half of the third millenium, at the same time taking on some of the more distinctive artefact types found in other areas. The contents of the Yorkshire round barrows are one example. Since so many of the core areas are linked by sea, connections between quite distant groups would not have been difficult to establish and may even account for early dates from two sites in England, which otherwise would seem anomalous (Pearson 1979: 280; Manby 1980a: 47). At the same time it looks as if the

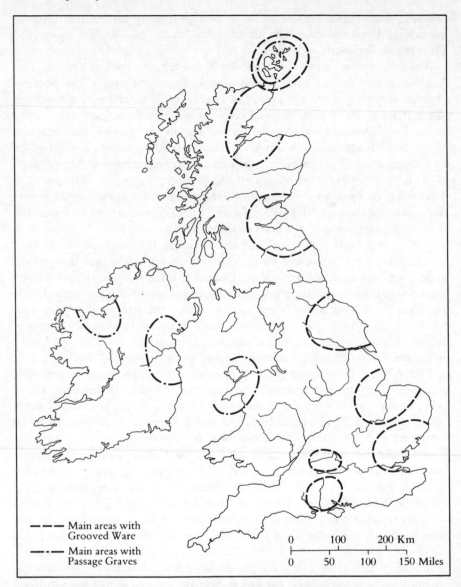

Fig. 3.5 Outline distributions of Grooved Ware and Passage Graves.

political geography of Britain underwent subtle changes during the Later Neolithic. Communities in the north may have assumed more importance as links between England and Europe lapsed. As we shall see, the position was to change only gradually. Once Wessex resumed its former importance, connections with the Continent were resumed.

So far the discussion has been based on radiocarbon dates. Now it is worth widening the discussion to admit the evidence from another source. The making of axes has been studied for many years, with the result that the lifespan of successive production sites is known in some detail. The accepted sequence illustrates the declining influence of southern England after about 2700 to 2500 bc, and the rise of other communities in the north. Only towards 2000 bc does the south resume much of its importance. In the Earlier Neolithic, the only clear evidence of flint mining comes from Sussex, where a number of centres were making axes and other items for exchange. Preliminary characterisation suggests that Sussex axes were widely distributed during this initial phase, even into areas in which flint mines were to develop later (Selkirk 1977). The production of axes for more local use is known in upland Britain, for example in Cornwall, Wales and north-west England, but this activity was not on a large scale (I. F. Smith 1979). During the Later Neolithic, however, significant changes can be seen in the patterns of distribution. There is no evidence that the Sussex mines remained important (Selkirk 1977), and the major expansion in axe production took place outside lowland England altogether. It was concentrated at two main centres, Graig Lwyd in north Wales and Great Langdale in Cumbria (I. F. Smith, 1979). Not only did the rate of production at these sites increase; it also seems as if the products of these centres were being distributed over much larger areas, including some which previously had been served by the Sussex mines. The direction of distribution was practically reversed. Only towards the end of the third millenium is there much evidence for developments in the south of England. Mercer has related these to the new energy devoted to building ceremonial monuments (1981: 35–6). The major flint mines at Grimes Graves in Norfolk developed at this time and were ideally placed for supplying both northern and southern England (*ibid*). Also, it is possible that the flint mines at Easton Down in Wessex came into being in the mid-third millenium and continued in operation after 2000 bc, but the published evidence is unsatisfactory (Stone 1932), As Grimes Graves developed close to the east coast, the production of stone axes in Cornwall also increased in scale, until this area seems to have supplied large areas of southern England (Cummins 1979; I. F. Smith 1979). In short, the changing sequence indicates the growing importance of northern England, followed by greater activity in the south.

THE NATURE OF INTERACTION

How are these patterns to be understood? In the final section of this chapter we need to say rather more about the character of the exchange system which linked such disparate areas, and we must stress the few common factors in their development.

At a purely local level, artefacts had been used to mark status divisions for some time before the adoption of Grooved Ware. The rather specialised contents of some Earlier Neolithic enclosures already prefigure the parallel assemblages of the later third millenium, just as the extension of exchange ushers in a range of new and distinctive patterns. One clue comes from Windmill Hill, for long regarded as the type site of the Earlier Neolithic. Not only was this site one of the last causewayed enclosures to be used, but the stone axes found here are quite different from the Cornish products which occur on most of the sites in Wessex. Two-thirds of the axes at Windmill Hill come from the Great Langdale quarries (I. F. Smith 1965: 110), and this development effectively symbolises the changes in orientation which were to take place during the Later Neolithic.

The same can be said of the pottery from Windmill Hill (*ibid,*: 43). Not only does the site contain a significant proportion of decorated vessels, but because of its rather late date it also includes a range of early Peterborough Ware. Here the divisions among Neolithic assemblages come more sharply into focus. Isobel Smith (1966) has shown how Peterborough Wares are a direct development from the decorated pottery of the Earlier Neolithic. Until the advent of Grooved Ware in different regions, these styles and their associations may have been used to mark important distinctions in society. As we have seen, Grooved Ware itself did not develop out of an existing tradition in lowland Britain, but spread into different areas in which Peterborough Wares or their counterparts were already well established. In each area it seems that the Grooved Ware assemblage took on some of the characteristic associations of the Peter-borough tradition, whilst developing others of its own. Grooved Ware is discontinuously distributed, leaving large areas of the country where the existing Peterborough tradition retained its status. It would be misleading to think that social developments were necessarily less complex in these areas. Some communities might have established long-distance links, where others chose to remain aloof. In such cases the Peterborough and Grooved Ware assemblages might have played equivalent roles.

It seems likely that during the second half of the third millenium a number of communities were changing. They were developing in comparative isolation and along radically different lines. One common feature of these communities is the way in which they established long-distance links with one another as they came near to their fullest devel-opment. It is possible that some of these groups were reaching the effective limits of expansion and chose to form long-distance alliances rather than pursue the uncertain option of colonising peripheral areas. This option did not exist in the Orkneys where the whole process started. Such long-distance connections can be traced both from portable objects and monuments. Artefacts could have been prestige objects associated with special types of transaction and even with ritual practices.

The symbolic role of these assemblages is very important. Whilst axes or maceheads may have travelled over considerable distances, it is unlikely that fragile pots did so, although their characteristic designs were shared in other media. The importance of such symbols does not depend on our ability – always frustrated – to provide a literal translation: rather, it is their association with power and prestige which is important in determining their diffusion. This is well illustrated by the use of designs found in passage grave art well outside the distribution of megalithic tombs. However, alliances are not maintained by the movement of museum pieces; the most important element may have been access to ritual knowledge and other information. Whilst this provides another channel for the spread of innovations, it can be demonstrated only by links between local monuments. Such alliances must be seen as a strategy which excluded outside groups and reinforced that exclusion by the manipulation of material culture. Equally, it was a network which may have been confined to those of high status. Such a process has been termed 'peer polity interaction' (Renfrew 1981).

What determined the characteristic distributions of these traditions and the elaborate monuments which went with them? The main evidence of social complexity is discontinuously distributed through a number of regions, which have been termed 'core areas'. Two factors seem to be especially important: agricultural land and sources of hard stone. Probably land was the most significant factor, since the Middle Neolithic 'standstill' might have been caused by over-exploitation of the soil. The main patterns of lithic exchange follow the changing economic fortunes of different areas, but they do not determine them.

The core areas are all noted for above average fertility. The Boyne Valley is extremely rich; the Orkneys have the best agricultural land in the Northern Isles; east Scotland is the most productive agricultural land north of the border, and nearly all the other core areas correspond to former deposits of loess (Catt 1978). The areas with significant concentrations of exotic axes are among the most fertile parts of England. On a smaller scale, Manby's work in Yorkshire suggests that the special items of the Later Neolithic are limited to the more productive parts of the settled landscape (1974: 100). Similarly, Alison Sheridan has shown that in the south the stone axes distributed in the Later Neolithic are associated with significantly more productive soils than those made in the preceding period (pers. comm.). At its simplest this suggests that social changes were most likely to happen among communities with access to productive farmland. This is hardly surprising in the wake of a possible recession.

This general statement can be amplified in two ways. First, it is becoming apparent that the Later Neolithic period did see agricultural intensification, although such evidence is confined to a very few areas. It has been well summarised by Whittle (1981) and by Burgess (1980a: 193–9), and takes three basic forms. There is evidence for plough cultivation, revealed by ard marks preserved beneath later earthworks. Pollen evidence suggests a resumption of land clearance some time before the introduction of metal artefacts (Bradley 1978a: 106), and we now have growing evidence for land enclosure at this time, extending from the pit alignments of north Northumberland (Miket 1981) to the ditched paddocks on the fen edge at Peterborough (Pryor 1978). At the same time, there is convincing evidence of feasting, an institution which would be unthinkable on any scale in a crippled economy. Surely this is the significance of the high proportion of pig bones on Later Neolithic sites (Tinsley and Grigson 1981: 226–8). This is often explained by a change to pastoralism (H. S. Green 1980: 189), but pig does not provide secondary products. It is pre-eminently a meat animal. The best reason for keeping a large number of these animals would be in order to indulge in meat consumption.

It would be wrong to leave this argument in such a schematic form. Pig does not occur in isolation and does not dominate the fauna on all Later Neolithic sites, even those with Grooved Ware. It is particularly interesting that pig was not the main animal on two extensively excavated sites which seem to have functioned as settlements, Fengate (Pryor 1978) and Skara Brae (D. V. Clarke 1976a; 1976b). For just this reason, the pig bones from Fengate are doubly important (Pryor 1978: 154–5, 185–6). They were almost certainly discarded on a single occasion, and were associated with a series of flint artefacts which had probably been used for butchery. The crucial point is that this material may have originated from a single episode of feasting on what was otherwise a working farm; but the sheer quantity of bones in this deposit suggested to the excavator that meat had been provided for more people than were living in the settlement. Here we can suggest that feasting was a strategy for building personal prestige. It is conceivable that in areas which lacked agricultural promise, similar strategies could have been based on the export of fine artefacts, but this is even harder to demonstrate. It is true that most of the axe quarries were in areas of extremely marginal land, and the presence of so many elaborate monuments can hardly be coincidental, when usually they are found in areas with high agricultural yields. Grimes Graves may be a significant exception to this pattern, since the Neolithic inhabitants of the area would have had access to the rich grazing land on the fen edge.

It is very important to recognise that both Peterborough and Grooved Ware assemblages do occur in what seem to be domestic contexts, although they are rarely found together. There is no evidence that Grooved Ware was a domestic ceramic, whilst Peterborough Wares played a role in burial ritual (*pace* Burgess 1980a: 41), nor can we invert this scheme. Rather, they may each be thought of as high status or special purpose assemblages which were broadly equivalent to one another in different parts of the country. In the same areas, on the other hand, the adoption of the Grooved Ware tradition could have involved the down-grading of the Peterborough assemblage. The process of ceramic change will be discussed more fully in Chapter 4, but the major difference is that in most areas the Peterborough tradition developed *in situ*, whilst the Grooved Ware assemblage was intrusive. In either case the exclusive character of certain associations extends to the domestic level.

In conclusion, we can suggest that it was on the basis of agricultural wealth, feasting and control of lithic artefacts that different elites were able to develop after the Neolithic standstill. These particular resources did not dictate one particular road to advancement, but allowed very different strategies to be followed. The convergence came about because isolated elites gradually formed alliances with one another, with the result that the Grooved Ware assemblage created a crucial link between groups who had little in common initially. At that stage there was scope for the emulation of characteristic forms of burial or ceremonial monument. It would be wrong to suppose that alliances, once created, were necessarily lasting. The very fact that political dominance ultimately passed from northern Britain back into Wessex surely reveals such a system as unstable and possibly competitive. Indeed, by the time that Wessex had regained its former importance, the Orkneys were starting to lose their dominant position.

Nowhere is the changing balance of power more clearly seen than in the oscillation between exchange systems based on Cornish and Cumbrian axes. A recent simulation study leads us to believe that these two systems were in direct competition with one another (Elliott, Ellman and Hodder 1978). There is some similarity between the areas over which each of these axe groups predominated and the boundaries of the different styles of ritual monument (Fig. 3.6). For example, the Cornish axes predominate in the areas with Burl's group 1, 2 and 3 henge monuments, and Langdale axes where group 4, 6 and 7 henges are found (Cummins 1980; Burl 1969; Fig. 1). This division in the axe distribution is strikingly similar to Burl's distinction between an eastern tradition of ceremonial monuments and the area with sites in his Wessex and south-western traditions (Burl 1976: Fig. 13). Given the changing political geography of the Neolithic, it is no surprise that Wessex should regain its importance at the time when cross-channel contacts were being renewed.

This is not the occasion to embark on another dissection of the Beaker Folk, even though they are so prominent in death. Suffice it to say that the types of empirical pattern discussed in such detail for Neolithic Britain are precisely the same as those faced by scholars studying the Beaker cultures in Europe. It is interesting that just as Beaker specialists are deciding that their evidence is best explained by the spread of prestige objects (Shennan 1982a), British scholars should be faced with similar problems in discussing the Grooved Ware complex.

It seems likely that these two traditions came together towards the end

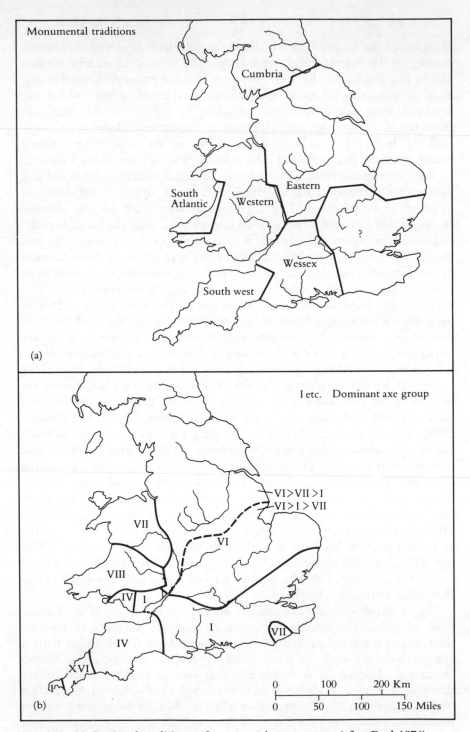

Fig. 3.6 (a) Regional traditions of ceremonial monuments (after Burl 1976).
(b) The major regions of Later Neolithic Britain as defined by the distributions
of stone axes from different sources (after Cummins 1980).

of the third millenium bc. It was as the importance of Neolithic Wessex increased that continental contacts were resumed, and Beaker pottery and metalwork were introduced into this country (Lanting and van der Waals 1972). There is some reason to suspect that at first Beaker pottery was used alongside Peterborough Ware (C. Richards, pers. comm.), but whatever the reason, its appearance must mark a further step in the widening of political alliances. More interesting still is the way in which Beaker pottery now spread through the British Isles. Lanting and van der Waals consider that only one group of Beaker material came to Britain direct from the Continent. This was introduced into Wessex from parts of the Rhineland and then spread gradually across the country – Beaker pottery and its associations seem to have moved between the core areas along *existing* lines of exchange. In time they were to take over as the main high status assemblage, but that development can be reserved for the next chapter. At this stage it is enough to say that before the first metal dagger was buried, some objects already served as weapons of exclusion.

4 Unnecessary pyramids
– *Monuments and graves*
(2000–1300 bc)

'When a country is overstocked with people, as a pasture is oft overstocked
with cattle, they had wont in former times to disburden themselves by sending
out colonies, or by wars; . . . or employing them at home . . ., as those
Egyptian Pharaohs . . . did, to task their subjects to build unnecessary
pyramids, obelisks, labyrinths, channels, lakes, gigantic works all, to divert
them from rebellion, riot, drunkenness.'

Robert Burton, The Anatomy of Melancholy

'A realist, he has always said:
"It is Utopian to be dead,
For only on the Other Side
Are Absolutes all satisfied
Where, at the bottom of the graves,
Low Probability behaves." '

W. H. Auden, New Year Letter

INTRODUCTION

As these two quotations suggest, the archaeology of the second millenium
is written with the evidence of monuments and graves. The burial mounds
have produced most of the finer objects, and the other monuments
dominate what remains of the contemporary landscape. This chapter asks
why these two types of information should have assumed so much prominence. Can the archaeologist investigate the role of ritual activities and,
if so, how are these sites to be understood today? Are there any absolutes
in the archaeology of death? Were pyramids really necessary?

To some extent this account complements the interpretations in Chapter
3 and will overlap parts of the same time period, but true to the thematic
character of this book, our discussion will espouse a different approach
from its predecessor. Although prestige objects remained of central
importance throughout the second millenium, they will not be discussed
in detail, since the essential features of such artefacts have already been
considered. Similarly, although public monuments and elaborate burials
were often mentioned in the earlier chapter, these form the main subject

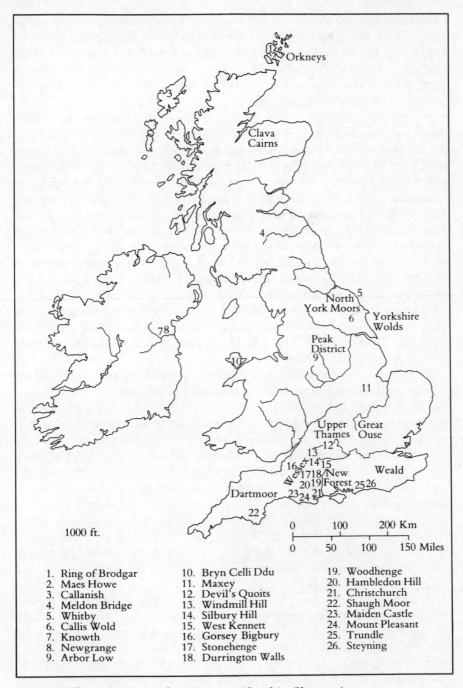

Orkneys

Clava
Cairns

3

4

5
North
York Moors
6   Yorkshire
         Wolds

Peak
District
9

11

78

10

Upper | Great
Thames | Ouse
12

13
16 14 15
17 18 New   Weald
20 19 Forest 25 26
23 24 21

West Kennett

Dartmoor

22

1000 ft.

| 0 | | 100 | | 200 Km |
| 0 | 50 | | 100 | 150 Miles |

1. Ring of Brodgar	10. Bryn Celli Ddu	19. Woodhenge
2. Maes Howe	11. Maxey	20. Hambledon Hill
3. Callanish	12. Devil's Quoits	21. Christchurch
4. Meldon Bridge	13. Windmill Hill	22. Shaugh Moor
5. Whitby	14. Silbury Hill	23. Maiden Castle
6. Callis Wold	15. West Kennett	24. Mount Pleasant
7. Knowth	16. Gorsey Bigbury	25. Trundle
8. Newgrange	17. Stonehenge	26. Steyning
9. Arbor Low	18. Durrington Walls	

Fig. 4.1 The main sites and regions considered in Chapter 4.

of this account and much of what is said here has some application to the Later Neolithic. This overlap is inevitable, since the period divisions applied to British prehistory fail to make a clean break. Grooved Ware belongs to the Later Neolithic but for some writers the adoption of Beaker pottery has marked the start of the Bronze Age. Often the two groups of material were in use at the same time.

At first sight there is a more pragmatic reason for highlighting monuments and funerary ritual, for not only do these provide the raw material for the prehistorian; they dominate the evidence from domestic settlements which are all but absent (Fig. 4.1). In practice, the rarity of elaborate settlements cannot be the result entirely of faulty fieldwork or of natural destruction: surely these settlements were evanescent in the first place. There are numerous well preserved living sites known from the succeeding period, and it is becoming increasingly difficult to believe that their predecessors crowded into the areas in which there has been no work. It seems much more likely that the state of our evidence reflects the actual priorities of society, that burial mounds and ceremonial centres were always more elaborate and more lasting than the settlements, and that they also absorbed a far larger share of the energy budget. It is often suggested that settlement may have been fairly mobile and could have involved a greater reliance on livestock (Bradley 1978a: 112–13). Until more evidence is found, it seems unwise to adopt this notion.

As in the Later Neolithic, it is almost impossible to present any chronology without engaging in discussion of the functions of the artefacts; we need a basic time scale in order to place the different monuments in perspective. There is no doubt that during the second millenium, metalwork took on many of the functions played by the prestige objects of the Later Neolithic, but this time it is far more difficult to find links between grave goods and other artefacts. The clearest sequence comes from the metalwork, with a distinctive Beaker-associated industry, which has its own sequence of development (Burgess 1978), and then two phases of grave goods known mainly from the burials of Wessex (Gerloff 1975). These phases are referred to as Wessex 1 and 2 (Table 4.1). Some hint of the special character of these metal objects comes from their depiction in rock art, including the famous carvings at Stonehenge (Simpson and Thawley 1973; Schmidt 1979).

At the same time there has been the temptation to define an equally straightforward ceramic sequence, running from 'native' Neolithic wares, through Beakers to other styles, in particular Food Vessels, Collared Urns and the pottery of the Deverel-Rimbury tradition. These schemes have met with significant difficulties. They do not agree particularly well with the available radiocarbon dates, which show that several different styles could have been made at the same time (Burgess 1980a: 84–98), and the contextual evidence suggests that different ceramics played rather special-

Table 4.1 Terminology and chronology used in Chapter 4 in relation to major types of monument. Calibration of radiocarbon dates after Clark (1975)

	2000	1900	1800	1700	1600	1500	1400	1300	1200	1100	1000 bc
Terminology	*Final Neolithic* Early		Middle		*Early Bronze Age* Late Beaker Wessex 1? Wessex 2?				*Middle Bronze Age*		
Henges	(Timber)		(Stone)								
Complex burials	?——?——										
Land clearance								– – –			
Agricultural intensification									–?–		
	2520	2385	2230	2095	1975	1835	1710	1595	1495	1385	1250 BC

ised roles. The changing character of these roles suggests that different styles could have changed their status, beginning as special purpose ceramics and gradually diffusing down into the domestic sphere. Miller has suggested (1982: 89) that this type of pattern may be the result of emulation:

The process of emulation . . . results in items changing their symbolic association, and in new items being adopted, in a dynamic process that proceeds quite apart from any actual change in the principle of hierarchy or even in the relative positions of the respective groups . . . If an individual or group wishes to improve its relative position within the hierarchy, it may seek to emulate the group above it by adopting certain products or styles associated with the higher group. If the group above wishes to maintain its superior position, it must either seek to prevent this, or to have new symbols of its differentiation adopted in order to maintain the previous contrast.

An interpretation of the British evidence is given in Figure 4.2.

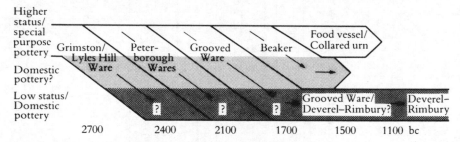

Fig. 4.2 The changing status of different ceramic styles during the second millenium bc.

It suggests that virtually all the ceramic styles of the second millenium could have played rather specialised roles. In southern England, for example, Beakers appear initially in burials or public monuments, rather than settlement sites (Whittle 1981). Middle period Beakers are more common in henges, where they seem to take over the role of Grooved Ware, but are also found with rich graves. In the late Beaker period, however, the same styles play an important part in settlements where they may have taken over from existing types of domestic pottery. As Beakers became less important in other spheres, Food Vessels and Collared Urns were first used as grave goods. Neither of these types is common on settlements in the south (Burgess 1980a: 86–97). Finally, with the disuse of Beaker pottery even in settlements, new developments took place. The main domestic wares anticipate the Deverel–Rimbury tradition and perpetuate coarser elements of the Grooved Ware repertoire (Barrett 1976). As Miller's scheme suggests, it seems as if most styles of pottery were adopted for use in special circumstances, but as these distinctive styles became more widely available their exclusive character was threatened. New types were developed to take over their original roles, whilst the older styles entered the domestic sphere. The downgrading of special purpose artefacts would provide a stimulus for fresh developments; existing social distinctions needed re-assertion through the creation of new ceramic styles. This process places greater emphasis on context than on chronology. Thus 'Beaker settlements' may not belong to the period of rich Beaker graves, and people who were buried with Collared Urns may rarely have used them in life.

MONUMENTS AND· GRAVES

Having equipped ourselves with a time scale, we can turn to the monuments. Here the changes are easier to recognise, but the evidence does not speak for itself, and we must approach it with suitable questions. The most important of these is provoked by the quotation from Robert Burton. Why do societies build monuments which consume enormous amounts of labour and yet have no practical function – the 'unnecessary pyramids' of his text and of my title? In a recent paper, Cherry (1978) has considered the role of such monuments in early states. He has pointed out that they occur mainly in two phases. The first period of monument building takes place whilst societies are at a formative stage, and helps to bind them into a coherent organisation. Monument building is both a celebration of existing complexity and a way of uniting the different forces in one society by providing a common focus for their activities and aspirations. After this initial burst of energy, there may be a reduction in the intensity of public works, until a second phase of monument building takes place as the fabric of society decays. In the latter case it can act as a way of focussing the communal will and effort on a single act of integration. Cherry provides two examples of this process, Minoan peak sanctuaries and Egyptian pyramids, the latter the very example discussed by Burton in my first quotation. The earlier peak sanctuaries were built as the state was coming into being and their construction slackened once work on the palaces commenced (*ibid.*: Fig. 1). The second group of sanctuaries is of later date and belongs to a final period of decline. Similarly, the size and complexity of Egyptian pyramids diminished with the increasing stability of the state (Rathje: 1975). The sites were no longer so elaborate or time-consuming, and stone was replaced as a building material by mud brick.

Cherry relates this type of pattern in the archaeological record to Webster's suggestion (1976) that complex societies may pass through a period in which sanctions are enforced through ritual and ceremonial, rather than political coercion. He suggests that so-called theocracies form an intermediate stage in the evolution of ranked societies. In such cases authority lacks a recognised secular basis and power is validated directly through reference to the supernatural. Such societies may initiate elaborate monuments to the supernatural, and in Cherry's view the building of such massive structures may have political implications in justifying and displaying the role of a powerful minority. One is reminded of the theory, put forward by Jones and Kautz (1981), that 'crisis cults' were a decisive factor in the emergence of the state.

These different ideas imply that the development of large ritual centres may precede the emergence of identifiable elites in the archaeological record. Communal monuments hide the individual hand; single burials reveal it. Until we have investigated considerably more settlements, funerary ritual seems to be the most promising area for discussion. Here there is no shortage of analytical techniques, although it soon appears that the surviving information from British sites is hardly sufficient to support much interpretation. Too little of the necessary information has been collected in the field, and in some ways our questions come a century too late.

Although a vast number of barrows have been dug, everything depends on the assumptions with which the burial record was approached. Early excavators were not greatly concerned with social interpretation, and few undamaged sites remain available to us today. The most widely adopted approach to burial sites develops from the work of Binford (1971), who suggests that the complexity of the mortuary ritual reflects the social position enjoyed by the deceased individual. Variants of this approach include attempts to 'rank' the dead according to the amount of energy expended in the funeral (Tainter 1978), or the variety and complexity of the surviving grave goods (O'Shea 1981a). Whilst the first approach places the emphasis on the work of barrow building, the second attempts to 'score' the different grave goods according to their rarity in the archaeological record. Such patterns need to be related to skeletal evidence concerning the age, sex and diet of the deceased, but in Britain such information is rarely available. Still less is it possible to take these approaches to an entire cemetery. Whilst a number of writers have commented on promising patterns brought to light by early fieldwork (e.g. Burgess 1980a: 295–325), Petersen has been unable to identify any clear trends among more recently recorded excavations (1981: 236–71).

There need never have been a consistent relationship between the world of the living and that of the dead. 'Scoring' of grave goods has proved to be a rather poor method of detecting rank (Tainter 1978), at least compared with studies of energy expenditure, but for either approach to have much meaning, the analytical results must be related in turn to the other activities of the survivors. If the funeral rites express differences among the dead, can these differences be identified in contemporary settlement plans? In Britain this question cannot be answered. Similarly, if we recognise contrasts in the scale of different mounds, can we relate these to the energy budget as a whole when we know so little about the Early Bronze Age economy? We may have separate cemeteries for different levels of a ranked society, but if these differences were expressed through different ceramic styles, we could easily miss the point in looking for a chronological sequence. Indeed, this may have happened already (cf. Whittle 1981; Bradley 1981a).

Although this chapter will offer some comments on the clearest patterns in the funerary record, the opportunity for more detailed study has been missed, and is unlikely to occur again. For this reason we must be content with a rather wider approach to the problem. We can start from the obvious contrast between the few, geographically restricted burials of the Later Neolithic and the far larger number of furnished graves which are found in the second millenium. Again, there appear to be differences in the rate at which funeral offerings were made – more in certain Beaker phases than in others and more again in Wessex 1 than Wessex 2. Why did a society which was able to produce wealth items put these in the ground in some phases more often than in others? These questions have been considered by Parker-Pearson (1982), who has made a close study of recent British funerary practices. He suggests that the schemes described above do not make sufficient allowances for the reasons for choosing either simple or complex funerals. They assume that burial rites always reflect the organisation of the society undertaking them, but such studies do not show why these rites should change through time. Parker-Pearson suggests that funeral rites can be a way of focussing the attention of the living on the status of the dead, but that normally this will happen when there is good reason for making a public statement. He argues that this occurs mainly in cases of competition, threat or ambiguity. Kossak (1974) has taken a similar view in his analysis of 'display graves', suggesting that these burials were deposited at times of military, social or political change, or during phases of drastic culture contact, and applies this argument to a number of outstandingly elaborate burials in European prehistory. The same idea was expressed by Childe (1945). This approach again allows changes in 'ritual' activity to be related in a rational manner to other developments in the archaeological record. How well do these ideas work in studying the second millenium?

THE EVIDENCE OF MONUMENTS

So far as larger public monuments are concerned, this discussion gives rise to several expectations. They should have been built on a considerable scale, using a large labour force, and should contain elements which suggest communication with, or access to, the supernatural world. They should appear in regions or in periods in which furnished burials do not play a prominent part, and where a chronological sequence can be studied, the emergence of single graves with indications of individual status should be found at a later date. Following Parker-Pearson, one would expect the burials of this formative period to be unusually rich.

As mentioned in the previous chapter, there is no horizon of 'public' monuments, and the sequence of development varies between different parts of the country. The major henge monuments belong to a period of significant changes. Their implications have been most fully discussed in two areas of the country, Wessex and the Orkneys. The first point is to establish the scale of these sites, for unless they can be shown to have made considerable demands on labour, the basic theory cannot be taken further. There are suitable estimates from both of these areas. Renfrew (1979: 212–14), working in the Orkneys, obtained estimates of at least 80,000 man hours for the construction of the Ring of Brodgar, a figure which can be compared with those for building megalithic tombs, which range from 10,000 to 100,000 man hours. There are no figures for the construction of second millenium barrows in this area. In Wessex the largest henges have already been the subject of considerable discussion. The figures used here are taken from a recent study by Startin and the writer (1981). In contrast to Renfrew's earlier analysis of these sites (1973), this paper concludes that the building of the main henge monuments involved a far greater investment of manpower than most earlier sites, apart from the enclosures at Hambledon Hill, and possibly the Dorset Cursus. There is little evidence for steadily increasing control over human labour in this region. Rather, the building of sites like Durrington Walls marks a radical departure. The ditch alone may have required about 500,000 man hours. The detailed construction of these sites also differs from that of their predecessors (Startin and Bradley 1981). The work may have taken place under closer direction and co-ordination. It is likely that the work force was larger and that it was engaged in construction over a much longer period. For example, the contemporary monument at Silbury Hill may have been built continuously, despite several changes of design, and was never completed (Atkinson, 1970). To set these estimates in perspective, they are higher than the labour requirements of Iron Age hill forts, even though the latter sites were built at a time when the population was significantly greater. Such figures are more than a hundred times higher than those for a typical round barrow (W. Startin, pers. comm.). In a sample of seventeen societies practising simple crop agriculture, each individual contributed an average of only 800 man hours a year (Leach 1976). There is a very striking contrast with the other estimates, and to this extent at least we are entitled to consider the building of the henges as a distinctive phenomenon.

How much evidence exists for the non–utilitarian nature of these sites? The case can perhaps be divided into positive and negative evidence. The positive evidence is actually rather ambiguous, for the simple reason that we should not expect past societies to make the same distinctions between the domestic, social and religious as we do now. Even so, two features of these sites suggest a range of special functions which is hard to accommodate if we regard them as exclusively secular centres. First, a small proportion of these sites incorporate significant astronomical alignments, as do the passage graves at Newgrange and Maes Howe (Patrick 1974; Burl 1981: 124–6). The best known example of this pattern can be found at Stonehenge (Atkinson 1956), but this relationship is not peculiar to that site, and similar arrangements may have existed at timber monuments, for example the Later Neolithic complex at Meldon Bridge in southern Scotland (Burgess 1976a: 171–2). It is customary to question the reality of such evidence, arguing that a knowledge of astronomy goes beyond the likely capacity of the contemporary population. This view is largely a measure of our ignorance, and betrays an ethnocentric attitude to the question. As Thorpe (1981) has shown, simple astronomical observations are found very widely in the ethnographic record and are not limited to complex societies. Practices which were within the capacity of hunter-gatherers should not have been beyond the powers of communities in this period. He also observes that simple astronomy need not involve the construction of lasting monuments or the existence of specialist groups. We cannot use this evidence alone to postulate a priesthood, still less a social structure borrowed from the Maya state (*pace* McKie 1977: 209–11). Much depends on the extent to which we are prepared to accept the claims for more complex procedures, including the existence of lunar observations (Thom 1971) and the prediction of eclipses (Heggie 1981: 100–4). Here the basic argument is much more tenuous and claims are probably exaggerated, but once we have accepted the reality of even the simplest observations, like the orientation of Stonehenge on the midsummer sunrise, the question is no longer one of acceptance or rejection, but simply of degree.

The second argument for the specialised role of certain centres concerns the possibility that some of the stone and timber circles found there embody specialised methods of surveying, involving the layout of complex geometrical figures and the use of a standard unit of length (Thom 1967). Provided the surveys employed in modern studies identify the original ground plan correctly, the major issue becomes the statistical significance of our analyses (Kendall 1974; Heggie 1981: 32–82). It seems that whilst the complexity of these designs has been overemphasised, they did exist and used a regular unit of length, perhaps the human pace (Kendall 1974: 258). It does not follow that a site with a complex ground plan must possess a ritual character – there have been similar claims for Iron Age brochs (McKie 1975: 85–90) – but the cumulative evidence is reasonably impressive.

So too is the negative evidence mentioned earlier. Some sites are perhaps too clean to have functioned as ordinary settlements, examples being

Maxey and the Devil's Quoits, where large scale excavations have taken place. On other sites timber circles seem to have been replaced in stone. Unless there had been a complete change in the function of henge monuments, this development weakens the case for interpreting the timber circles as houses. Indeed, some of the henges were interchangeable with other types of monument which could not have been settlements. For example, Burl suggests that the large stone circles of western Britain may have been the counterpart of the major henges in other areas (1976: 26). The specialised role of stone circles is shown at two important sites where they are found with passage graves. There was one such circle around the great tomb at Newgrange (M. O'Kelly 1982), and at Callanish in the Outer Hebrides a small passage grave was inserted into an existing stone circle (Ashmore 1981). A comparable sequence is known at Bryn Celli Ddu on Anglesey where an important henge monument was buried beneath another passage grave (C. O'Kelly 1969).

These sites introduce our second question. How far was there a dichotomy between the evidence for corporate monuments and that for single burials? There is some divergence between the areas with Later Neolithic henge monuments and those with individual graves of the same period. The Yorkshire Wolds contain the highest proportion of Neolithic single burials, but the main henge monuments are some distance away. In Wessex, on the other hand, henges were of even more importance, but Later Neolithic single burials are not very common, despite the high rate of excavation over the last two centuries. Few of the round barrows are earlier than the Beaker ceramic phase. The contrast with the Wolds is very striking. Wessex contains about 70 per cent of the earthen long barrows in Britain, but only 7 per cent of the Neolithic round barrows or ring ditches (Kinnes 1979). As we have seen, where burial monuments and henges did exist in close proximity, the burial rite rarely emphasised the role of the individual. For example, the poorly dated Clava Cairns of northeast Scotland do incorporate single cremations, but these were without any grave goods (Henshall 1963: 29). The link with other types of monument is strengthened by the presence of stone circles around the mounds. The Clava Cairns seem to be aligned on major phases of the moon (Burl 1981b).

This link between public monuments and undifferentiated burials can be taken one stage further, for it seems likely that the location of henges in Wessex was influenced by the presence of earlier enclosures and long barrows. These mounds had covered undifferentiated burials, similar to the later deposits in the Orkneys. It is often assumed that this geographical relationship implies that henges are the direct replacements of earlier monuments (Ashbee 1970: 104–5; Renfrew 1973: 548–9). Alternatively, we can suggest that the location of these sites some centuries later refers to the ancestors as a source of influence. The same reference to archaic traditions can be seen in the sporadic re-use of causewayed enclosures or the deposition of artefacts around much earlier long barrows. It also appears in the re-use of Mycenean tombs in Archaic Greece (Snodgrass 1980: 38–40). Specialised deposits were placed in the enclosure ditch at Hambledon Hill (Mercer 1980: 37), whilst major settlements seem to have developed outside several other enclosures. Significantly, the interiors of these sites were little used, or were kept rather clean. Examples of this pattern are known at Windmill Hill (H. S. Green 1980: 168), Maiden Castle (Care 1982) and the Trundle (J. Gardiner, pers. comm.).

In summary, it seems as if most henges did play a special role in ritual activity and that they were not simply elaborate settlements. They were built on a massive scale and their construction clearly made extravagant demands on human labour. Generally speaking, the distribution of these sites avoided areas with rich graves. Some of the monuments were sited near to earlier burial places. In this case we can suggest that the presence of the dead contributed to the power of the living.

Having defined the basic relationships in the archaeological record, it remains to see how they changed through time. Here the evidence of the Beaker assemblage is very helpful. Although there no longer seems much reason to envisage a phase of immigration – at any rate on a scale which is archaeologically detectable – this material has one great virtue. It begins as a high status assemblage and so it plays a prominent role on the very sites being considered here. Beaker pottery has the added advantage that it has a fairly well defined sequence, whereas the internal development of Peterborough and Grooved Wares remains to be worked out.

As mentioned earlier, the role of Beakers changed through time, although the details of these patterns may vary according to which of the available typologies is employed. The present account is based mainly on Case's chronology, which has the virtue of simplicity (Case 1977); the more detailed sequence put forward by Lanting and Van der Waals (1972) still remains to be tested and may prove to be too elaborate. Since there is general agreement that the earliest Beakers are found in Wessex, the evidence from this region provides a useful starting point. Four contexts can be considered: two types of older monument (causewayed enclosures and long barrows) where fresh deposits were now being made; the new ceremonial centres, and elaborate individual burials. The first Beakers are found in the later levels of causewayed enclosures and long barrows, and also as occasional finds in henges. In Wessex they do not appear in rich graves. In the middle phase they played a far more prominent role in henges and became important finds in burials. By the time that they featured prominently in the domestic record, their status was probably diminishing. Whilst late Beakers remained quite important as grave goods, they played a smaller role on the henges (Table 4.2).

Although the burial evidence shows less patterning in other areas, it is worth extending this scheme to cover the entire country (Table 4.3). Among the sites where large amounts of early Beaker material have been

Table 4.2   The changing associations of Beaker pottery in Wessex

	Early phase (%)	Middle phase (%)	Late phase (%)	
Long barrows	28	36	36	(percentage of all
Causewayed enclosures	43	14	43	occurrences on each type of
Henge monuments	28	50	22	monument)
Complex burials	—	62	38	

Table 4.3   The changing associations of Beaker pottery nationally

	Early phase (%)	Middle phase (%)	Late phase (%)	
Long barrows	40	30	30	(percentage
Causewayed enclosures	60	10	30	of all occurrences on each type of
Henge monuments	29	50	21	monument)
Complex burials	2	49	49	

found were three much older burial monuments: the massive round barrow at Callis Wold in Yorkshire (Coombs 1976), and the great passage graves at Knowth (Eogan 1976) and Newgrange (M. O'Kelly 1982). Other finds from the latter site include a bronze axe and possibly debris from feasting. One indication of the special role of Beaker pottery is the unusually high proportion of finely decorated vessels in certain collections, including those from the later silts of the causewayed enclosure at Windmill Hill (I. F. Smith 1965: 80), and from the henges at Gorsey Bigbury (ApSimon, Musgrave, Sheldon *et al.* 1976) and Mount Pleasant (Wainwright 1979a: 86–8). The small quantity of Beaker pottery within Durrington Walls has a similar distribution to the prestige objects considered earlier. It is worth adding that Beaker vessels may be the first ceramic types in Britain with a sufficiently complex design structure to carry individual or group symbols (S. van der Leeuw, pers. comm.).

The basic sequence of artefacts and monuments can be amplified in two ways. In the initial stages it seems as if Beaker material was playing a rather similar role to other finds from earlier monuments. Again communities were using traditional sites as a way of establishing their own position. Just as some of the henge monuments seem to have been located amidst much earlier communal tombs, the deposition of Beaker pottery in these places reveals a conscious emphasis on tradition, which is the more misleading for following an interval during which they had not been used. Another sign of this reference to the past is the fairly frequent discovery of isolated human bones in Beaker settlements. Despite this link, there are surprisingly few secondary burials of this date in earthen long barrows.

Beaker burials in Wessex show another significant pattern. The first examples, which date from the middle Beaker phase, do not occur in the area around Stonehenge, and only late Beaker burials are known close to the monument (Whittle 1981: 321). These patterns led Whittle to observe that 'at an early phase richer Beaker burials and major henges were in some sense in competition or . . . the users of each were involved in activities contradictory to each other' (*ibid.*: 329). Similarly, Shennan (1982a: 156) suggests that this contrast reflects the differences between two separate ideologies:

It may be . . . that what we are seeing is the replacement of an ideology in which the existence of heirarchy was legitimated by the provision of monuments and ritual 'beneficial' to the whole community, by one in which inequality was more openly expressed and presented as natural by the consumption of prestige items and ritual symbols by powerful individuals.

Adopting the finer chronology suggested by Lanting and Van der Waals, we may be able to trace this changing relationship in even greater detail, although the closer the chronological sequence the harder it is to subject it to independent checks. Burgess' recent analysis suggests an alternation between the richer burials and monument building (1980a: 107). He argues that the major series of Beaker burials in Dorset and Wiltshire belongs to their steps 2 and 3 and that the next group of elaborate graves dates to the Wessex 1 phase, which overlapped step 7. It seems possible that the main Beaker activity at the henges took place in between these two phases during a period in which burials were rather simpler. Something of this interplay can be seen in Table 4.4.

Table 4.4 The sequence of henges and complex burials in Wessex

Types of site	Ceramic associations	Estimated dates
Henge monuments with timber circles	Grooved Ware	2050–1850 bc
Burials avoiding areas with large henges	Beakers (steps 2 & 3)	1950–1800 bc
Reconstruction of existing henges	Beakers (mainly middle period)	1800–1600 bc
Burials, no longer avoiding henges	Beakers (step 7), Collared Urns and Food Vessels	from 1600 bc

The character of Beaker activity at henge monuments is rather difficult to interpret and varies in intensity from Mount Pleasant with a substantial amount of this characteristic pottery (Wainwright 1979a: 86–8) to Stonehenge with a small number of sherds (Whittle 1981: 305). Also, it seems to have been during this period that some of the henge monuments were rebuilt in stone, including Stonehenge itself. This development is not confined to Wessex, even though its chronology is best known in that area. Nor was the construction of stone circles always associated with Beaker pottery, since some examples date from the third millenium (Burl 1976). It is usually supposed that such circles were direct replacements of timber monuments on these sites, but this interpretation is much too simple. Although the building of stone circles provides a clue to the character of their wooden prototypes, we must not exaggerate the evidence of continuity. On sites where radiocarbon dates provide a close control, it seems likely that the stone settings were erected some time after the timber uprights had rotted. For example, the posts at Mount Pleasant would have lasted roughly eighty years, but the timber circles on this site were built around 2000 bc and the stone setting three centuries later. Molluscan evidence shows that the site became overgrown during this interval (Wainwright 1979a: 230).

The reconstruction of certain sites in stone created a uniformity which had not existed previously. Some important timber monuments were not replaced – for example, the Southern Circle at Durrington Walls (Wainwright and Longworth 1971: 23–38) – whilst stone circles were built on other sites where timber settings may never have existed. There were further contrasts. The forms of the stone monuments need not reflect the layout in the timber phase. Whilst the timber circles at the Sanctuary were replaced by stone circles (Cunnington 1931), similar structures at Mount Pleasant were replaced by a cove and three standing stones (Wainwright 1979a: 28–31). Nor is there a consistent relationship between the complexity of the monuments in these separate phases. The Aubrey Holes of Stonehenge 1 form an accurate circle, whilst the stone monument of phase 3a involves more complex geometry (Atkinson 1956; Thom and Thom 1978: 138–62). Woodhenge contained a series of oval rings in its initial phase (Hogg 1981), but apparently these were replaced by only two stones (Cunnington 1929: 14). It seems as if the main function of the stone-built monuments was not to reproduce the original site in a more durable form, but to enhance, commemorate or even renew the relationships expressed in its initial construction. If this reasoning is correct, such a process might be compared with the reuse of existing enclosures and long barrows.

The sheer scale of activity at the henge monuments cannot be ignored. The labour requirements of some of these stone settings far exceeded those of their simpler prototypes. To build the original earthwork at Stonehenge required only 11,000 man hours, but Stonehenge 2 would have taken about 360,000 man hours to construct and in fact was left unfinished (Startin and Bradley 1981). Even if draught oxen had been used for some tasks, the impact on the energy budget would have been considerable, especially as it was in the Beaker phase that the bluestones were introduced from south-west Wales. Stonehenge 3a may have replaced this monument without a significant interval and required about 1,750,000 man hours, between three and four times the amount of work needed to dig the ditch of Durrington Walls several centuries earlier (*ibid.*). There is a date of 1720 ± 110 bc for this phase at Stonehenge (BM 46). Such estimates give the impression of an 'inflationary' spiral in the labour requirements of the large monuments.

True to Cherry's original model, this peak of monument building seems to have ended at about the time that Burgess' second group of rich burials was being deposited, towards the beginning of Wessex 1. As Burgess has noted, there is an air of finality about the treatment of existing public monuments and soon the majority were abandoned altogether (cf. Burl 1981a: 193–4). The changes of plan at Stonehenge are not dated very closely, but at Mount Pleasant a gigantic palisade was constructed around the hilltop in the seventeenth century bc, and was burnt or partly demolished before its timbers had rotted (Wainwright 1979a: 48–64). Similarly, the ditch of the henge monument at Arbor Low, which may have been left unfinished, contained a Beaker arrowhead in its lowest level. Stones were laid out on this site prior to building a large circle, but their ramps were never constructed and the site was abandoned (Gray 1903). The Beaker period also sees the last use of megalithic tombs. For example at West Kennett, a chambered long barrow containing middle Beaker pottery was filled in completely (S. Piggott 1962 *passim*). Only two major sites in Wessex, Stonehenge and Mount Pleasant, seem to have been maintained after this date. From this stage onwards individual burials appear to have played a more prominent role. The same development is expressed by the construction of new round barrows on top of existing long mounds. This practice is fairly widely distributed, but with one exception, which contained a late Beaker, all the newly-built mounds are associated with Food Vessels, Collared Urns or 'Wessex' daggers. Similarly, a round barrow containing a Food Vessel was built on top of the henge monument at Arbor Low (Gray 1903). In each case it seems that individuals were taking over sites formerly associated with the community.

This change can be seen in other spheres and most of the patterns described in the previous chapter came to an end at about this time. Grooved Ware was playing a less important role in the henge monuments, where it had been replaced by Beaker pottery. Peterborough Ware was also going out of fashion; this tradition seems to have merged with the Beaker series, producing a distinctive domestic coarse ware (Whittle 1981) as well as a range of fine pottery for use in burial rites. With these developments, the evidence for parallel assemblages comes to an end (cf. Fig. 4.2). The same also applies to the long-distance exchange of stone axes (I. F. Smith 1979). If these developments show the break with the past that Burgess suggests (1980a: 80), they may result from a change in the ways in which power was exercised and displayed. Undoubtedly, the transition could have been sudden and even dramatic, but we cannot write political history from such vague patterns.

THE EVIDENCE OF BURIALS

The second part of the basic model places a greater emphasis on the burial record and it is to this evidence that we now turn. We need to ask two questions of this material. How far are we entitled to suggest that individual position and attainments were reflected in funerary rites, and how far can we identify changes in the scale and complexity of burial ritual during the remainder of the second millenium?

As Petersen's work has shown, generalisations based on early fieldwork are difficult to sustain (1981: 236–71), but there may be strength in numbers, so this account relies mainly on two extensively studied areas, the Wessex chalk and the Yorkshire Wolds (Burgess 1980a: 295–324). Exceptions can still be found to practically every point.

Although Early Bronze Age barrows differ considerably in size, form and complexity, normally the earliest burial occupies the central position and contains the most elaborate artefacts, although in some cases these graves were disturbed or re-used at a later stage (*ibid.*). Despite increasing evidence for a dual rite, cremation is normally secondary to inhumation, where the latter was practised at all. If the earliest burial was a cremation, usually later inhumations are absent (*ibid.*). Cremations may be subsidiary to inhumations even within the same feature. It may have been important to retain the bones of certain individuals, whereas those of others could be destroyed. Rowlands (1980: 51) has suggested that this distinction between two different ways of treating the body has a wider significance: 'It is quite feasible that inhumation: survival of the bones: continuity as a prerogative of high rank may be contrasted with cremation: burning and destruction of flesh and bones: destruction of the individual identity: low rank'.

The same distinction between dominant and subordinate positions within one barrow may be recognised in the distribution of different types of urn. Although normally this pattern is treated as evidence of sequence, radiocarbon dates show that communities would have had the choice of several different vessels at any one time. Thus in Yorkshire Collared Urns are usually secondary to Food Vessels (Manby 1980b: 316), and in Wessex Deverel-Rimbury pottery is secondary to both of these types (Bradley

1981a). When more than one style occurs in a peripheral position, they may have been buried on different sides of the mound. At Steyning, Deverel-Rimbury deposits were found on three sides of a small barrow and a Collared Urn on the fourth (Burstow 1958), and at Latch Farm, Christchurch, a Collared Urn was found alongside a series of Deverel-Rimbury pots, and an Enlarged Food Vessel was recovered from the opposite side of the mound (C. M. Piggott 1938). The same principle applies to the burials of different groups in Yorkshire, where ninety percent of the male graves were from central positions within a round barrow, whilst children were often buried in its northern sector (Pierpoint 1980: 226).

The central burials tend to contain higher quality artefacts than those around them, and may be buried in coffins or receive other special treatment (*ibid.*). Often they are in deeper graves than the other burials. It is normal for mounds and even individual graves to have received a series of later burials (Petersen 1972). Barrows of only one phase are rare in modern excavations.

There is less sign of a consistent relationship between the form of the covering mound and the character of the graves underneath it. In Wessex there is a rather weak connection between the distribution of the most impressive grave goods and the location of the large barrow cemeteries, although this does not mean that the largest mounds necessarily contained the richest material. In Yorkshire such a relationship applies more readily to large isolated barrows, often those situated in prominent positions (Pierpoint 1980: 239). On the other hand, it was in the late Beaker phase when attention was being paid to the provision of elaborate burials that round barrows in Wessex increased in size. It may have been at the same time that specialised forms of mound, the bell and disc barrows, were first adopted (Ozanne 1972; Bailey 1980: 19–25). Again, there is no direct connection between the forms of the more specialised mounds and the contents of the burials associated with them, but it is clear that in Wessex as a whole they do contain a higher proportion of 'rich' graves than other barrows. Over half of the burials in Piggott's list of 'rich' graves came from major cemeteries, and often more than one rich grave was found in each of these groups (cf. S. Piggott 1938: 102–6). All these features suggest that important distinctions *were* being made between different individuals, especially from the late Beaker period onwards. The frequent presence of more than one body in the same grave warns against too free a use of the term 'single' burial (cf. Petersen 1972).

If the complex sequence in many mounds has led to their description as 'cemetery barrows', the evidence of *barrow cemeteries* is still more complex. Such sites have already attracted a large amount of interest and speculation. They show different densities of barrows and a great variety of ground plans, and vary in size from four mounds to over forty. Some contain specialised types of mound, notably bell and disc barrows, whilst others are less conspicuous and show fewer superficial contrasts. Where there is sufficient dating evidence, it appears that cemeteries developed over a long period, the first deposits being buried during the Beaker period and the last dating from Wessex 2 or even later. There can be signs of a horizontal sequence, with the later barrows towards the edges of the group, but there is no evidence that early mounds were always supplanted by others. Rather, the earliest mounds can show the most phases of renewal, whilst later barrows were used less intensively. The essential feature is expansion rather than replacement.

None of these patterns is easy to explain. The fact that these cemeteries developed only gradually has persuaded some writers to interpret these sites as dynastic burial grounds. Indeed, Stephen Green has compared the rate of barrow construction during the second millenium with the average lifespan of different rulers documented in the ethnographic record (1974: 133). The very compact distributions of these cemeteries have also been discussed. Green has defined a series of different territories in the area around Stonehenge, using the barrows themselves as boundary markers (*ibid.*: 134–5), but other writers have thought that they contained the burials of communities who lived much further afield. Fleming, for example, has argued that the areas with the main cemeteries in Wessex may have been used by pastoralists who congregated there during the summer months (1971).

Some of the greatest barrow groups occur in Wessex, where the biggest cemetery on the Dorset Ridgeway contains about forty mounds (Fleming 1971). The larger cemeteries in Wiltshire are of similar size, whilst those on the upper Thames gravels contain as many as twenty barrows (Benson and Miles 1974). These large groups are unusual and over most of southern England, the one part of the country where comprehensive lists are available, the cemeteries contain fewer than ten mounds and sometimes fewer than five. There are rather larger cemeteries in East Anglia (Lawson, Martin and Priddy 1981).

Atkinson (1972) has suggested that the burials of this period may account for the entire population, but it is hard to reconcile such low estimates with the demands which would have been made by contemporary agriculture. The point is reinforced by estimates of the rate at which new barrows were built. In the Great Ouse Valley, Stephen Green estimates that one was constructed every six years (1974: 132), and even amidst the nucleated cemeteries of the Dorset Ridgeway the rate may have been no higher than a new barrow every four or five years (Royal Commission on Historical Monuments 1970: 427). For this reason it is possible that mound building was a special event.

Developments were not especially uniform in different parts of the country. The Wessex barrow cemeteries, in which a substantial share of the richer grave goods was buried, consisted of mounds of above average proportions (Fleming 1971). Despite the presence of bell and disc barrows in these groups, there is no consistent relationship between the number of specialised mounds and the size of the whole cemetery. In the regions with larger cemeteries, the barrow groups are more closely spaced than they are elsewhere. The main groups in H. S. Green's study of the Great Ouse valley were located about 10 km apart (1974), whilst those on the upper Thames gravels occur at intervals of about 4 km (Benson and Miles 1974). The smaller cemeteries on the chalk of Dorset appear at intervals of roughly 5 km (Fleming 1971), but in some areas, especially close to Stonehenge, the interval can be as little as one km (Royal Commission on Historical Monuments 1979). We can summarise these points by saying that the more extensive cemeteries contain a disproportionate share of rich graves and elaborate mounds, and also that they are closer together. In several parts of the country, the greatest concentration of cemeteries is found near to existing henge monuments. These cemeteries continued to develop long after the constructional phases on such sites had ended. At present it is not possible to tell whether these patterns reflect the distribution of settlement as a whole. They may represent a separate landscape of the dead. This question could be investigated by careful fieldwork. Whatever the outcome, these patterns do seem to indicate that communities were able to display their power as much through formal cemeteries as individual graves.

Due to the poor quality of the data, this discussion has covered a wide time-span. Now we must consider the second of our questions – can any chronological patterns be recognised in the scale and character of burial rites? There has been so much discussion of the nature of Early Bronze Age grave goods that it would be tedious to offer a full discussion of this material. Just two key points need emphasis: the scale of the exchange networks through which these items were passing; and the evidence for fluctuations in their supply or deposition. Lastly, these patterns can be related to what is known about the development of settlement.

The objects in the more elaborate graves can be divided into two groups: those which developed from the repertoire of the British Later Neolithic; and others which have an international character. Many of the latter group belong to a west European tradition in which basic styles of copper, bronze and gold objects were widely copied and exchanged. Such extensive patterns could develop only after the integration of southern England with the European mainland through the extension of the Beaker network; the scale of the larger system overshadows the detailed differences in the orientation of contacts. In the Beaker phase these were probably towards the Rhineland and the Low Countries – the similarity between the domestic pottery of the Netherlands and eastern England provides a striking instance of this link (Gibson 1982). In Wessex 1 the closest connections were with Brittany, and appear in the burial record (Gerloff 1975). Similarly, the closest relations in Wessex 2 were with graves in Central Europe (*ibid.*).

Within this community of tradition some very specific links can be identified, for example the Armorico-British daggers of Wessex 1, which were made of foreign metal (Ottaway 1974), the Tumulus Culture pins imported during Wessex 2 (Gerloff 1975: 110–12) or the introduction of Baltic amber (Shennan 1982b). Less direct relationships are indicated by artefacts which may have been made in Britain. The case of faience beads illustrates this point. Although it was once believed that these had a common source in Egypt, it is now suspected that they were also made in several areas of Europe, including Scotland (Newton and Renfrew 1970); but whilst this evidence precludes their dissemination by long distance trade, it does not explain the appearance of this class of material at this specific time. Southern England was only one area which saw the rise of ranked societies during the second millenium bc, and there is no reason to doubt that elites in quite distant regions were in contact with one another. Thus occasional links with the Mediterranean should occasion no surprise; they are an indication of the scale of this system, but they cannot explain its development, since they appear only in its later stages. 'Links' with Mycenae like the Bush Barrow grave group are of some chronological interest but otherwise they add little but local colour (cf. Renfrew 1968).

The artefacts that were travelling at this time may have played similar roles to the Neolithic prestige objects considered earlier. The main difference is that they were deposited in graves more often than the latter types. Some items, like the goldwork of this period, may even have been made specifically for funerals (Coles and Taylor 1971: 13), whilst other types – daggers and axes – can be depicted on carvings in burial cists (Simpson and Thawley 1973; Schmidt 1979). It would be wrong to suppose that the special significance of these objects resulted in an even supply. The rate at which these items were made or imported may have fluctuated, with the result that in some phases characteristic types were imitated in more accessible materials. Thus in the Beaker phase metal daggers were imitated in flint, and goldwork was copied in jet; whilst in the later Wessex period faience beads, bronze pins and bronze daggers were all being copied in bone. Significantly, the latter were depicted within their sheaths, emphasising the non-utilitarian character of these finds (Kinnes 1978). Overall, there were probably more grave goods in Wessex 1 than Wessex 2, when there is far greater evidence for the production of copies. Appropriately, the earlier daggers were made from continental metal sources, whilst the later examples used a succession of British ores (Ottaway 1974). Again, copies of metal types were more common in highland areas than in the south, where continental sources were more accessible. Even in lowland

England, the main use of elaborate grave goods came just after the abandonment of henges. This is to be expected from the original model.

BURIALS AND THE DEVELOPMENT OF SETTLEMENT

There is another way of looking for changes in the burial record, one which allows a direct comparison with settlement evidence. So far the discussion has proceeded entirely in terms of the conventional typological sequence. This has given problems. For example, until recently it was assumed that the late Wessex Culture could be placed in the middle of the second millenium (Renfrew 1968), but when a series of Wessex 2 graves were dated, the results tended to be much later than had originally been expected, and fell between about 1300 and 1000 bc (Barrett 1980a; 82). More recently, dates for Wessex 1 graves have become available, and overlap with those from late Beaker burials (Burgess 1980a: 107). The effect is to open a gap in the radiocarbon sequence in which there is little evidence of complex deposits anywhere in England. It is tempting to question this result, arguing that these difficulties arise from irregularities in the calibration curve, or that the early group of dates is created by sampling old timbers taken from coffins or pyres. Neither argument really alters the problem. There is no shortage of dates in the interval between 1550 and 1300; the difficulty is that these do not come from elaborate burials. Similarly, it is inconsistent to doubt the 'early' dates because they could be based on old wood, but to accept 'late' dates, which in at least two cases are on samples from coffins or pyres. Many more determinations are needed in order to check this observation, but at the moment it appears that deposition did not proceed as evenly as the stylistic sequence might imply. This suggestion is not easy to test, although it is worth pointing out that typology is a way of dating production and radiocarbon a method of fixing deposition (Kristiansen 1978a). The interval between these two processes need not be of fixed duration. As our model suggests, funerals may have been less elaborate in periods of greater stability.

One feature of interest is that the peaks of deposition just suggested bracket a period of expansion in the settlement pattern. The mid-second millenium saw a widespread phase of colonisation, shown in the utilisation of areas which are now heathland and moorland. These include the New Forest, Dartmoor, the Wealden sands, the Derbyshire gritstone and the North York Moors (Bradley 1978a: 115). This expansion has long been recognised in the widening distribution of round barrows, especially those associated with Collared Urns, and latterly by the identification of contemporary houses and fields. This widening of the settled landscape was originally attributed to 'Urn Folk' (Childe 1940: 145–62); although this view has gone out of fashion, no explanation has taken its place.

The broad dating of this development is confirmed by pollen analysis, and by investigation of a number of settlements. For example, the main period in which the East Moors of Derbyshire were settled was between about 1600 and 1500 bc (Hicks 1972), and the main settlement of the North York Moors has dates between about 1500 and 1400 bc. The main colonisation of Dartmoor also took place in the mid-second millenium; indeed, the well-known settlement at Shaugh Moor itself began life about 1500 bc (Wainwright and Smith 1980). Much of the newly settled land is adjacent to areas in which complex burials have been found. Relationships include those between the Wessex chalkland and the New Forest, the South Downs and the Weald, the limestone and gritstone of Derbyshire, and the Yorkshire Wolds and the North York Moors. Since there is no independent evidence of population growth, we should consider whether this phase of expansion was related to the economic needs of the core areas. If so, the first group of elaborate burials could mark the consolidation of authority which made these changes possible.

Apart from food, the newly settled land could provide other commodities. Shale ornaments were made on the Derbyshire gritstone (Beswick 1975), and the settlement of the North York Moors allowed access to the source of Whitby jet (cf. Shepherd 1981). Similarly, Dartmoor could have supplied the metal requirements of a wider area. However, it should not be supposed that these changes amount to a shift in the location of settlement; more probably they represent the *extension* of existing subsistence patterns into more marginal areas, where traces of those activities can still be recovered today. Their subordinate status may be reflected in the burial record. The mounds and cairns in the newly settled regions are less elaborate than those in the core areas, and the range of associated material is usually much more restricted. This applies not only to pottery styles but also to the size of the monuments. This point can be illustrated by the contrasting character of the burial monuments on the Derbyshire limestone and on the surrounding moors (Table 4.5; cf. Marsden 1977; Hart 1981: 56–7; Hawke-Smith 1981: Fig. 5.4). In view of the restricted range of grave goods in the latter area, it is worth considering the idea put forward by Service (1971: 157–8) that 'chiefdoms . . . tend to expand by

Table 4.5 The contrasting character of burial monuments in different parts of the Peak District

	Limestone ('core area')	Gritstone ('periphery')
Size of barrows	Larger	Smaller
Range of grave goods	Wider	More limited
Metalwork in graves	More frequent	Less frequent
Fine flint in graves	More frequent	Less frequent
Jet in graves	More frequent	Less frequent
Main ceramics in graves	Beakers, Food Vessels	Collared Urns

a sort of budding off of families that have low potentiality in the inherit-ance scheme . . . To the extent that the spatial distribution of growth is unimpeded, there is a tendency for distance from the original centre to correspond to rank differences among the local groups'.

The extension of settlement into these areas makes the important point that the regions with complex burials cannot be treated in isolation. The extension of political relations into continental Bronze Age societies meant that such areas might become increasingly dependent on a wider hinterland if they were to maintain their new role. A similar expansion of settlement can be seen in Europe, where for the first time it is possible to distinguish between core areas and a dependent periphery. The fortunes of these two areas cannot be treated separately. Communities on the periphery of ranked societies may have lacked much freedom of action, whilst the core areas themselves drew on the economic reserves provided by their new neighbours. Burial rites could play quite different roles in these two zones, reinforcing the power structure at the centre, and at the same time playing down social differences in the newly settled areas.

THE END OF EARLY BRONZE AGE SOCIETY

The interpretation in this chapter now has four separate elements: the construction of public monuments; the provision of conspicuous burials; land clearance and the exploitation of exchange. All four of these can be brought together in studying the last centuries of the second millenium. Before that time, the system had shown a basic stability, but by 1000 bc it had been swept away. The very different patterns which followed are discussed in Chapter 5. Here we need to consider the sources of instability and to ask how far the responses which they drew conform to the original model.

The empirical evidence is well known. From a landscape whose most prominent features were the burial mounds, we move into a period in which their place is taken by field systems, farms, land boundaries and hill forts; and from a society whose basic structure was expressed through ritual and ceremonial to one in which food production and warfare played a more visible role. There is no sign of an elite burial rite and no evidence for the continued use of ceremonial centres. Most of the older core areas lost their distinctive character and were reduced to a marginal position around the edges of new centres of power.

Why did these changes come about? Which were the unstable elements in the Earlier Bronze Age system? Four features appear to be relevant to these questions: changes in the settled landscape, brought about by human misuse of the soil; climatic change; fluctuations in the intensity of prestige trade with the core areas and changes in the orientation of exchange between different regions of the country. These factors can perhaps be combined into two basic approaches. If natural and anthropogenic factors affected the business of food production, it would be difficult for an elite to maintain its position and to engage in external trade; and if the supply of special artefacts was impeded, the same groups would find it much harder to maintain their traditional status.

The evidence for environmental change is ambiguous, because it is difficult to decide how much of the evidence results from climatic variation rather than anthropogenic factors (Bradley 1980: 59). In either case the chief impact of these changes was felt in the more marginal areas settled in the mid-second millenium. In these regions there is evidence for widespread podsolisation and for the development of peat bogs. To some extent changes in their soils may have been accelerated by over use, with the result that they became increasingly acid and poorly drained. At about the same time there is evidence for a change towards a cooler, wetter climate which might have occasioned a retreat from the more exposed upland areas (A. Harding 1982). Regions in which the scale of activity slackened include Dartmoor, the heathlands of southern Wessex, the Derbyshire gritstone and the North York Moors. It is not necessary to distinguish between the contributions of these two factors. On Dartmoor, for example, the major phase of settlement took place before the main development of the peat, and climate may have been a major cause of change (Smith, Coppen, Wainwright and Beckett 1981), whilst on the North York Moors the soil was capable of sustaining a second period of use during the Iron Age (Spratt and Simmons 1976), and the damage does not seem to have been lasting. It may have been hard to maintain crop production if the growing season was reduced.

At the same time, there are signs that the supply of prestige items was failing. Grave goods were more widely copied in other materials; daggers were no longer made from imported metal, and when they were finally buried some of them were completely worn out (Bradley 1980: 62). As these developments took place in some areas, other regions were assuming a more prominent role. Objects which might once have found their way into Wessex barrows were being deposited in the Thames valley and East Anglia, where rapiers now succeeded daggers (Fig. 4.3).

Again there can be no single reason for this change, which is easier to observe than it is to explain. The growing importance of these lowland regions may be related to their agricultural potential, especially at a time when the core areas were flanked by tracts of wasted land. The lower Thames may have had more to offer than areas whose economic structure was in jeopardy. At the same time, the collapse of the earlier system may owe something to more distant developments. As mentioned earlier, southern England was at the edge of a network of ranked societies which extended over much of Europe and perhaps reached the Mediterranean. It was at the height of Britain's own difficulties that the structure of

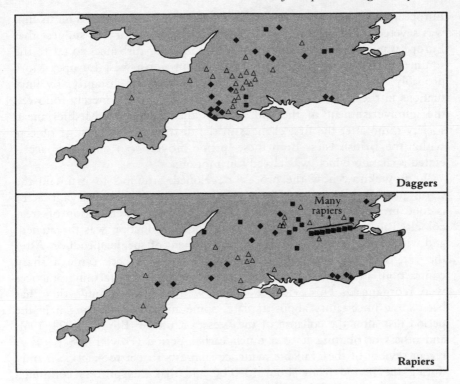

- ■ finds from regions mainly of Class 1 (good quality) land
- ◆ finds from regions mainly of Class 2 (medium quality) land
- △ finds from regions mainly of Class 3 (poorer quality) land

The two bar charts show the contrasting distributions of these artefact types in relation to the three land classes and the changing ratio of grave goods to river finds.

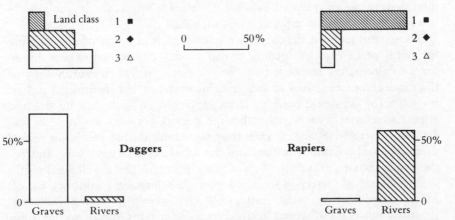

Fig. 4.3 The distributions of bronze daggers (after Gerloff, 1975) and rapiers (after Rowlands, 1976), in relation to the agricultural potential of the regions in which they were found. Land quality is graded from 1 to 3.

European exchange networks was disturbed and the Mediterranean link was severed (cf. Burgess 1980a: 155–7). It is unnecessary to suggest that Europe was overrun by marauders, or even that disturbances so far to the south provoked a single response throughout north-west Europe. More probably, the period of crisis was reflected, however distantly, by fluctuations in the scale of exchange. Just as climatic change merely followed the impoverishment of the soil, so too the collapse of Mediterranean society came after the first changes in the distribution of prestige objects within the British Isles. Both these 'prime movers' can only have accelerated a change which was already in motion.

We now know how the process developed: attempts to maintain the status quo failed. How were those attempts made? The first relevant factor is food production. We have argued that with the deterioration of areas colonised in the mid-second millenium, food production was threatened, and with it any arrangements for the movement of surplus produce. After the extension of the existing agricultural regime, there came a sharp contraction, and only at this stage does it seem likely that farming practices were reorganised. This evidence is very well known, although there has been some uncertainty about its date, some authorities locating it in the period just after the collapse of the Wessex Culture (Burgess 1974: 196), and others attributing it to a much earlier period (Fowler 1981: 40). A recent review of the available evidence suggests that it took place mainly during the period from about 1300 bc and that this process continued unbroken into the first millenium (Bradley 1980). For that reason its detailed intepretation is treated in the next chapter. For present purposes, we can suggest that intensification began as an attempt to maintain the existing social system by achieving higher levels of production in these areas which still remained fertile. In the earlier phase food production was increased by the *extension* of existing practices. Only when it was already too late were there attempts at *reorganisation*.

The second factor is the use of complex burials as a way of emphasising the status of an elite. According to our model, one would expect this to form an alternative response to these pressures. In fact the chronology of the more elaborate graves shows just this evidence. As mentioned earlier, the dates for Wessex 2 barrows have proved to be unexpectedly late and appear to cluster over a rather limited period between about 1300 and 1000 bc (Barrett 1980a: 82). Thus they were built during the major period of change and continued in use until the whole system gave way. Indeed, the last elaborate graves in Wessex may postdate the development of a different kind of society in the south-east. A beleaguered minority cut off in an isolated enclave, communities in Wessex were maintaining traditional practices when these were effectively obsolete. This surely accounts for two very striking observations: the worn-out condition of the latest grave goods, which could have consisted of artefacts which had gone out of fashion (Bradley 1980: 62), and the building of extremely late bell barrows which no longer contained burials at all (Horsey and Shackley 1980: 41–2). These mounds take the sequence down to 1000 bc.

Lastly, there are the ceremonial centres. As mentioned earlier, only two of these sites, Stonehenge and Mount Pleasant, are known to have lasted into the late Wessex period. Significantly, Mount Pleasant was abandoned about 1300 bc (Wainwright 1979a). By that time Stonehenge could have been the sole survivor of a class of monument which had existed for more than a millenium. It had made the greatest demands upon manpower and represented the most elaborate undertaking of this whole society. Cherry's theory predicted that elaborate monuments might be constructed in two distinct phases, during the formative years of social evolution and also in the final period of decline when the whole structure of society needed to be reinforced. The sequence at Stonehenge is doubly symbolic (Atkinson 1956). In the later years of the Wessex Culture a fresh attempt was made to construct a really complex monument, but significantly this ambitious conception had to be abandoned in favour of a simpler design. The transition between Stonehenge IIIb and IIIc is dated to 1240 ± 150 bc, the period in which so many other changes were taking place (1–2445). Finally, in phase IIIc the monument was completed, but now it no longer expressed the aspirations of its original builders.

This chapter and its predecessor have discussed 'the Age of Stonehenge' (cf. Burgess 1980a). Surely it is significant that the completion of that monument was to be its last act. We began by comparing the building of henges with the construction of pyramids. The most appropriate conclusion comes from Byron's 'Don Juan':

'What are the hopes of man? Old Egypt's king
Cheops erected the first pyramid
And largest, thinking it was just the thing
To keep his memory whole, and mummy hid;
But somebody or other rummaging,
Burglariously broke his coffin lid:
Let not a monument give you or me hopes,
Since not a pinch of dust remains of Cheops.'

5 The embarrassment of riches
– The consumption of fine metalwork
(1300 bc– 700 BC)

'. . . It was nothing more than the fact that every human being's dislike of every other human being's attempts to get on – a dislike in which today we are all agreed – in that country crystallised earlier, assuming the form of a sublimated ceremonial that might have become of great importance if its evolution had not been prematurely cut short by a catastrophe.'

Robert Musil, *The Man Without Qualities*

'Halsey Edge was a tall scrawny man of fifty-something, with a pinched yellow face and no hair at all. He called himself 'a ghoul by profession and inclination' . . . and he was very proud of his collection of battle-axes. He was not so bad once you had resigned yourself to the fact that you were in for occasional cataloguings of his armoury – stone axes, copper axes, hammer axes, adze axes, Mesopotamian axes, Hungarian axes, Nordic axes and all of them looking pretty moth-eaten.'

Dashiell Hammett, *The Thin Man*

The results of field archaeology often have a cumulative effect. After a long period in which interpretations remain largely intact, a series of chance discoveries breaks new ground. During the last decade this has happened with the Later Bronze Age. For nearly twenty years this period lacked any real identity, but now it is revealed as a major time of change (Table 5.1). The main monuments of the second millenium went out of use, and the landscape was remodelled around the needs of intensive agriculture. Barrows were replaced by houses, and henges were replaced by hill forts. Field systems have been identified over large areas of the countryside. As a result of intensive fieldwork, the number of dated settlements is higher than anyone would have expected (Fig. 5.1).

The artefact evidence has increased at much the same rate, but is strangely dissociated from these sites. For years there was practically no link between the field evidence and the elaborate metalwork, and for this reason some of the settlements were dated to a later period. With the identification of a ceramic sequence running in parallel to the sequence of metalwork (Barrett 1980b), it might be supposed that the problems were

Table 5.1 Terminology and chronology used in Chapter 5 in relation to major types of monument. Calibration of radiocarbon dates after Clark (1975)

	1300	1200	1100	1000	900	800	700	600	500 bc
Terminology	*Middle Bronze Age*				*Late Bronze Age*				
	MBA 1	MBA 2			LBA 1	LBA 2	LBA 3		LBA 4/ EIA 1
Industrial phase	Acton Park	Taunton			Penard		Wilburton Ewart Park		Llynfawr
	Later Bronze Age								Iron Age
Complex burials	– – – – –								
River metal	– – – –							– – – – –	
Main periods of hoarding									
Defended sites		?			?		?		
Mucking type enclosures			?			?		?	– – –
Rich riverside settlement?			?			?			
	1595	1495	1385	1250	1100	975	880	800	700 BC

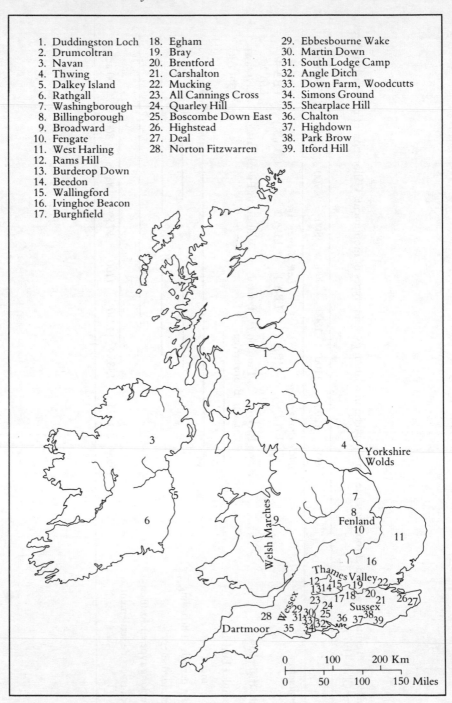

1. Duddingston Loch
2. Drumcoltran
3. Navan
4. Thwing
5. Dalkey Island
6. Rathgall
7. Washingborough
8. Billingborough
9. Broadward
10. Fengate
11. West Harling
12. Rams Hill
13. Burderop Down
14. Beedon
15. Wallingford
16. Ivinghoe Beacon
17. Burghfield
18. Egham
19. Bray
20. Brentford
21. Carshalton
22. Mucking
23. All Cannings Cross
24. Quarley Hill
25. Boscombe Down East
26. Highstead
27. Deal
28. Norton Fitzwarren
29. Ebbesbourne Wake
30. Martin Down
31. South Lodge Camp
32. Angle Ditch
33. Down Farm, Woodcutts
34. Simons Ground
35. Shearplace Hill
36. Chalton
37. Highdown
38. Park Brow
39. Itford Hill

Fig. 5.1   The main sites and regions considered in Chapter 5.

at an end, but the only result was that two independent bodies of information were now available for study where only one had existed previously. Few connections could be found between the two halves of the evidence. As a result, different reconstructions could be offered, the metalwork with its weapons and personal ornaments suggesting a society with differences of wealth and rank (Coombs 1975), and the settlement evidence implying a largely undifferentiated pattern outside the areas with early hill forts (Cunliffe 1978b: 11–30). This chapter will be an attempt to integrate these two types of information.

Despite the real advances achieved in recent fieldwork, there can be no doubt that it is the metalwork which should dominate the discussion. There are great numbers of bronze hoards in the country, and over 250 gold finds, even excluding Ireland (J. Taylor 1980). In the British Isles as a whole there are about 2,600 weapons of Later Bronze Age date (Burgess and Coombs 1979). Whilst this period has produced an armoury worthy of Halsey Edge, the question that should have been asked at the outset – how so many objects made their way into the archaeological record – has been eclipsed by the recognition that here is a ready-made body of material for chronological, stylistic, spatial and technical analysis. In taking this material as 'given', metalwork specialists have failed to come to grips with its real complexity. The mere fact that this metalwork exists has been enough to start an academic industry, in which there has been too much concern with points of detail and too little with the significance of these objects to their makers. This chapter will emphasise the central importance of this material and the circumstances in which it was deposited.

Such a study must cover themes which have been highlighted in earlier chapters. The discussion of Deverel-Rimbury cemeteries brings in ideas first considered in relation to Earlier Neolithic tombs. We shall be concerned with elements of a prestige goods economy, as we were in analysing Later Neolithic society, and to a lesser extent the roles of burial monuments will also be considered again. The present discussion has a different emphasis from these accounts. Whilst these theories do apply to Later Bronze Age material, the extraordinary number of metal artefacts raises problems of its own. At an empirical level, it is hard to integrate such specialised deposits with the uniformity of the settlement evidence, and at a more theoretical level, the separation of finer artefacts from occupation sites and burials requires analysis in its own right.

During the period from the fall of the Wessex Culture to the beginning of iron working, the archaeological record sees the appearance of various largely new types of deposit. As mentioned earlier, the major paradox is that in a period which until recently was best known for its metalwork so few bronzes should have been discovered in settlements. Even those that have been found are usually small personal items or fragments of scrap (Needham and Burgess 1980). The remaining deposits take four main forms: grave goods, hoards, river finds and single finds. Each of these has been interpreted in a different way (Bradley 1982b).

Grave finds become increasingly rare during this period. They have been supposed to reflect the social identity of the dead person, although this need not be the case. Some communities *conceal* differences of rank in funeral rites, for example the Neolithic farmers considered in Chapter 2. Alternatively, great displays of wealth may help to emphasise social position during times of uncertainty, the approach suggested for the Earlier Bronze Age. Hoard finds become more prominent during the first millenium, but normally are interpreted in practical terms. They consist of two or more pieces of metalwork buried together on one occasion, and are classified according to their assumed owners or functions. The first approach divides this material into the so-called founder's hoards, merchant's hoards, craftsmen's hoards and personal hoards (Evans 1881: 457–9), whilst the second method distinguishes between secular hoards and votive hoards (Levy 1982). Groups of material in the first category have been considered as personal possessions, or as metalwork in various stages of the production cycle from initial manufacture to the collection of scrap for remelting. The second class is sometimes regarded as sacrifices or funeral offerings, an interpretation more common on the Continent than in Britain. Most often, these deposits are not explained at all, and are used as steps in building a chronology. It is a moot point whether this can be achieved using deposits of unknown character.

The third group of finds comes from 'wet places' – rivers, lakes and peat bogs. These objects have provoked more discussion than the others. They consist mainly of weapons, but their integrity as a class has been questioned and different writers have considered whether their composition has been biased during their recovery (Bradley 1979; Ehrenberg 1980): could the process of dredging favour only the larger artefacts, or could such finds have been eroded from settlements on dry land? With greater knowledge of settlement finds, these objections seem less helpful (Needham and Burgess 1980). There has been considerable debate concerning the interpretation of this material. Does it result from chance losses at fords or from accidents during navigation? Do river finds reflect the sites of battles? If they were deliberate deposits, were they sacrifices to water deities? There is a danger of neat equations – for example, Burgess has pointed out how such finds become more frequent with the climatic deterioration of the first millenium bc (1974: 197). Again, it seems possible that these finds assumed the same roles as grave goods, which are remarkably rare throughout this period. Only the single finds escape this controversy. Despite their frequency and often their fine condition, these have been regarded simply as chance losses.

Such a complicated scheme raises more problems than it solves, and by proposing anecdotal explanations for most of the finds, it separates them from the mainstream of prehistoric studies. There are several reasons for believing that such an extensive body of artefacts requires a more searching analysis, if only because so few of these ideas reflect the quantity and quality of such finds. Metalwork which took a long time to make can hardly have come to us through the incompetence of so many boatmen and the forgetfulness of so many smiths.

There is the further problem that these categories are not self-sufficient. The contents of these different groups may change with time or may alternate from one region to another. Similarly, objects in two different categories sometimes prove to be interrelated. Since these characteristic patterns exist across much of north-west Europe, it is unnecessary to provide many examples here (cf. Bradley 1982b). One case in which the form of deposition changed concerns the way in which weapons were deposited. In the Early Bronze Age most of the daggers are found in graves (Gerloff 1975), whereas many of the Middle Bronze Age rapiers are known as river finds (Rowlands 1976: 396–422). Weapons also provide an example of regional patterning: it is well known that Late Bronze Age swords are found mainly in rivers in southern England (Ehrenberg 1980) and in hoards in Scotland (J. Coles 1960). A case of complementary patterning is illustrated by the finding of apparently male weaponry in these rivers and of supposedly female ornaments as hoards and single finds on dry land (Bradley 1982b: 115). If the analytical categories overlap, it is premature to treat hoards, single finds and settlement finds as elements of a 'utilitarian' system, and grave goods and river finds as parts of a 'ritual' tradition. It is even less satisfactory to offer intuitive interpretations of the first group and to leave the rest in limbo, declaring that questions of religious belief are beyond the limits of inference. These different types of deposit may sometimes be interdependent and if we are to investigate them at all, we must develop theories which embrace the similarities as well as the differences. As a first step, let us suggest that the common element is that these deposits were made consciously and voluntarily. It is harder to show that they were meant to be recovered, the crucial problem in the law of Treasure Trove.

Taking this broader approach, we can find two basic interpretations of the deposition or destruction of 'wealth' items. One considers these processes as a method of controlling the supply of objects and thus of maintaining their value; the other sees the act of deposition as the important feature. Each presupposes a different kind of society.

The first approach owes most to modern economic analysis. It assumes that bronze artefacts were valuable as well as useful, and that their value was determined by fluctuations in supply, which would make them either more or less abundant. This seems a reasonable approach, since the raw material was introduced into lowland Britain from outside. In Denmark, Kristiansen (1978b) has tried to identify such fluctuations from the amount of wear on surviving artefacts, and has shown how the supply of bronzes was most stable in areas with a productive economy. Where the supply was erratic or inadequate, artefacts would be used over longer periods and would become more worn. These objects might be recycled, but they would rarely be discarded. When too many bronzes were available, there would be different problems. Due to the length of the exchange networks, there may have been no control over the production areas, and the only way of maintaining the value of bronze would be by reducing the amount in circulation. At such times, metalwork could be deposited in large amounts. The supply could have been regulated at different levels in society – by the smiths who would see no advantage in unnecessary over-production, or by an elite who would be unable to maintain their position by gift-giving if the value of those gifts fell too sharply. In this scheme the destruction of metalwork is a way of preventing inflation.

Kristiansen has suggested that many bronze hoards in Denmark were actually funeral offerings (1978b), and if his calculations on wear rates are accepted, it would appear that episodes of increased supply resulted in more lavish offerings being made to the dead. The difficulties with this model should be evident. It assumes a fairly uniform economy, which could be anachronistic, and in particular it requires a measure of co-ordination which might be beyond the scope of contemporary society. Secondly, if we assume that the scale of ritual practice was conditioned by the economics of the bronze trade, there is a danger of imposing our own values on Bronze Age society and of treating this activity entirely as superstructure when other theories suggest that it played a central part in political relations. Lastly, there is some ambiguity concerning the levels at which control of the metal supply was exercised – partly by the smiths and partly by their patrons. Smiths may not have possessed such freedom of action. This point requires clarification, although it might suggest why different forms of deposit could have been employed within the same society (cf. Bradley 1982b: 112–16): control was taking place at several levels.

The main weakness of this approach is that it fails to relate supply and deposition in a satisfactory manner. On the other hand, it does suggest that the destruction of such material was intended to control its circulation. We can take this element from Kristiansen's scheme and investigate its application in other models. An approach which places more emphasis on subsistence has been advocated in papers by Flannery (1968), Ford (1972) and O'Shea (1981b). They distinguish between the different responses to economic uncertainty shown by mobile societies and more sedentary communities. Whilst mobile societies usually change their location in response to economic stress, this is not possible with groups who depend on stable agriculture. These writers suggest that in good years such societies may invest part of their economic surplus in special artefacts, which can be passed on to their neighbours in order to create reciprocal relations. The intention is to form alliances with groups who can supply food in periods of crisis. O'Shea describes this arrangement as 'social storage'. In his words it consists of 'the use of tokens as a means of storing food value'. This system runs the risk of inflation. As O'Shea says (1981b: 178)

The very stability which allows tokens to be accumulated threatens to destroy their value . . . The food value which can be obtained through the reconversion of valuables is strictly limited by the system's ability to produce and mobilise surplus. If too many valuables exist relative to the potential of the system, the value of such tokens will decrease . . . Because these items usually are consumed at a slower rate than food, such an imbalance is inevitable unless some mechanism exists to remove or further transform these tokens.

Not surprisingly, one mechanism for effecting this change is the destruction of these objects.

This theory has its limitations, since it makes little allowance for the uses of these objects within different communities, merely rationalising their functions in economic terms. The basic hypothesis is fairly easy to test. We can make a prediction concerning the kinds of pattern which this arrangement should leave in the archaeological record: the destruction of these items should occur in times of economic success but such objects should have been used in different ways in regions whose own economy was more stable. These questions will be discussed in detail later, but it is worth remarking that this approach might explain why the same artefacts could be deposited under different circumstances in nearby areas, for example the changing relationship between grave goods, hoards or river finds in parts of north-west Europe (cf. Bradley 1982b: 112–16). In some regions these may have been used as prestige goods, or as status objects, whilst in others they acted as 'tokens' and could be destroyed.

The third theory with an emphasis on regulating the metal supply has been mentioned in discussion of the Later Neolithic. This is Meillassoux's idea that the special character of prestige items is safeguarded by regular destruction (1968). Unlike the model just considered, it places more weight on the *social* roles of different artefacts. Rowlands (1980) has already commented on what seem to be similar patterns in the European Bronze Age, and it is worth stressing again how social control could be exercised through control over the distribution of special items. The danger, in Meillassoux's opinion, is that the number of special purpose items in circulation may increase until they threaten to spread into the general economy and to lose their exclusive character. If they do so, they need to be 'sterilised'. It is worth quoting from his account of marriage payments (1981: 71–2; my emphasis):

To prevent exchange-value from creeping into its circulation, it is necessary either that some central power produces bridewealth and regulates its circulation, or that the bridewealth payments be destroyed when their claims are extinct . . . In the context of a domestic society with no centralised power, the first solution is impossible. So destroying or neutralising bridewealth . . . is the only way to restore [its] original function . . . Some bridewealth payments which have been honoured [do] continue to exist and circulate. Indeed the communities which accumulate most goods are suspected of recovering them after having used them; social pressure can be exerted to make these communities destroy or neutralise them in some way . . . The destruction of wealth is thus the logical solution to a contradiction arising out of bridewealth circulation; *to eradicate incipient value from objects expected to remain neutral and economically dormant.*

This theory offers one explanation for the link between different categories of deposit and the supposedly 'invisible' funeral rites of the Later Bronze Age. Special items have to be destroyed when the relationships which they express come to an end. The European literature shows many instances in which items which had served as grave goods in one period appear in different contexts in the next phase (cf. Bradley 1982b: 112–13), and it would be worth extending this approach to some of the 'votive hoards'. Some Danish hoards, for example, contain sets of personal insignia which could have been accumulated over the lifetime of one or more individuals (Levy 1982). This theory might also apply where objects were discarded when they could still have been used. The main problem with applying this theory to the archaeological record is the quantity of material requiring explanation. This factor may restrict Meillassoux's interpretation to quite specific instances.

All three of these theories have been concerned with the need to withdraw material from circulation in order to preserve its character – its economic value in one case, its special uses in another. None of these approaches has considered the dramatic forms which destruction seems to have taken. The deposition of river finds may have been a spectacular event and, whatever the motives for discarding bronzework, there must have been a powerful embargo on its recovery. Another way of looking at this problem is to place the main emphasis on the act of destruction and to see this as the significant transaction. If so, it might be easier to appreciate why certain locations should be used so frequently for this purpose, for example stretches of the Thames in Greater London (Needham and Burgess, 1980). Burgess and Coombs suggest that there was a relationship between the deposition of metalwork and periods of instability in Bronze Age society (1979: v). If they are correct, we can suggest that the public discarding of fine bronzes might have been employed in building personal status. If river finds did take on the functions of grave offerings, funeral rites would be one occasion for this to take place. There are obvious analogies to this competitive approach to social relations in the ethnographic literature, for example the Big Man feasts of New Guinea (Strathern 1971), or the potlatches of North America (Rosman and Rubel 1971). They represent a kind of ritualised conflict, in which social prestige is accumulated through a display of wealth and generosity. The potlatch itself took place at rites of passage and could provide an occasion for contesting the succession when a leader died (*ibid.*).

It would be quite wrong to adopt this interpretation because it offers a ready-made analogy. There are two ways in which this outline must be amplified. Chapman (in prep.) points out that many examples of competitive consumption are found in societies in which a colonial government has forbidden warfare. These practices form a type of surrogate conflict. Although Musil was writing about the Austro-Hungarian empire, his words are appropriate here: 'every human being's dislike of every other human being's attempts to get on . . . [assumed] the form of a sublimated ceremonial'. The contrast between institutionalised consumption and actual warfare should be visible in the archaeological record. One possible example can be seen in southern Germany or north-west Bohemia, where the use of hill forts and hill settlements alternated with phases during which large numbers of bronze artefacts were deposited (Bradley 1981b: 232; Bradley 1982b: 119).

A second point is that many of the deposits considered here are supposedly of 'ritual' character. In Kristiansen's scheme surplus bronzes went into 'votive hoards' (1978b), and in Flannery's presentation of the social storage model one way of destroying special items was their deposition at the pyramid of La Venta (1968). It may be that so-called 'gifts to the gods' have a special character. This is suggested by Gregory's recent re-analysis of the potlatch and similar institutions (1980). He points out that most forms of competitive consumption concern gifts between rival individuals and their supporters and that the rules of reciprocity mean that the imbalance created on one occasion can be redressed on others. This pattern has been described as 'alternating disequilibrium' (Strathern 1971: 222). 'Gifts to the gods', on the other hand, serve rather different functions. They enhance the prestige of the person making them, without the risk that the equivalent gift will be returned. In this way they allow the continuous accumulation of prestige. Since these sacrifices cannot be recovered, such offerings also deplete the overall supply, making it more difficult for other contenders to trump the original effort. We can accept the reality of ritual activity without supposing that it lies entirely outside the scope of archaeological interpretation. Religion can function as economy and economy as religion (cf. Friedman 1979: 304–17).

All these patterns are contained within a broader model of Later Bronze Age society recently suggested by Rowlands (1980). Working from a reconstruction of the patterns of alliance suggested by Indo-European kinship terms, he suggests that the movement of fine metalwork, cattle and other commodities were linked to a wider European system in which exchange formed part of a process of social competition (Rowlands, 1980: 46–7):

Relations of dominance and hierarchy depend directly on the manipulation of relations of circulation and exchange and not on control of production *per se*. But circulation and exchange cannot be separated from the production of surpluses needed for such transactions and hence the resources required to produce them . . . Since alliances are established through exchange, involving material goods, women and symbolic knowledge, success depends on maintaining the flows of these resources. However, alliances in themselves do not bring prestige, but instead form the support base for local leaders to compete with each other in ceremonial displays of feasting and fighting, in the recitation of heroic deeds, and in claims to ritual and genealogical ties with the ancestors and the supernatural world.

Not all the elements of this scheme can be tested against the archaeological record, but the problems of deposition do assume a central role in discussion. Here, perhaps, we can recognise the final traces of alliances and exchange; we can infer something of the production and distribution of fine artefacts, and can come a little nearer to working out their uses. The remainder of this chapter will move in this direction, using the alternative models suggested earlier. It will attempt to investigate the relationship between the evidence of consumption and indications of social change provided by more orthodox sources: subsistence patterns and settlements.

The final section of the last chapter drew attention to important changes in political geography towards the end of the Wessex Culture. At the same time, there were signs of competition between communities in the older core areas and other groups nearer to the coast. The changing relationship between these areas will form the main framework of discussion. Wessex and the Thames Valley have more settlements and also more metalwork than most parts of Britain. How were the two types of evidence related to one another?

THE MIDDLE BRONZE AGE IN WESSEX AND THE THAMES VALLEY

After dominating the settlement pattern of the second millenium bc, Wessex became a rather marginal area. The occupation sites show less variety than those in the Thames Valley (Barrett and Bradley 1980a), or in another chalkland region, the Yorkshire Wolds (Manby 1980a). Metalwork is less abundant than it is in other areas and the ceramic sequence shows little change (Barrett 1980b). In contrast to the Thames Valley and parts of eastern England, Deverel-Rimbury pottery was used in Wessex for 300 years after it had been replaced elsewhere. The basic settlement sequence appears to be fairly simple, with the reorganisation of land use on the chalk perhaps developing from agricultural changes in areas nearer to the coast (Barrett and Bradley 1980a). Although some field systems were already in use during Wessex 2, other areas of intensive Bronze Age activity were not occupied until later. For example, the enclosure at Shearplace Hill was probably settled from the Wessex 2 phase onwards (*ibid.*), but the radiocarbon dates for sites in Cranborne Chase and the Marlborough Downs suggest that settlement did not develop there until 1000 bc or later (Barrett, Bradley, Green and Lewis 1981: 219–34). There may have been a hiatus whilst major changes in agricultural practice took place on the more sheltered lowland soils. It may not have been until ponds and wells had developed that year-round settlement of the higher downland was feasible (cf. Bradley 1978a: 117).

The evidence for agricultural change is so well known that a detailed account is not needed. The main feature of the chalk downland is the development of regular field systems, not unlike the parallel reaves which were being built on Dartmoor at this time (Fleming 1978). Their planning and execution must have made considerable demands on manpower. This development was particularly significant since these fields showed only a limited respect for existing barrows, and by the middle of the first millenium some of these had already come under the plough (Bradley 1981b: 25–6). The contemporary houses were probably distributed among the fields. Only later did they cluster around individual enclosures.

The latter sites provide some indication of the agrarian character of this system. Ellison has shown that the extent of Middle Bronze Age enclosures is directly related to the amount of good farm land in the vicinity (1981a 424–5). This has two implications: first, these sites must have produced their own food and were not sustained by produce introduced from outside (Peebles and Kus 1977); and secondly, the economy must have attained a fairly even level of production. Ellison's study includes a number of large enclosures, which she regards as a separate class. Three of these sites, Norton Fitzwarren (Langmaid 1971), Rams Hill (Bradley and Ellison 1975) and Highdown (A. E. Wilson, 1940; 1950) occupy sites later used by hill forts, and Rams Hill possessed a defensive rampart from the 11th century bc (Bradley and Ellison 1975). The latter sites also made more demands on manpower. These enclosures show the same relationship to productive land as the smaller sites. For this reason, it is unlikely that their occupants were sustained by tribute. It seems as if the precocious development of these centres may have been a function of their favourable location.

If there are other divisions to be recognised in the settlement pattern, they take a different form. The development of small enclosures within existing field systems did not involve the nucleation of settlement since the earlier homesteads could be just as extensive (Barrett and Bradley 1980a: 189–92; Barrett, Bradley, Green and Lewis 1981: 224). Two other features seem more important: the increased scale of the surrounding earth-works, and the occasional evidence of 'feasting' on these sites. The recently excavated site at South Lodge Camp is instructive in both these respects (*ibid.*). The enclosure is no larger than other settlements on the chalk, but is surrounded by a ditch two metres deep. Its interior is dominated by one round house, associated with Deverel-Rimbury fine ware. There is evidence of large-scale meat cooking in this area. Half the site seems to have been left free of buildings and was occupied by storage pits. These few details apart, there is little evidence for differentiation in the settlement pattern.

The contemporary burials confirm this initial impression. Some are known in flat cemeteries, and where they were deposited in newly built barrows the latter were unusually small (Ellison 1980a). Many of the burials occupied the flanks of existing mounds. There are three elements to the planning of the cemeteries. The burials include few grave goods apart from pots. If metalwork is discovered, often it belongs to the cemetery as a whole rather than any one deposit. The cremations them-selves can be segregated into clusters, whose age and sex composition is consistent with the burial of family groups (Ellison 1980a: 122). Contem-porary settlements may be composed of units on much the same scale (Ellison 1981a: 417–21). At South Lodge Camp two neighbouring barrows appear to show some significant differences, and a large mound containing primary and secondary cremations has produced a series of urns, whilst a small satellite mound is associated with unurned cremations (Barrett, Bradley, Green and Lewis 1981: 226).

Two further features of these cemeteries are important: the contrast between single burials and groups of cremations, and the relationship between cemeteries and settlements. It seems possible that a number of Deverel-Rimbury cemeteries developed around barrows which had orig-inally been built to cover only one burial. Such barrows are more widely distributed than the cremation cemeteries, which accompany only a few of these mounds. This development mirrors the character of the settlement pattern, with an initial phase in which houses were dispersed around the fields, followed by the building of more elaborate enclosures, perhaps housing only one family (Bradley 1981a: 100–102). The decision to group the burials in a cemetery seems to have been influenced by the quality of the available land (*ibid.*). As in the Neolithic period, there seems to be an association between the adoption of collective burial and the control of valuable resources. This is apparent in coastal areas of Wessex, where numerous cremation cemeteries have been found.

The second point concerns the relationship of these cemeteries to settle-ments. Until recently, it was supposed that Bronze Age burials would not be found close to occupation sites. Since the discovery of a cremation cemetery near the Deverel-Rimbury settlement at Itford Hill (Holden

1972), the position has changed radically, and twenty-five examples of this relationship have been identified (Bradley 1981a). There seem to be a number of common features worth exploring. The cemeteries are usually located within 500 metres of the settlements. They seem to be placed behind the living areas themselves, and again the cemeteries contain one or more clusters of burials.

Having considered Earlier Neolithic burial rites in such detail, there are two lessons to apply in this case. The linking of burials and critical resources is a tactical statement which may have more to do with the problems of land tenure than the realities of descent. Similarly, the undifferentiated character of such burials may present a misleading impression. We can approach these questions from several angles. First, we should note that the remarkably 'egalitarian' layout of these sites is at odds with other characteristics of Middle Bronze Age society in Wessex. The presence of one metal object in each cemetery contrasts sharply with the discovery of more elaborate artefacts elsewhere in the region. The sheer scale of land clearance may result from central direction, but there is little sign of ranking in the burial record (for an alternative view of land clearance, see Fleming 1982b). The more elaborate character of some enclosures makes the same point. Individual identity is being suppressed in the burial rite and the existence of a number of *groups* is emphasised in its place. Apart from the central position of male cremations at Itford Hill (Holden 1972) and Simons Ground, Site G (White 1982: Fig. 28), the sexes no longer received separate treatment.

This emphasis on the group is particularly revealing, since it developed during a period of agricultural intensification. A rather similar pattern has been identified in the ethnographic record (Goody 1976). Goody recognises a strong correlation between the adoption of plough agriculture and the inheritance of land through both the male and female lines. This is accompanied by the practice of endogamy. Both are devices which are designed to keep land within the community. Due to the demands made by productive agriculture, it is important that such a resource should not be alienated. Goody also emphasises the growing significance of the family as the basic unit of labour. It would be wrong to adopt this scheme too literally – the plough had been in use since the third millenium – but the combined emphasis on agricultural growth and on 'family' groups is certainly provocative, particularly when burials were being located so near to settlements. The group's control over its land may have been reinforced by the presence of its ancestors.

If this is correct, the Deverel-Rimbury sites make a statement about the priorities of contemporary communities but need not reflect their social organisation. Here the evidence of metalwork is probably decisive. Each site can be accompanied by one metal item which may not be associated with the burials themselves (Ellison 1980a: 124). Possibly it stands for the group rather than one individual. At the same time deposits of much finer metalwork can be found in apparent isolation, notably the ornament hoards of the Taunton industrial phase (Rowlands 1976: 224–73). Three of these hoards were found in barrows and a number of other examples are reported as being found with human bones (cf. Burgess 1976b; R. Taylor pers. comm.). Outside the main area of Deverel–Rimbury cemeteries, there are at least seven such hoards which could have accompanied burials (*ibid.*). One hoard which was not found with human remains is of special interest here. This famous hoard from Ebbesborne Wake in Wiltshire comes from a Celtic field system (Shortt 1949), but it may be even more significant that its findspot is only 200 metres from a cremation cemetery (M. Green pers. comm.). Similarly, the Stump Bottom hoard was found near to the contemporary settlement on Park Brow in Sussex (Anon., 1926). It seems likely that such deposits consisted of personal equipment which had evidently been worn. Following Meillassoux (1968), bronze ornaments could have been special items that needed to be destroyed once their role was finished. It may be significant that another ornament hoard came from Norton Fitzwarren where it had been buried just outside the defences (Langmaid, 1971). By analogy with continental finds, the ornaments may be female equipment, and their distribution and associations certainly avoid those of contemporary weapons (Fig. 5.2).

The hoard from Norton Fitzwarren has its counterpart in another hilltop enclosure of this period. The ditch at Drumcoltran in south-west Scotland contained an important hoard of bronze rapiers (F. R. Coles 1893: 105–6). Weapon hoards are not common in the Middle Bronze Age and have a mainly coastal distribution which excludes Wessex (Coombs 1975: Fig. 4). Elaborate weapons are rarely discovered in settlements, but single finds of rapiers and basal looped spearheads are known from the same parts of the downland as these sites. Otherwise they are more common as river finds (Fig. 5.2; cf. Rowlands 1976: maps 16–18). Since two dirks have been found with human skulls (Burgess 1976b), we can suggest that these objects might have been deliberate deposits – the 'male' equivalent of the ornament hoards (cf. Bradley 1982b: 115).

It is worth highlighting one other pattern shown by this material. Ellison (1980b) has argued that the three large enclosures at Norton Fitzwarren, Martin Down and Highdown were in areas with an unusual number of these artefacts, and that the frequency of such objects fell with increasing distance from these sites. She sees this as a reflection of exchange patterns radiating from a central location, but this seems most unlikely unless all these ornaments were chance losses. This case recalls Pierpoint's study of the Rudston area during the Neolithic (1980: 271–5), and these finds could be re-interpreted as deliberate deposits made in areas of special significance. There may be a similar relationship between the enclosures at Martin Down and Rams Hill and finds of contemporary weapons, some

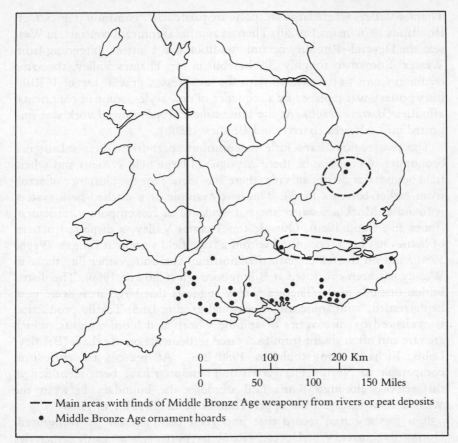

Fig. 5.2 The distribution of Middle Bronze Age ornament hoards in relation to the main areas with finds of contemporary weapons from rivers (data from Rowlands, 1976).

of them in rivers (Ellison 1980b: Fig. 3).

Putting these arguments together, we can see how different metal deposits may reflect the preoccupations of contemporary society, but how each might have illuminated a separate aspect. The finds from cemeteries reinforce the close relationship between the population and its land, whilst deposits in different locations reveal other dimensions of that society. We need not think of every ornament hoard as a surrogate burial, since they may represent the deposition of special items in other circumstances, but it is particularly revealing that some of these deposits should be found near to the more elaborate enclosures. A ranked society need not express that ranking in every context.

The distribution of ornaments almost avoids our other study area in the

Thames Valley, where large weapons are particularly common (Fig. 5.2; cf. Rowlands 1976: maps 16–20). There is another significant contrast: in Wessex, the Deverel–Rimbury ceramic tradition had a history extending from Wessex 2 down to roughly 700 bc, but in the Thames Valley, the same tradition seems to have ended with the last Wessex graves. Deverel–Rimbury pottery was replaced by a sequence of new styles, some of continental affinities (Barrett 1980b). At the same time European metalwork was imported into this area (Barrett and Bradley 1980b).

The two regions have little in common apart from their subsistence economies. As in Wessex, there are signs of large field systems and where field boundaries do not survive, there is evidence for the clearance of scrub from earlier barrows (*ibid.*). The best example of a ditched field system is found at Mucking, where there is evidence of contemporary settlement (Jones and Bond 1980). Outside the Thames Valley, a dispersed pattern of houses has been recognised within a large field system at Fengate (Pryor 1980), and on the fen edge further north an enclosure rather like those in Wessex has been excavated at Billingborough (Chowne 1980). The distribution of finds in the Thames Valley suggests that large areas were now being settled, with some use of seasonal grazing land. Textile production is evidenced by discoveries of spindle whorls and loom weights, which are rare and often absent from excavated settlements on the chalk (Bradley, Lobb, Richards and Robinson 1980: 288). At present no enclosures comparable to Norton Fitzwarren or Highdown have been identified in this region, although Rams Hill straddles the boundary between the Wessex downland and the upper Thames basin (Bradley in press).

It is in the burial record that important contrasts can be recognised. During the currency of Deverel–Rimbury pottery, a series of cemeteries had been established, whose organisation was similar to that of sites in Wessex (Barrett and Bradley 1980b: 251). Apart from a few isolated cremations, this collective burial rite seems to have lapsed around 1000 bc, at the same time as Deverel–Rimbury pottery.

Again, there is reason to doubt whether simple cremation cemeteries reflect the full character of contemporary society. The emphasis in the funeral rite is on the undifferentiated group and normally bronzes are excluded from the burials. It is interesting to consider the relations of these cemeteries to other classes of material. The only weapon type in these sites is the small side-looped spearhead, which is also found in settlements. This type of spearhead has a wide distribution, whereas the more elaborate spearheads of the same period are known mainly close to rivers, or in the rivers themselves, where they are found with other types of weapon (Ehrenberg 1977; 1980).

In fact the cemeteries and river finds have rather similar distributions (Barrett and Bradley 1980b: Fig. 3), but quite different contents. How can we explain this? Evidence from an earlier period may be relevant here. It was during Wessex 2 that the middle and lower Thames Valley first played a prominent role, and at this stage a precocious metal industry may have developed (*ibid.*: 250). Although bronze daggers were available in this region, they were rarely placed in graves. Unlike their counterparts in Wessex, they seem to have been deposited in water. This might well suggest that the earliest river metalwork was the counterpart of the most elaborate grave goods on the chalk.

If these two ways of depositing weaponry were equivalent to one another, there need be less evidence for social change than is commonly supposed. The main context in which fine metalwork was deposited altered from land to water, and appear to have done so whilst dagger graves were still being used in Wessex. The sheer concentration of metalwork has no counterpart in the latter area. This contrast is emphasised still more by the spectacular way in which metalwork was consumed (Ehrenberg 1980; Needham and Burgess 1980). Its deposition in rivers would provide an opportunity for social display, whether or not this took place at funerals. It is impossible to tell whether the river deposits were originally accompanied by bodies, although this seems quite likely – for example a dirk was found in the River Wreake together with human skull fragments (Burgess 1976b: 101).

Subsequent developments in the Thames Valley are especially informative here, since the deposition of weaponry in the river continued on an increasing scale after the cremation cemeteries went out of use. Although the barrows of Later Bronze Age Wessex were less impressive than those of earlier periods, they were *permanent* monuments to the dead. Once the deposition of metalwork in the Thames became important, the building of barrows in this area seems to have ceased. In Wessex some effort was made to commemorate the dead, but in the Thames Valley they lacked a permanent memorial. The death of important individuals may still have entailed a lavish display of wealth, but there may not have been the same emphasis on continuity. Despite the extravagant amount of metalwork entering the rivers, it is impossible to tell whether these had been the personal property of the deceased, or a wider range of offerings provided by the living. This question can only be considered where there is some evidence of associations. In the Middle and Late Bronze Ages Burgess (1976b) has recognised a number of human burials accompanied by a *single set* of weapons, whilst some of the intact weapon hoards recovered from peat bogs contain much larger accumulations of material, and may have been created by a number of individuals. Following Gregory's interpretation, they could be represented as sacrifices to the gods, but may have as much to do with rivalries among the living as with the relations of the living and the dead.

In both the study areas, deposits of metalwork emphasise aspects of contemporary society which are not obvious from settlements or cemeteries. The range of surviving material reveals different priorities in these two areas: an emphasis on continuity, ancestry and land holding in Wessex, and on discontinuity and competition in the Thames Valley. In Wessex, the prevailing burial rite minimised differences of status; the existence of these distinctions is suggested mainly by single finds and hoards. In the Thames Valley, on the other hand, these differences may have received more emphasis through the deposition of river metalwork. Here, social collapse may have been averted as the Wessex Culture ended, and the main changes could concern the manner in which elaborate artefacts were deposited (cf. Coombs 1975: 76). If so, a further contrast with Wessex is apparent, for in the latter area there seems to be evidence of decreasing social complexity, and formerly low status ceramics were the only artefacts which remained unchanged after the superstructure had given way.

Two features seem to confirm the contrast between these two regions. The burial rite in Wessex makes little distinction between the sexes, although the ornament hoards do seem to be female equipment. These are not common in the Thames Valley. Similarly, the distinctively 'male' finds which are known in the latter area hardly occur in the rivers of Wessex (Fig. 5.2). It is possible that this highlights more basic contrasts of social organisation. In both areas different artefact styles have mutually exclusive distributions. This may be one indication of competition between different communities (Ellison 1980b: Fig. 2; Bradley and Hodder 1979). It is particularly revealing that these different styles were not shared between our study areas. Both examples suggest significant differences between the populations of the two regions.

Having established the basic character of these systems, it is worth commenting that each seems to have had its counterparts in other areas of the country: the Thames Valley has much in common with the fenland (Pryor 1980), and Wessex shares other features with Sussex (Drewett 1980) and the south-west (Fleming 1978; Johnson 1980). Further north, the Yorkshire Wolds present a rather different sequence, which may combine elements of both systems (Manby 1980a). We must now return to our two study areas and ask how these different patterns developed during the Late Bronze Age.

THE LATE BRONZE AGE IN WESSEX AND THE THAMES VALLEY

The characteristic feature of the Wessex sequence is its continuity. The existing pattern of Deverel–Rimbury settlement remained substantially unchanged for centuries, with the result that our chronology depends on those sites with radiocarbon dates. The main indication of change during the Middle Bronze Age was the emergence of distinctive enclosures. This development continued during the Late Bronze Age. It can be seen on the Marlborough Downs (Gingell 1980), from re-analysis of Pitt-Rivers' classic site at Angle Ditch (Barrett, Bradley, Green and Lewis 1981) and still more clearly at Down Farm, Woodcutts, where the enclosure developed around two existing houses (*ibid.*). There is evidence for craft production on some of these settlements. There are signs of bronze-working in the Middle and Late Bronze Ages (Barrett and Bradley 1980a: 195–6), and quern production is also evidenced on the Marlborough Downs (Gingell 1980: 215) and possibly in Cranborne Chase (M. Green pers. comm.).

The burial evidence shows a similar continuity and there were no major changes in funerary practice until the end of the Bronze Age, when cemeteries disappeared altogether. The distribution of single graves with metalwork moved further into northern and western Britain and avoided Wessex entirely (Fig. 5.3; cf. Burgess 1976b). There is no longer a concentration of ornament hoards or weapon finds to complement the metalwork from the cemeteries, but this problem might be resolved if, like the pottery, some metal types had a longer history in this region.

There are three main areas in which there is evidence of change: the development of larger open settlements, the construction of land boundaries and the building of hill forts. The first development is little understood, but large open settlements dating to the Late Bronze Age have been found in several areas. Examples are known at Burderop Down (Gingell 1980) and perhaps All Cannings Cross in north Wiltshire (Cunnington 1923), Beedon in Berkshire (Richards 1978: 75–80) and at Chalton in Hampshire (Cunliffe 1973a: 178). Burderop Down includes evidence of metalworking and quern production. Large scale excavations have not been undertaken on these sites, but the fine pottery from All Cannings Cross suggests that the settlement may have been fairly rich. More work will be needed in order to find out whether any of these sites were of high status.

The large open settlement at Beedon is flanked by a boundary earthwork and provides rare dating evidence for an element of the linear ditch system, which extends from the Berkshire Downs as far south as Cranborne Chase. These ditches have often been described as 'ranch boundaries', but their actual purpose is unknown (Bowen 1978). They cover large areas of the downland, sometimes defining land units which extend from the river valleys into the higher chalk, in the same manner as Saxon estates (Bradley 1978a: 48). Where they come into contact with existing field systems, they often cut across them, putting them out of use (*ibid.*). At Boscombe Down East and Martin Down, they are closely related to earthwork enclosures (Bowen 1961: Fig. 3a). It is tempting to see this development as an indication of greater stock management. However, the layout of some of these units could be as consistent with an equitable division of arable and pasture

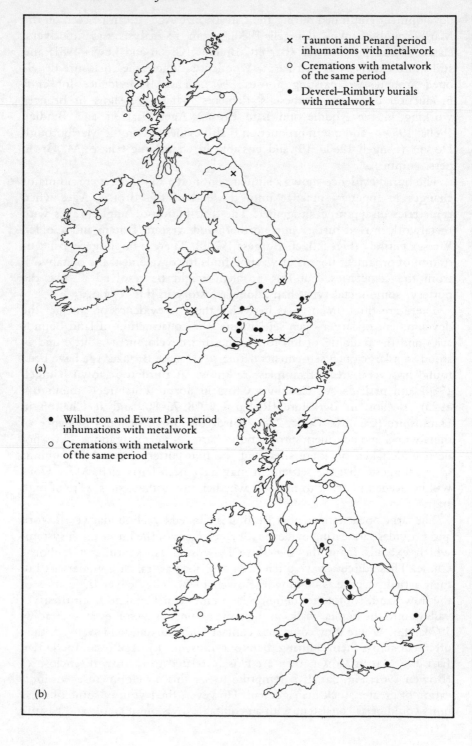

× Taunton and Penard period
   inhumations with metalwork

○ Cremations with metalwork
   of the same period

● Deverel–Rimbury burials
   with metalwork

(a)

● Wilburton and Ewart Park period
   inhumations with metalwork

○ Cremations with metalwork
   of the same period

(b)

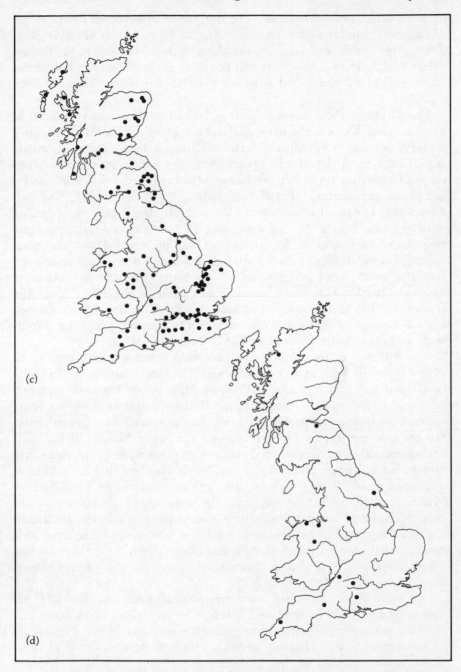

Fig. 5.3 (a) and (b) The distribution of successive groups of Later Bronze Age burials with metalwork (after Burgess, 1976b); (c) The distribution of Later Bronze Age weapon hoards (after Coombs, 1975); (d) The distribution of hill forts and/or hill settlements with radiocarbon dates earlier than 600 bc.

between different communities. The northern and southern limits of the distribution of linear ditches correspond to the limits of ceramic style zones during the Middle and Late Bronze Ages (Ellison 1980b: Fig. 2; Barrett 1980a: Fig. 3). In each case there was one large enclosure on this boundary, Rams Hill to the north and Martin Down to the south (Ellison 1980b: Fig. 2).

The dating of these developments is central to their interpretation. In most areas of Wessex, the only artefacts are sherds of Deverel–Rimbury pottery, but this is not closely datable (Barrett 1980b). The earliest date could come from the Martin Down enclosure which contained a worn razor of uncertain type, but the linear ditch on the site was not directly linked to this feature (Pitt-Rivers 1898: 198; Bowen 1961: Fig. 3a). Boscombe Down also contained Deverel–Rimbury pottery, together with two Late Bronze Age vessels (Stone 1936). At the opposite extreme, two linear ditches in Berkshire, where the pottery follows the same sequence as the Thames valley, both include sherds of the ninth to seventh centuries BC (S. Ford pers. comm.; J. Richards pers. comm.). Another ditch at Quarley Hill has a *terminus ante quem* in the Early Iron Age (Hawkes 1940). It does not seem likely that these ditches form a chronological horizon, but comparable earthworks on the Yorkshire Wolds seem to belong to the same period (Manby 1980a: 327–8).

Whilst these ditches cut across earlier field systems, they seem to be earlier than hill forts or hill settlements. The best example of this relationship is the Iron Age site at Quarley Hill, which occupies a pivotal position in relation to several different land units (Hawkes 1940). These hilltop sites raise many problems. They may produce finds of metalwork, but they do not appear to be related to the larger Middle Bronze Age enclosures, although the defended settlements must represent an equivalent investment of labour. Like those in the Welsh Marches, they seem to have developed from 700 bc onwards, although most of the early hill forts in Wessex straddle the Bronze Age/Iron Age transition. Their sheer scale can be very striking, but it is difficult to decide their role in the settlement pattern. They tend to be located towards the boundaries of ceramic style zones, and also on the edges of the linear ditch system. Some sites contain a high proportion of post-built structures, whose most likely interpretation is as granaries (Cunliffe 1976a: 347).

Although these sites had some residential function, Cunliffe has suggested that their most plausible role is as centralised food stores and that the occupants of these more complex sites may have engaged in redistribution (*ibid.*). The role of such sites will be considered in more detail in the next chapter, but at this stage we must relate their development to the other changes in the settlement record. There could be a connection between the imposition of new boundaries on the landscape and centralised supervision of the food supply. If so, this might be another sign that competition for land was the dominant concern of communities in Wessex. Gent (1983) has suggested a way of testing Cunliffe's interpretation, although this analysis perforce combines formally Late Bronze Age and Early Iron Age sites. In the Middle Bronze Age, it will be remembered that Ellison found a linear relationship between the size of different enclosures and the productivity of the surrounding land (1981a: 424–5). This suggested that all the sites played an autonomous role in food production. Gent has shown that the same relationship did not exist among the first Wessex hill forts, where the size of the different sites bears no relation to the amount of fertile land in their vicinity. If these sites had stored produce introduced from a larger area than they could exploit themselves, there might be a closer relationship between the size of the hill forts and the economic potential of the whole region. This appears to be the case (Gent 1983). The first hill forts in Wessex show a linear relationship between their size and the amount of good agricultural land within 7.5 km. This result suggests that some early hill forts or hill settlements might have played a role in centralised storage and could have had a larger sphere of influence than other sites. It is not clear whether the produce stored there was to be consumed on the spot, redirected among the local population or exchanged over greater distances.

How far are these changes reflected in the deposition of metalwork? It is the *absence* of specialised deposits which is probably significant here. If the Deverel–Rimbury cemeteries express the links between communities and their land, it is significant that such an 'egalitarian' structure should no longer be found once the process of enclosure was complete. The dating of the land boundaries is unsatisfactory, but it does seem clear that the cemeteries had gone out of use by the time that hill forts were being built (Bradley 1981a: 104) – the two systems were contradictory. It is less evident how the dead were treated, but isolated human bones are known from a number of Late Bronze Age sites, for example those at Ivinghoe Beacon and Egham (Cotton and Frere 1969: 192; Longley 1980: 79). The rarity of bronze deposits in Wessex may be equally significant.

In the Thames Valley there are also signs of change, although these take a different form (Barrett and Bradley 1980b). The basic distribution of settlement remained much the same, and quite a number of sites show lengthy sequences. As in Wessex, there is evidence for some very extensive settlements, including Burghfield on the Kennet gravels, where occupation was scattered over at least ten hectares and ran discontinuously from the Deverel–Rimbury phase to the Iron Age (Bradley, Lobb, Richards and Robinson 1980: 256–85). There are signs that the different sites had different economic emphases with the result that they were able to make use of virtually all the land (*ibid.*). Metalworking was practised on many of these settlements, together with textile production. Until about 600 bc, the large number of grain storage pits, compared with sites on the chalk, suggests the flourishing state of the economy. There is limited evidence for field boundaries and for a series of ponds (Barrett and Bradley 1980b).

Apart from the economic evidence, there is little in common between this sequence and developments in Wessex. There are no traces of large-scale land divisions and the importance of defended sites remains a matter for discussion. The major development in this area appears to have been a distinct type of 'fortified' round house (T. Champion 1980a: 233–43). It seems that early hill forts like Ivinghoe Beacon occupied a more peripheral position.

The sites described by Champion have no counterpart in Wessex at this early date, although they are related to other sites in Kent, East Anglia and Yorkshire (*ibid*; Manby 1980a: 321–4). For some time writers have suggested that there ought to have been a class of higher order settlements to go with the elaborate metalwork found in the Thames valley during this period (e.g. Rowlands 1976: 207–8; Bradley 1979), but these sites have been recognised only recently. Their discovery was delayed for two reasons. It was thought that the finds of weaponry should be interpreted as evidence of warfare (e.g. Coombs 1975: 75), and so early hill forts figured prominently in the discussion. The main distribution of defended sites is different from that of the weaponry. Most of the weapons come from rivers discharging into the North Sea or from Ireland, whilst the majority of hill forts have been identified in Wessex or in the Highland Zone of Britain. Although there are Bronze Age finds from a few hill forts in the Thames Valley (Needham and Burgess 1980), these may not date the defences to this period. The second reason for confusion has been the resemblance between major Bronze Age enclosures and much earlier henge monuments (cf. Collis 1977a). The important site of Mucking South Rings was originally interpreted as a henge (Jones and Bond 1980: 471), and the same applies to the enclosure at Thwing on the Yorkshire Wolds (Manby 1980a: 321–3). It was after excavation at these sites that re-interpretation of earlier work has made much progress, and now it is possible to identify a whole series of circular enclosures, some of considerable proportions, which seem to have been built from the tenth century bc onwards (T. Champion 1980a: 233–43). The most extensively excavated contain a single round house, twelve metres or more in diameter. Examples include Mucking South Rings (Jones and Bond 1980: 473–5), Thwing (Manby 1980a: 321–3) and West Harling sites 2 and 3 (Clark and Fell 1953). Also, it is clear that some of these sites were engaged in metal production, including examples at Mucking, Highstead, Carshalton and Deal (T. Champion 1980a: 233–43). The current work at Thwing is especially relevant, since this excavation has yielded well preserved faunal remains. A major deposit of bones comes from the terminals of the inner ditch and accounts for roughly forty cattle and pigs which apparently had been slaughtered for food (Mounteney 1981: 83). This may be further evidence for the special role of feasting. It is not clear if these sites were really isolated, or whether they comprise the more obvious nucleus of larger settlements. Certainly Mucking North Rings was surrounded by an array of other features. Apart from their smaller size, one characteristic which distinguishes them from hill forts is the absence of ancillary buildings. Given the scale of these sites, it is tempting to think of them as the settlements of an elite. They were far too small to be defended against attack, but Mucking North Rings is one of the few sites with evidence for weapon production (Barrett and Bradley 1980b: 263).

Two Irish sites may shed some light on the English enclosures, especially since there were close contacts between the two areas. The recently excavated site at Rathgall was particularly rich and included an important workshop which had been making bronze artefacts. Outside the one large house, there were a series of trough-shaped hearths remarkably like those found with the burnt mounds of this period. These were probably used for cooking meat (Raftery 1976). The other site is at Navan, where a sequence of enclosed round houses has been investigated (Selkirk 1970). This began life towards the end of the Bronze Age, but despite the considerable size of the one internal building, the early enclosure has been interpreted as a farm. This seems particularly unlikely since the site later developed into a ceremonial monument. Significantly, it appears in the epic literature as the royal capital of Ulster. Nearby was an artificial pool containing Late Bronze Age sword moulds, together with human skull fragments (Lynn 1977).

The discovery of these sites helps to account for an anomaly in the distribution of metalwork within the Thames Valley. The major finds of bronzes cover only parts of the area in which contemporary settlements have been excavated (cf. Bradley, Lobb, Richards and Robinson 1980: 292–3; T. Champion 1980a: 229). This may be because such items are the result of higher status activities attached to these remarkable sites. Perhaps the ordinary settlements did not participate in these practices, although they may have supplied an elite with food and other products. This striking distinction within the settlement pattern is best illustrated around the confluence of the Thames and the Kennet. Most of the ordinary settlements are on the Kennet gravels, but the river finds come from the Thames near to another of these distinctive enclosures at Marshall's Hill, Reading (Fig. 5.4).

The number of river finds remained fairly constant during the Late Bronze Age and only in the Ewart Park industrial phase were they complemented by further deposits on dry land (Needham and Burgess 1980: Fig. 7). Despite the emphasis on weaponry among the finds from lowland England, the evidence for armed conflict is very limited, and most of the defended sites avoid this area altogether. For this reason we might envisage a contrast between ritual and actual conflict of the type considered earlier.

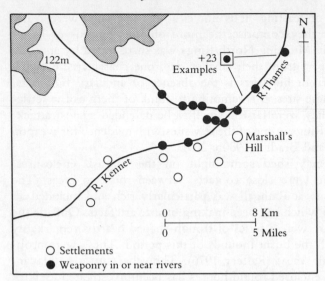

Fig. 5.4 The distribution of weapon finds around the confluence of the Rivers Thames and Kennet, in relation to the position of the Marshall's Hill enclosure and the sites of contemporary settlements (metalwork after Ehrenberg, 1980, with additions; the settlement distribution incorporates material compiled by Liz James).

In the Thames Valley conflicts may have been mediated through competitive rituals including the destruction of fine weapons, whilst in the areas with more hill forts there could have been actual warfare. The same distinction can be seen in the distribution of the Late Bronze Age burials with weapons, which avoids the Thames Valley completely (Burgess 1976a Fig. 2). Like the hill forts, they belong mainly to the end of this period and for the most part their distribution complements that of the weapon hoards (Fig. 5.3). Some of these weapon hoards come from bogs in the Welsh Marches, one region in which early hill forts *are* found (Coombs 1975: Figs. 13 and 14). Again, the question arises whether such deposits were individual 'grave goods' or larger collections of offerings. Two deposits are informative here, although neither is from the Thames Valley. The Broadward hoard, which was found in draining a bog, contained a large number of weapons associated with animal bones (Burgess, Coombs and Davies 1972), whilst the 'hoard' from Duddingston Loch contained parts of nine swords, twenty-three spearheads and a bucket, which had been burnt and broken before they were deposited. This metalwork was discovered with human and animal bones (Callender, 1922, 360–4). In each case a large number of people may have been responsible for accumulating these deposits.

It remains to consider how so much metalwork was produced and obtained. Despite growing evidence of metal production in areas as far apart as Devon and the Shetland Islands, the majority of this material seems to have been deposited in areas a long way from the original sources of the metal. The movement of these objects must have been a complex procedure. Rowlands has suggested that weapons and tools might have been made and distributed separately and could even have belonged to different spheres of exchange (1980: 36–7). Occasional hints of these processes can be discovered, but so far they defy analysis. For example, possible shipwrecks have been identified in the English Channel, containing cargoes which may have been scrap metal shipped from France (Muckleroy 1981; R. Taylor 1980). Studies of the character and sources of Bronze Age moulds are taking place (e.g. Needham 1980), and so are analyses of the metal itself (e.g. Northover 1982). Until these are complete, there is little point in speculation. Few of the existing patterns seem to be consistent with one another; the elaborate pooling and recycling of scrap metal hardly agrees with other evidence of bronzeworking and is hard to reconcile with the scale on which fine metalwork was being exchanged with communities in Europe.

Most writers are agreed that such complex patterns of movement must have involved sites of special character, engaged in controlling the 'trade routes'. Possible sites in the Thames Valley have often been suggested, usually from concentrations of river finds (Rowlands 1976: 207–8; Bradley 1979). It was only with the chance discovery of a riverside complex at Egham that any insight was gained into the character of this occupation (Needham and Longley 1980). Although work is still in progress, certain characteristics of this site may act as clues to the location of similar complexes. Occupation appears to have taken place on an island in the Thames, situated at the confluence of the river and one of its tributaries (S. Needham pers. comm.). The river bank had been reinforced by wooden piles and formed a consolidated waterfront at which boats could moor. The site contained an unusually high proportion of continental artefacts. Since only limited areas of the island were available for excavation, structural evidence is extremely meagre, but the surviving artefacts are remarkable for the high quality of both the metalwork and the pottery. There is evidence of craft production on the site, notably bronze-working, antler working and the making of textiles. The position of this site on an island means that it cannot have been self-supporting and that its subsistence requirements would have been met from other sites on the mainland. Quite large amounts of meat were being consumed, and the faunal remains suggested that 'eating was more probably a community affair than a family process' (Longley 1980: 79). Possibly the island was only part of a high status settlement controlling the movement of metalwork and other commodities along the river. Its situation on an island may have guaranteed its neutrality and this part of the settlement might have been used specifically for exchange.

The discovery of this site is important for two reasons. It sheds considerable light on collections of ostensibly domestic material from other parts of the Thames shoreline, which again includes fine pottery and metalwork, sometimes with continental imports. Such sites include Brentford, Wallingford and Bray (Barrett and Bradley 1980b). Rather similar evidence has been found in flood deposits at Washingborough in the Witham valley near Lincoln (Coles, Orme, May and Moore 1979), whilst there are older accounts of 'pile dwellings' associated with bronze artefacts in the Thames Valley (Needham and Longley 1980: 422–30), East Anglia (Bradley 1979: 4) and Yorkshire (Manby 1980a: 325). In Ireland it is possible that Dalkey Island, with its evidence of bronze production, occupied another 'neutral' location suitable for trade (Liversage 1968). It controlled the mouth of the Liffey and may have served the same function in the post-Roman period (Hodges 1982: 67).

The recognition of this complex has implications for long-distance connections. It is clear that some of the most elaborate bronzes, particularly weapons, have discontinuous distributions which link a number of widely separated areas on either side of the Channel. Clearly, the sea was no barrier, and items travelled in both directions (O'Connor 1980). The major river systems dominate their distribution, with notable complexes associated with the Seine, the Somme, the Aisne and the Oise, and further afield with the Rhine, the Main and the Maas. One of the closest links was between the modern sites of London and Paris. Given the new evidence from Egham, it is of interest that current work at Choisy au Bac has located a similar site at the confluence of the Aisne and the Oise (Agache 1979: 420–23). The complex patterns sketched for the Thames Valley have their mirror image elsewhere in Europe. The same applies to the deposition of this metalwork, which shows striking similarities in all of these areas.

DISCUSSION

This chapter started with a series of theories concerning the destruction of property. Having reviewed the complex sequence in the most informative areas of southern England, it remains to ask how these theories have fared.

This chapter has been restricted to the most distinctive of the bronze deposits and only the hoards with weapons or ornaments have been included. This decision was taken because we lack adequate criteria for deciding which of the other hoards could be offerings of personal property and which were the remains of metal production. In order to remedy this omission, the empirical data must be looked at afresh. Such work is now in progress (R. Taylor pers. comm.), but until it is complete, these deposits cannot be discussed to much purpose. Similarly, until wear on the artefacts has been analysed, Kristiansen's model cannot be tested. At best we can observe one pattern, reminiscent of some of his conclusions. Whilst nothing can be said about use rates in relation to agricultural practices, it seems clear that in some areas there is a relationship between the quality of different objects and the character of the land in which they were deposited. Thus in Wessex, gold ornaments may be buried in more productive land than those made of bronze, whilst in Lincolnshire weapons are associated with better soils than finds of tools (Gardiner 1980), but to say that success depended on agriculture is to leave out the most characteristic features of this period.

Subsistence featured prominently in the 'social storage' model, and here the basic theory allowed us to make two predictions: that the destruction of metalwork should be found mainly in periods of economic stability, and that it should have taken place mainly in areas in which returns were unpredictable. There are problems of definition here, but it seems rather unlikely that these ideas can explain the role of Late Bronze Age artefacts. The greatest economic uncertainty would occur in areas which were subject to climatic fluctuations, and this would be the case in highland areas rather than the lowlands. As the previous examples have shown, the main metal deposits come from the more productive areas of the country and tend to avoid those regions in which uncertain harvests would have been a problem. Such fluctuations were more probably resolved through control of the food supply (H. Gent pers. comm.). Again, the theory proposes that the destruction of bronzes should have been most frequent in periods of stability. We have no direct way of testing this suggestion, but an indirect approach is worth trying. Perhaps the building of hill forts in different areas provides one indication of the periods of conflict. If so, we could identify these as the phases when bronzes should remain in circulation, and the intervals in between as times when they could be destroyed. In fact, the two periods of 'hill fort' building, in the Taunton and Ewart Park phases, are those which saw the deposition of most of the hoards (Burgess 1980b: 244; Burgess and Coombs 1979: v–vi).

The other ideas have been discussed in sufficient detail already: Meillassoux's theory that prestige objects are destroyed in order to preserve their restricted role; Gregory's interpretation of votive offerings as an arena for winning prestige; and Chapman's contrast between the promotion of actual warfare and the substitution of surrogate conflict. All of these theories have been helpful in considering specific cases, although none of them has an overall application. Rather than repeat what has been said already, let us draw two lessons from our discussion.

First, all three of these theories show that once again we are considering societies in which certain artefacts took on wider meanings and functions. The patterns of deposition show a remarkable formality and also a striking resilience over a long period of time. For some years fieldworkers have hoped to locate settlements containing the types of elaborate artefacts known in these specialised deposits. This expectation may well be false. If we emphasise *deposition* as a topic worthy of study in its own right, we may find that certain types *could not* be discarded in burials or settlements. Their absence need not be an accident of archaeological fieldwork; it could be the defining characteristic of those types, and the strongest clue to their functions.

Secondly, the opposition between control of land and control of prestige trade is matched by the equally fundamental distinction between one society which experienced fragmentation and conflict and another with sufficiently powerful sanctions to transfer the same antagonisms into ritual. This contrast mirrors the changing scale of the two systems. Wessex was a relatively peripheral area and developments here had no real impact in the outside world. The Thames Valley, on the other hand, was one of a series of rich core areas engaged in political relations with several areas of Europe.

In a sense the Later Bronze Age sequence can be viewed as a set of widening circles, or perhaps as. a Chinese Box composed of overlapping and steadily more encompassing relationships. The scale of these different systems varies from the English county to the nation state. The patterns in these different areas are both separate and interdependent and, at the largest scale of all, the different sequences interlock.

On the most limited scale there are deceptive regional contrasts, like those between Wessex and the Thames Valley. At one level we find two divergent sequences, distinguished from one another by characteristic artefact styles and by radically different forms of deposition. At this scale there are already regional schools of metalworking whose distributions prefigure the documented tribes of the late pre-Roman Iron Age (Eogan 1974; Burgess 1980b: 249–51). On another scale, the contrasts between the economies in these different areas amount to a 'regional division of labour' and suggest economic and political relationships growing up within a larger social system (cf. Rowlands 1980). Such contrasts in subsistence and craft production may reveal a pattern in which the Wessex chalkland changed from a dominant position in the second millenium to a role in which it provisioned a core area in the Thames basin. Indeed, the role of the impressive hill forts seems rather different once it is realised how far they were located on the boundary between these two different systems. Textiles, for example, were made mainly in the Thames Valley, whilst the downland could have seen large scale cattle raising.

At the second level this type of system would provide a means by which food or craft production could be converted into power and prestige. The main agencies here were feast giving and the destruction of wealth. These particular processes may have been hidden behind a variety of beliefs, but surely served to provide a tangible benefit. At the same time competition for status and power may have been directed into the formation of long distance alliances, revealed in the archaeological record by the movement of weapons and ornaments (*ibid.*). Such a pattern was probably vulnerable, and position may have needed constant re-assertion, with the result that in the core areas the same rituals were enacted repeatedly as special items were exchanged and consumed. The emergence of local elites may have removed them from participation in food production, and those who occupied sites like Thwing or Egham may well have been supported by tribute from a wider region. Monopoly control over the movement of fine metalwork may have constituted a sufficient power base for this purpose, especially if it involved the patronage of bronzesmiths and control of their products.

At the final level, this system was international and sites like that at Egham have their counterparts in other regions of Europe. As the system extended and alliances bridged larger areas, it also became more vulnerable to outside processes of change. This applies particularly to fluctuations in the supply of raw materials, which may have come under increasing pressure as the demand for prestige items grew (T. Champion 1975). Thus, as the system itself expanded, the pressures at its base became more insistent. In time, there were problems in maintaining a flow of fine metal, and it was here that the collapse of the Bronze Age system began. Since such a wide network of political connections had developed, fluctuations of this kind could be impossible to control. To paraphrase Robert Musil, the sublimated ceremonial might have become even more important, but its evolution was cut short.

6 Continental drift
– The scale of the social system (700 BC–43 AD)

'Was it not . . . a true answer that Solon of Greece made to the rich King
Croesus of Lydia, when he showed unto him a great quantity of gold that he
had gathered together, in ostentation of his greatness and might? . . . Solon said
to him . . . "Why, sir, if another come that hath better iron than you, he will
be lord of all your gold." '

Francis Bacon, Speech to the House of Commons, 1606

'*Cleopatra*: Is it true that when Caesar caught you on that island, you were
painted all over blue?
Britannicus: Blue is the colour worn by all Britons of good standing. In war we
stain our bodies blue; so that though our enemies may strip us of our clothes
. . ., they cannot strip us of our respectability.'

George Bernard Shaw, *Caesar and Cleopatra*

INTRODUCTION

The title of this chapter is a reference to the competing interpretations of
Britain's place within Iron Age Europe. For many years it was axiomatic
that Iron Age culture in Britain had been imposed on the native population
by settlers from overseas (Clark 1966), but now there is room for doubt.
Many of the developments explained by this idea no longer seem to have
taken place together, and any Early Iron Age horizon is increasingly
difficult to find (Barrett 1980b). At the same time renewed research on
Later Bronze Age society has claimed some of this evidence and has
modified our understanding of the whole character of the native population (Barrett and Bradley (eds) 1980). This has further reduced the case for
outside influence. It remains a conspicuous irony that writers who reject
the 'invasion hypothesis' in studying the Early Iron Age should be so
unwilling to take the same attitude to the later part of this period. This
weakens their entire approach, as their critics have been quick to point out
(D. W. Harding 1974: 9–10). Both schools have developed entrenched
positions, and as so often happens, the major issues have been lost between
the battle lines.

At one level the debate is between two different views of British geography and two competing historical analogies. The seas around the British Isles may be thought of either as a barrier or as a link, and each conception could be illustrated from different historical periods. Proponents of the invasion hypothesis have been influenced by literary evidence for mass migration from the Late Iron Age onwards and have been prepared to project the same patterns back into earlier periods (e.g. Hawkes 1972). Their critics, on the other hand, doubt whether early communities may have possessed the technology and social organisation which large scale migration entailed (T. Champion 1980b). Neither school discusses the equally important effects of isolation and fragmentation. If the scale of the social network began to change at the end of the Bronze Age, this would have had equally far-reaching effects. There also seems to be a reduction in the amount of continental contact during parts of the Iron Age, and in particular between the fifth and second centuries BC. Once again this may be related to changes in the character of insular society.

Two further points must be made at the outset, if only to avoid confusion. By the Iron Age large sections of our chronology can be fixed by historical events or by cross-reference to areas which have a well-researched sequence. For this reason all dates are presented in calendar years. Radiocarbon determinations referred to in the text have been calibrated accordingly. Secondly, a major gap in this account is the lack of any discussion of the Arras Culture of the Yorkshire Wolds. This is one element in Iron Age society that does appear to be the result of European influence (Stead 1979), but so much modern fieldwork is currently being prepared for publication that any account of this material would be premature and uninformed. For this reason we will be concerned with areas mainly in southern England where there is already enough evidence to discuss (Fig. 6.1).

In Parts 1 and 2 of this chapter we will consider the social patterns which gradually developed as long distance contacts were relinquished, and in Part 3 we will see how these new arrangements broke down again as contacts with Europe were renewed (Table 6.1). This sequence has a fearful symmetry: it is another irony that the Late Iron Age should have so much in common with the Late Bronze Age.

PART 1 – FRAGMENTATION AND SOCIAL CHANGE
700–400 BC

For Gordon Childe the adoption of iron working had drastic social implications (1942: 182–3). He observed that the most significant contrast between bronze and iron technology lies in the difficulty of making and distributing bronze objects, compared with the ease of obtaining iron. Since copper, tin and their alloys are not widely distributed in Europe, the

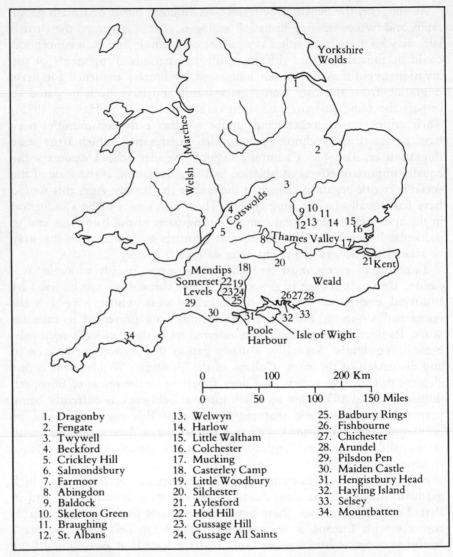

Fig. 6.1 The main sites and regions considered in Chapter 6.

1. Dragonby	13. Welwyn	25. Badbury Rings
2. Fengate	14. Harlow	26. Fishbourne
3. Twywell	15. Little Waltham	27. Chichester
4. Beckford	16. Colchester	28. Arundel
5. Crickley Hill	17. Mucking	29. Pilsdon Pen
6. Salmondsbury	18. Casterley Camp	30. Maiden Castle
7. Farmoor	19. Little Woodbury	31. Hengistbury Head
8. Abingdon	20. Silchester	32. Hayling Island
9. Baldock	21. Aylesford	33. Selsey
10. Skeleton Green	22. Hod Hill	34. Mountbatten
11. Braughing	23. Gussage Hill	
12. St. Albans	24. Gussage All Saints	

production of bronze objects must have made considerable demands. Long distance exchange networks were needed, not only to accumulate the different raw materials, but also to distribute the finished products. The restricted distribution of these sources lent itself to control of the metal supply by powerful elites.

In his view iron working did not raise the same difficulties. It posed only limited technical problems and the raw material could be obtained in most areas, although this did not prevent certain regions from developing a

Table 6.1 Iron Age chronology in relation to major developments described in Chapter 6

700	600	500	400	300	200	100 BC	43 AD
Early Iron Age			*Middle Iron Age*			*Late Iron Age*	
Ha.C	Ha.D	La Tène	1 imports				
Period of fragmentation:			Period of isolation:			Period of incorporation:	
Contraction of style zones			Reduction of overseas 'trade'			Renewal of overseas 'trade'	
Regional settlement traditions			Reduction in number of defended sites			Complex burials	
Local forms of deposition			'Developed' hill forts			Larger nucleated settlements	
Peak of 'early' hill forts			Nucleated 'villages'			Agricultural intensification	
Destruction of hill forts			Craft specialisation			Federation and inherited kingship	
700	600	500	400	300	200	100 BC	43 AD

powerful position through their control of the most abundant resources. Childe argued that the general adoption of iron undermined the complex social formations which had built up around the distribution of bronzes. There were fewer restrictions on the supply of metalwork and for this reason the Iron Age was more 'democratic' (*ibid*.: 183). He has been followed in this view in a useful study of social change on the island of Gotland (Nylen 1974).

In Britain, however, this interpretation creates as many problems as it solves, and the first part of this chapter will provide an alternative reading of the evidence, taking the inception of iron working as its starting point. In order to do this, we must ask two questions: what is the most likely explanation for the change of metal technology, and to what extent did this change coincide with changes in the scale of social and economic systems?

Champion (1975) also stresses the complexity of the bronze trade, but he suggests that there may have been a direct relationship between the increasing scale of production and its eventual curtailment. With growing demand, it may have been more difficult to assemble the necessary raw materials and to distribute the finished products. The end of the Bronze Age may be marked by a major peak of production, and Champion argues that at this stage it was necessary to experiment with a more accessible material, one which had been known for some time but little used. Thus the importance of iron depended on its accessibility rather than its technological superiority (cf. T. Champion 1980c).

It is equally important to consider the role of the finished products within Bronze Age society. One effect of any increase in bronze production might have been to threaten the distinctive character of special purpose artefacts. As we saw in the previous chapter, one reason for the destruction of fine metalwork may have been as a safeguard against inflation. Indeed, there was apparently a peak of metal deposition during the final phase of the Bronze Age. Another way of protecting the distinctive character of the exchange system would be to develop a range of new forms with a more restricted circulation (cf. Bradley 1980: 70). This pattern has been observed in the development of second millenium ceramics (see p. 70), and the same considerations may have provided a stimulus for the earliest use of iron. Significantly, this material was used first to reproduce traditional types of bronze artefact.

It is much more difficult to trace changes in long distance relations, since these are generally identified through the contents of special deposits, like the river metalwork discussed in Chapter 5. At first sight there is a reduction in the number of metal finds of continental origin or inspiration. The number of bronze swords entering the archaeological record fell by more than two-thirds between Late Bronze Age 3 and Hallstatt C (Burgess 1968; Cowen, 1967), and when the sword was replaced by the dagger during Hallstatt D the number of finds fell by nearly 50 per cent (Jope, 1961). Although all these finds come from similar contexts, this pattern is rather deceptive since the number of weapon deposits in Iron Age Europe decreased at much the same time (I am grateful to Sara Champion for advice on this point). It was only after 400 BC that cross-Channel connections may really have lapsed (D. W. Harding 1974; Cunliffe 1978a: 152–7).

Childe's interpretation placed great emphasis on the *fragmentation* of society which, he suggested, would have come about with the use of more accessible sources of metal. Again this is a difficult point to discuss since there is no clear indication of the intensity of iron production during the mid-first millenium BC. The apparent decrease in bronze working may be partly a product of changing modes of deposition, whilst iron objects are less likely to survive in the archaeological record than those made of a more durable material. Again, it is perfectly possible that less metal of any sort was used at this time.

Even making allowance for these uncertainties, there remains a series of developments which suggest that Childe's approach was basically correct, although undoubtedly he placed too much emphasis on the 'democratic' character of Iron Age society. The evidence for fragmentation takes three basic forms: a growing regionalism in artefact styles, settlement types and modes of deposition; a greater self-sufficiency in the economies of different settlements; and much greater evidence of conflict, expressed in the building, and even the destruction, of a significant number of hill forts.

We have already mentioned the changing frequency of Iron Age weapons, the majority of which have been found in rivers. Their falling numbers may well be part of a much more general pattern, but the same can hardly apply to the local changes in their distribution, which contracts sharply between Late Bronze Age 3 and Hallstatt C, and further still in Hallstatt D. The later material is concentrated in the middle and lower Thames Valley to the virtual exclusion of other regions. It is not easy to interpret these changes. It may be that a greater proportion of Iron Age imports and their British counterparts were controlled by communities in the Thames Valley and that this material was no longer available to groups elsewhere. Alternatively, people in this area could have maintained a traditional type of ritual which had lapsed in other areas. This may also apply to communities in Wessex and East Anglia, who seem to have deposited bronze hoards after this practice had been discontinued in other parts of the country. These two groups of metalwork avoid the Thames Valley entirely.

There may be a parallel trend in the ceramic evidence. Although distinctive style zones seem to have existed at the end of the Bronze Age (Barrett 1980b), there seems to be a tendency for these to increase in number and definition during the Early and Middle Iron Age. It is possible that they also became smaller. It is particularly interesting that some of these style zones should correspond to local forms of metal deposition. For example, the last bronze hoards in Wessex are found in very much the same area as early furrowed bowls (Cunliffe 1978a: 33). The distribution of East Anglian hoards is rather similar to that of a second ceramic tradition (*ibid.*: 37), whilst Professor Harding has placed considerable emphasis on the possible links between a distinctive style of fine pottery in the Thames Valley and the distribution of early daggers, mainly in the river (1974). Such patterns should not be exaggerated, but this may be another case in which communal boundaries were emphasised at times of stress.

In a short account of Iron Age society it is quite impossible to do justice to the full range of settlements, but it is clear that many distinctive local types first developed between about 700 and 400 BC. This occurred extremely widely. For example, in northern Britain this pattern can be seen with the palisaded sites of the borderland and southern Scotland and also with the first brochs and wheelhouses on the west coast. In the south it accounts for many of the more characteristic types of enclosure on both the uplands and the river gravels, and for practically all the major groups of hill forts, apart from those in the Weald and on the Atlantic seaboard. Whilst many of these settlements represent a new departure, they also mark the beginning of quite sustained local traditions.

Recent excavations in central southern England suggest that these newer sites may have been more self-sufficient than their Bronze Age predecessors. In the latter period it seems that certain economic activities had been confined to different parts of this area. Indeed, this provides one indication of the importance of regional exchange. Textile production, for example, was most prominent close to the Thames and its tributaries, and is hardly evidenced in Wessex, where the development of linear ditches suggests another type of economy. By the fifth century BC all trace of this important distinction had been lost. Loom weights, weaving combs and spindle whorls were virtually ubiquitous; the linear ditch system had probably come to an end; and storage pits and raised granaries were distributed throughout both of these areas. The subsistence economy had a strikingly uniform character, with an agricultural regime based on fairly intensive mixed farming and very little sign of industrial production directed towards a wider region (D. W. Harding 1974; Cunliffe 1978a). The evidence is limited severely by our poor knowledge of developments in eastern England, although it does seem likely that the initial Iron Age settlement pattern there consisted of self-contained units, not unlike those in other areas (Drury 1978a).

Apart from these economic considerations, we can make some general remarks about the character of the sites occupied in this period. It has always been apparent that Iron Age settlements can show a long period of use, but sometimes they seem to have changed their outward form. At times they remained the same size but became rather more elaborate, assuming the character of an earthwork enclosure or even that of a more massive hill fort. Open settlements might be enclosed at a later stage, and in some cases we find a substantial change in the scale of the surrounding ditch or palisade (Cunliffe 1978a: 161–75, 217–27). Such evidence provides an impression not only of self-sufficiency but of growing ostentation. To take one famous example, it was perfectly possible for an elaborate settlement like Little Woodbury to develop from a palisaded enclosure into a small hill fort (Bersu 1940).

Such hill forts are the third key feature of this period, for not only do they exhibit a rapid increase in numbers; certain of these sites could show signs of actual conflict. This evidence is difficult to use, since the available dates leave a great deal to be desired. The first sign of drastic change is provided by the widespread development of defensive sites. To judge from those cases on which radiocarbon samples are associated with the defences themselves, this seems to have reached a peak between about 700 and 450 BC (Fig. 6.2; of Avery 1976: Fig. 5). The newly constructed sites were distributed very widely and may even include examples near to the Thames Estuary, where hill forts are rarely found (Morris and Buckley, 1978: 21–7). It seems likely that this peak of activity overlapped the change of metal technology. At all events the new sites are essentially similar to those first built during the Late Bronze Age (cf. p. 118).

It is harder to discuss evidence for actual aggression. This interpretation is based mainly on the significant number of defensive structures which seem to have been burnt down during this relatively limited period. This occurred in several different areas of the country, including the Cotswold

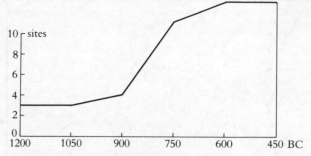

Fig. 6.2 The chronological distribution of Late Bronze Age/Early Iron Age hill forts with radiocarbon dates associated directly with their defences. The dates have been calibrated after Clark (1975).

scarp (S. Champion 1971), the Welsh Marches (Savory 1976), northern England (Challis and Harding 1975), and parts of Scotland (McKie 1976), where a number of the 'vitrified' forts are dated to this period. The first problem is that we cannot tell whether these ramparts were destroyed by hostile action. The case must rest entirely on the chronology of these events, and this evidence has to be qualified. The radiocarbon dates from burnt ramparts refer to the age of the wood used in their building and not to the date at which they were destroyed. For this reason the destruction of these sites may have taken place over a longer period than is immediately apparent. For a rampart to have burnt at all, it must have contained a quantity of timber, and since such ramparts went out of fashion during the Iron Age period the evidence for destruction may be biased towards the earlier sites. Even so, the burning of so many Early Iron Age defences is difficult to discount entirely, especially since the evidence for 'skull fetishes' – possibly a sign of head-hunting – seems to be strongest during this period (C. Wilson 1981: 147). One very striking feature is the way in which hill forts with evidence of burning divide into two regional groups (Fig. 6.3). This distribution pattern is not the result of biases in excavation, as the rarity of similar sites on the chalk makes clear. Nor is it a distribution of vitrified limestone ramparts, for comparable evidence of burning comes from much later sites with different defensive structures.

Cunliffe has identified two successive forms of hill fort in southern England: an 'early' type which became established at various times during the Late Bronze Age and Early Iron Age; and 'developed' or 'planned' hill forts which are found from about 400 BC onwards (1978a: 268–78, and pers. comm.). The latter sites will be considered in the second part of this chapter, and only the early hill forts concern us now. Although they include a wide variety of different sites, one common characteristic is the number of four-post structures that they contain. There are strong argu-

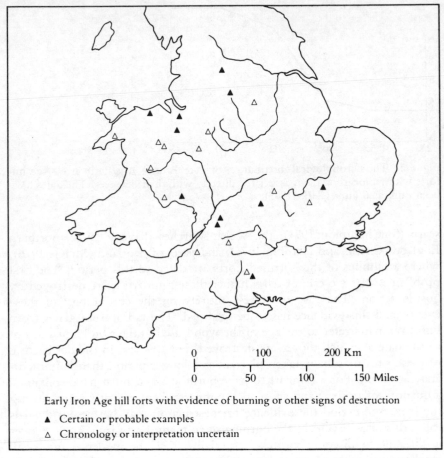

Early Iron Age hill forts with evidence of burning or other signs of destruction

▲   Certain or probable examples

△   Chronology or interpretation uncertain

Fig. 6.3   The distribution of early hill forts with possible evidence of destruction.

ments for interpreting most of these buildings as raised storehouses (Gent 1983).

One of the major problems of Iron Age archaeology concerns the role of the defended sites, for their construction and operation seems difficult to reconcile with the fragmentation and self-sufficiency suggested for the settlement pattern as a whole. There are a few clues to their pre-eminent position. From the Bronze Age onwards, the building of hill forts required a significant amount of labour, and some of the earliest Iron Age examples contained one or more large round houses like those on Late Bronze Age sites in eastern England. The sheer number of storage structures on some of these sites raises problems. Certain hill forts perhaps contained more storehouses than a resident population would have needed. Also, they seem to outstrip the likely capacity of the site as a productive unit. Recent work by Henry Gent (1983) has shed some light on this question. It seems clear that raised storehouses are unusually strongly represented on enclosed or defended sites and are correspondingly less common on open settlements. This does not seem to reflect a bias in discovery since the same contrast does not apply to round houses (*ibid.*).

The fact that some of these hill forts are so much more extensive than ordinary settlements provides one clue to their functions. As mentioned in Chapter 5, the scale on which the Late Bronze Age/earliest Iron Age hill forts in Wessex had been constructed appears to be related to the amount of good agricultural land within an area extending for about 7.5 km from these sites. Such an extensive region could not have been farmed efficiently from a single centre, and the provisioning of the sites must have involved relations with other settlements. Since excavation indicates that such sites were quite densely occupied, the overall extent of these enclosures should be some indication of both their population and their storage capacity.

So far, then, we have suggested that some of the early hill forts contained a disproportionate share of raised store buildings and that these sites were probably provisioned from a larger area than their occupants could have farmed directly. How is this pattern to be interpreted? Perhaps the most widely accepted idea is that such sites were engaged in the redistribution of agricultural produce and other commodities (Cunliffe 1978a: 331). Indeed, in Service's well-known formulation, redistribution was one of the essential elements of a chiefdom (1971: 133–45). In his opinion redistribution developed as a response to economic and ecological diversity. Certain centres assume a dominant role in the settlement pattern because an elite is able to accumulate food and other items and to redirect them within the community. This whole development depends on the existence of environmental differences, and without economic imbalances between communities there would be no role for these centres to fulfill.

This formulation has suffered a setback. Originally, it was developed to account for practices in Polynesia, but more recent research in Hawaii has questioned the value of Service's interpretation (Earle 1977a and b). Despite the existence of ecological variations between different areas, Earle has shown that most exchanges of subsistence goods take place through the kinship network or by barter and do not affect the social hierarchy. The goods that did pass up the hierarchy were not redistributed in the general interest but were employed to fund military and political expansion. Tribute was mobilised in order to supply an elite, who redirected these goods as part of a political policy. 'The redistributive hierarchy of the Hawaiian chiefdom functioned to mobilise goods to support the operation of the political superstructure; in short, redistributional mobilisation was a form of taxation' (Earle 1977a: 226). It is not clear that redistribution in Service's terms can be found in the ethnographic record.

It is difficult to see why the types of relationship that Service described should have become established in Early Iron Age Britain. During the Late Bronze Age there had been economic variations between different regions, and the hill forts could have been engaged in exchange. However, in the early part of the Iron Age the chief characteristic of the smaller settlements is their virtual self-sufficiency. There is little evidence of economic specialisation between different regions of lowland Britain and no real sign that it occurred between individual sites. Craft production is hardly in evidence, and there is little formal variation amongst the settlements of this phase. There seems to be little reason why a redistributive economy should have been needed and, indeed, it is difficult to see how it could become established. Hill forts may have been provisioned partly by the population of the surrounding area, but there seems little reason to suppose that the local inhabitants benefited from this arrangement beyond the military protection offered by these sites. Again, this evidence suggests a significant contraction in the social network.

PART 2 – ISOLATION AND SOCIAL CHANGE 400–100 BC

Around 400 BC close relations with the Continent seem to have lapsed. Apart from south-west England, few areas show much evidence for the continued introduction of European artefacts or for native production of copies. This applies mainly to items from the La Tène cultures of the mainland, but the same change can be seen with the more exotic objects introduced from the Mediterranean (Cunliffe 1978a: 152; Harden 1950; Harbison and Laing 1974). Similarly, British hill forts reached their fullest development during this period of relative isolation, whilst they became less significant in most areas of Europe (Collis 1975). The British hill forts show several significant tendencies. Their number started to fall, suggesting that certain sites may have been achieving a pre-eminent position at the expense of others, an idea backed up by our earlier suggestion of conflict. Some of the sites were deserted or continued in use as simpler farming settlements whose defences were no longer maintained. Newer sites, some of which were defended for the first time, took on a more prominent role.

Some of these sites show two important developments. There is evidence for fairly rigid subdivision of the defended area and also for considerable continuity in the maintenance of a coherent layout (Cunliffe 1978a: 273; Guilbert 1975). Where excavation has been on a sufficiently extensive scale, they appear to show an orderly division of the internal space between houses and storage facilities. The latter include raised granaries or storehouses, but unlike the examples on earlier sites, these were built on a massive scale and were maintained on a regular basis.

In some areas the changes affecting hill forts may not have been complete for a century or more after the break with Europe, and almost certainly they proceeded at different rates in different areas. Although they show a basic continuity with the patterns described in Part One, the later stages of hill fort evolution involved their fairly regular spacing across the landscape, as if each site dominated a territory of roughly equal extent. This pattern has been described in Wessex, Sussex, (Cunliffe 1978a: 275–8) and perhaps the Marches (Stanford 1972). The later stages of this development were roughly contemporary with the emergence of other nucleated settlements, chiefly in the lowlands where the hill forts were not common. A series of such sites has been recognised in recent fieldwork, but investigation is still at an early stage. Although they are best exemplified in eastern England, some of the excavated sites, like Beckford on the Warwickshire Avon (Britnell 1975) are found within the area dominated by hill forts. The same applies to sites on the Wessex chalk. In eastern England the nucleation of settlements into these 'villages' belongs mainly to the third century BC and is seen at sites like Mucking (M. U. Jones 1974), Fengate (Pryor and Cranstone 1978) and Little Waltham (Drury 1978b). Similar developments probably occurred on the Thames gravels at Abingdon (Parrington 1978), and in Northamptonshire at sites like Twywell (Jackson 1975). The same processes may have taken place further to the north. For example the partially excavated settlement at Dragonby in north Lincolnshire (May 1970) shows a marked resemblance to the crop mark complexes on the Yorkshire Wolds (cf. Loughlin and Miller 1979).

There are at least two ways of interpreting this evidence. It may have been a response to population growth, coinciding with an increased number of settlements in other areas. This has often been suggested from the evidence of field survey (Cunliffe 1978b), but the reasons for this development are rarely discussed. We might see population pressure as one feature favouring agricultural change, and even as a reason for using iron to make more efficient agricultural implements. Alternatively, population may have been a dependent variable. It is equally likely that the increase in numbers was *part* of the process of agricultural growth. There is some support for this idea in the ethnographic record. Macfarlane, for example, (1978: 658) observes that:

in most 'peasant' societies, where the family is the main unit of peasant ownership, consumption and social life, in order to maximise production, one must also maximise reproduction . . . Where . . . the basic unit of society is a family or kin-group each new child is an asset, contributing to the welfare of the group, increasing prestige and political power, as well as economic well-being.

If we adopted this approach, we should still need to account for agricultural change at this time. We shall attempt to do so later in this chapter.

Another view is that the nucleation of Middle Iron Age settlement resulted from the amalgamation of communities which already existed as smaller, more scattered units. One distinctive feature of these sites is worth mentioning at this point. In a number of cases the separate houses on these larger sites seem to be grouped together in a series of compounds or annexes, which form the main structural component of the settlement plan (Fig. 6.3). This pattern is not found on earlier Iron Age sites. It seems possible that each of these components was the equivalent to the social unit represented in the earlier pattern of settlement. Such units occur quite widely from the third century BC onwards. Apart from some of the 'villages' mentioned earlier, the pattern exists inside later defended sites, including Salmonds-bury (Dunning 1976), Pilsdon Pen (Gelling 1977: Fig. 5), and Hod Hill (Richmond 1968: Fig. 2). It is tempting to suggest that these changes result from political centralisation and follow the altered distribution of hill forts. They may be one response to pressures on settled land, but this process could also be a protective measure as the pattern of defended sites became more firmly established.

Alongside these developments there are signs of economic specialisation. These are not easy to date and changes may not have occurred at a uniform rate from one area to another. They include the centralised production of fine pottery, which may have started in the sixth century BC in Wessex and in the fourth century BC in the Welsh borderland (E. Morris 1981); the production of salt on coastal sites, which developed on a significant scale from the latter date, or even earlier (Bradley 1975); the making of glass beads from about 300 BC (Orme, Coles, Caseldine and Bailey 1981: 155–60 and 168); and the large scale exploitation of iron sources in the second century (Cunliffe 1978a: 295; Money 1978). There were similar changes in agricultural production. The period from the fifth century has been described as one of agricultural 'stagnation' (M. Jones 1981: 120), but by the third century there were important changes in crop species (F. Green 1981: 148) and in the second century sites on the chalkland began to specialise in different cereals from one another (*ibid.*). A major textile industry began to develop in the Somerset Levels from about 300 BC, and other sites including Farmoor (Lambrick and Robinson 1979) and Fengate (Pryor and Cranstone 1978) seem to have specialised in stock raising. One indication of growing specialisation may be the development of new types of settlement, including the banjo enclosure (Perry 1972). The practice of building land boundaries was also revived at this stage. Not only was a range of artefacts now being made for exchange; there is evidence for the standardisation of products. It seems possible that pots and salt cakes were now made to standard sizes, and the same applies to the iron ingots described as currency bars (Allen 1967). Not surprisingly, a system of weights seems to have developed at this time (Cunliffe 1978a: 273).

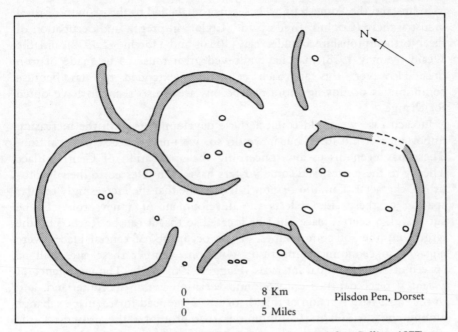

Fig. 6.4   Conjoined round houses at Pilsdon Pen, Dorset (after Gelling 1977).

It is easier to identify these changes than it is to explain them. There are several possibilities to consider. Obviously, it is very tempting to see the decline in long-distance contacts as the main stimulus to increased production. If so, it would be worth discovering the roles which continental imports had played in Early Iron Age society. Unfortunately, this has hardly been investigated, but if there had been some continuity of social practice from the Bronze Age, these artefacts could have been associated mainly with powerful individuals or communities. Once again, control over exotic artefacts may have been one element in building and sustaining a power base. If this were the case during the Early Iron Age, the stimulus for economic change could have come from above. It may be wrong to see the individual settlement as the level at which economic decisions were made.

On the other hand, a more traditional argument has its attractions. It is possible that at least some of these changes do result indirectly from population pressure. This would not create new consumer demands, but might have led to the settlement of increasingly specialised environments. It is often suggested that communities living in agriculturally unpromising areas will develop production for exchange in order to offset this disadvantage. This argument would be attractive in explaining developments in some areas of the country. For example, increased settlement of the

Mendips and the Somerset Levels seems to have led to the growth of rural industry there (Cogbill, Bradley and Taylor, in prep.), and occupation of the Northamptonshire boulder clays (Hall and Hutchings 1972) and the Weald (Money 1978) may have allowed greater use to be made of iron ores. However, this approach cannot be extended too far because communities occupying more prosperous areas also seem to have opted for change.

In each case we could connect these developments with the increasing importance of hill forts, but if we do so, we must proceed with caution. There has been discussion concerning the application of Central Place Theory to these sites, and some writers have even referred to their 'proto-urban' character (Cunliffe 1976b). It is possible that the increasingly regular spacing of these sites reflects the development of a new role. To be successful, a central place must be located so that it can be reached by the largest number of communities. If the occupants of central places were engaged in economic competition with one another these sites will be spaced at roughly equal intervals (Haggett 1965: 118). The emergence of a central place depends on economic variation within its hinterland, and in the most basic version of this theory it is the need for regular exchange among the surrounding communities that promotes the growth of the centre. In this respect the argument echoes our discussion of redistribution. Central Place Theory has been developed in the study of a free market economy and discussion of the spacing of different centres assumes that every community is able to deal with its produce as it wishes. In the Iron Age this seems most unlikely. If hill fort communities were being supported by tribute, settlements in the surrounding area would not be able to choose their economic allegiance (cf. Steponaitis 1978). There is no evidence for the existence of a free market at this time, and the more regular distribution of hill forts is not sufficient reason for making this assumption. In any case the theory usually implies a sequence in which craft specialisation precedes the development of the central place. This is incompatible with the archaeological evidence from southern England.

If the argument in Part 1 is accepted, some of the hill forts were already playing a powerful role before there are clear signs of economic specialisation in their hinterland. Indeed, the power of these sites must have depended to some extent on their ability to obtain tribute from nearby communities. Such communities would have had little scope for experiment on their own account. Over a longer period this system may have been inherently unstable, especially if individual settlements were growing in importance at the same time as the occupants of the hill forts were engaged in competition with one another. The relationship between hill forts and other settlements may have been essentially one-sided, and in times of conflict those providing the tribute could always shift their allegiance in return for protection from another source. Alternatively, certain sites might increase their own status and assume a defensive role themselves. For this reason it is worth asking whether the changes in the economy could have been the result of direct patronage from the centre. This sequence occurred in the Imerina kingdom of Madagascar, itself a 'hill fort society' (H. T. Wright, pers. comm.), and Clive Gamble has suggested that the Minoan palaces exercised a similar supervision over the rural economy (1981). By undermining the self-sufficiency of different communities, the elite were able to reinforce these groups' dependence on a centre. To this extent redistribution could serve a unifying role. As Gamble observes, 'the integration of a dispersed polity ... is achieved through *artificially created dependence* of ... far-flung settlements on the redistributive centre' (*ibid.*: 219, my emphasis).

The growing importance of hill fort communities as patrons and also as consumers is apparent by the Late Iron Age. It is worth considering the contexts of some of the metalwork of this period. No bronze swords of Hallstatt C have been found in hill forts (Cowen 1967) and very few of the later daggers come from these sites (Jope 1961). However, the later hill forts account for roughly a third of all finds of swords (S. Piggott 1950). In the same way, about a third of the currency bars have been found in hill forts, and these sites account for an even higher proportion of the hoards containing these objects (Allen 1967). Similarly, hill forts contain roughly a third of the bronze horse bits made during the Late Iron Age (Ward Perkins 1939), even though it is known that objects of this type were being made in ordinary settlements, before and after the Roman Conquest (Foster 1980; Davies and Spratling 1976). It might be objected that these figures are inflated by the amount of hill fort excavation which has taken place, but the proportion of glass beads on the same sites is substantially lower (Guido 1978: 45–59). Like the metalwork, these attractive items would not have been overlooked, even as chance finds.

Putting these arguments together, it seems that the period of isolation from Europe was one of decisive expansion in Britain. The major role played by the hill forts makes this contrast even sharper. It remains to be seen whether the decline of long distance relations was the only stimulus to economic change within Britain, but the timing of that development is remarkably striking. So are the changes that took place on the major hill forts. It remains to investigate the social role of the more elaborate artefacts, before and after 400 BC, but the long time scale provided by archaeology is already sufficient to favour some hypotheses at the expense of others.

Before considering the dramatic changes of the Late Iron Age, it may be helpful to sum up the main patterns revealed in the first two sections of this chapter. Although the process is little understood, the adoption of iron technology does seem to have come about at a time of real fragmentation. Indeed, it may have been the principal cause of change. We find the emergence of more clearly defined regional groups and evidence of increasing conflict. Regional exchange networks broke down, forcing the population to become more self-sufficient, and as a result this may have been a time of greater agricultural investment.

The major problem posed by these changes was the maintenance of a political superstructure. Initially, this may have been achieved by coercion and also by access to fine objects. We have seen that the occupants of the early hill forts may have been supported by tribute. However, once the supply of exotic artefacts failed, a more stable bond was required between the different levels in society. This could be achieved most effectively by the re-establishment of large scale exchange. Craft production may have been stimulated by patronage, and a social elite was able to use this new relationship to increase the dependence of the rural population on a few major centres. By this stage the situation was sufficiently stable for village communities to form through the amalgamation of smaller settlements. To some extent it may have been the increased stability of British society that persuaded European communities to resume cross-Channel contacts. As we shall see, soon this new development upset the balance that had been achieved.

PART 3 – INCORPORATION AND SOCIAL CHANGE 100 BC–AD 43

Until about 100 BC the main economic relationships of the inhabitants of Gaul had been towards the south. Mediterranean luxury goods had passed to native communities, who traded natural and human resources in return (Nash 1978). From the later years of the second century this profitable relationship was put at risk. The Romans formed an alliance with the Aedui of central Gaul and four years later they established the province of Gallia Transalpina (Brogan 1974). These changes in political geography had serious consequences for Gallic communities. At a time of growing contacts with the Roman world, a series of native 'city states' seems to have developed beyond the frontier (Nash 1978). At the same time the economic orientation of these early states was extended to communities further to the north (*ibid.*). The native states formed an effective buffer between Rome and the barbarians, but were quick to draw on resources that could be traded for prestige goods. One axis was represented mainly by the movement of wine, whilst the other included mercenaries and slaves. Since the northern boundary of these states was now at the Loire and the upper Seine, this system may have affected people as far away as the Channel coast.

It is not surprising that this drastic reorientation was to reach the British

Isles, and cross-Channel relations must have intensified with the threat of further Roman expansion within Gaul. Significantly, when this happened, between 59 and 56 BC, Britons took part in the resistance to Caesar. In spite of the prolonged isolation of Britain from the Continent, these developments had conspired to draw her back into Europe.

Apart from the threat of Roman expansion, there were good reasons why alliances with southern England should be increasingly desirable at this time. This may have been the first occasion since the Bronze Age that the British were producing enough food, raw materials and craft goods to engage in an export trade. It seems likely that exchange partners in Gaul were able to develop links with southern England, both to meet their own needs and to supply the states further to the south. At the same time the military threat posed by Rome meant that Britain could provide an important source of mercenaries.

The scant literary evidence fills out this sequence. There is Caesar's famous reference to the Belgae (Cunliffe 1978a: 68). Much energy has been spent in trying to identify this group in the archaeological record, but no completely satisfactory answer has been found. Caesar's comment is important because it summarises the sequence of events in one part of England. He says that the Belgae came first to raid and then to settle. This provides a helpful clue to the character of these contacts. The initial raiding may have been intended to provide livestock and captives for the markets to the south, a classic pattern around the periphery of emerging states (cf. Nash 1978). Perhaps colonisation came later, as political alliances were made. There is some evidence that this rapprochement resulted in the provision of miltary aid. The earliest coins in southern England have given rise to much controversy, but one particularly interesting idea is that most of the issues shared between Britain and Gaul had been used to pay mercenary troops (Kent 1981). In Gaul itself it seems that the coins of Gallo–Belgic E were minted to support the native resistance to Caesar. Similar support may have been given to groups in north-west France, and it is possible that their contacts with Wessex and south-west England were restricted by the Romans as an act of retaliation (Peacock 1971). It should not be forgotten that Caesar's intervention in British affairs was explained in Rome as a result of native participation in the Gallic Wars.

Britain was brought back into Europe at just the stage when insular society was experiencing changes of its own. These changes have been underemphasised in the literature because of Caesar's convenient reference to the immigration of the Belgae. We should remember that he had good reasons for emphasising the immigrant strain in the British population since he was seeking to justify a punitive expedition after British interference in Gaul. If we cannot recognise the Belgae in the archaeological record, we should be reluctant to make them responsible for too many changes in British society. Surely it was because of the social and economic changes which had taken place already that European communities were encouraged to form alliances.

There were three main axes of contact: between north-west France and south-west England; between the same area and Wessex, and between the region east of the Seine and south-east England. The first of these connections may have been of high antiquity, and it is by no means certain that any hiatus had occurred in the operation of this route (Cunliffe 1982). The main attraction was Cornish tin. This is mentioned by Pytheas about 325 BC, and certainly some of the decorated pottery in the south-west resembles types which went out of fashion in France by 200 BC (Avery 1973: 529). We know from Pytheas that the major centre of the tin trade was called Ictis, and was six days journey from the south-west. This has been identified as the Isle of Wight (Hawkes 1975: 29–31). The coastal site at Mountbatten near Plymouth may have had a similar function and has produced a notable collection of imports (Cunliffe 1982).

The second link is better known and connects the region of Armorica, the ancient equivalent of Britanny and Normandy, with southern Wessex (*ibid.*). The main British site occupied another liminal position, on a coastal promontory overlooking Christchurch Harbour (Cunliffe 1978c). Hengistbury Head may also have occupied a tribal boundary, but the evidence for this division comes from a later period. Interestingly, all the major occupations of this site took place in periods of close relations with the continent, the Early Bronze Age, the Late Bronze Age/Iron Age transition and the Late Iron Age itself. The main continental imports were wine amphorae and their contents, together with Armorican pottery and coins, whilst the site seems to have been involved in large scale industrial activity, including iron, bronze and silver working, shale working and the extraction of salt (*ibid.*). There is rather similar evidence from Poole Harbour not far to the west (Cunliffe 1982: Fig. 3). The inland connections of Hengistbury extend into Wessex, the Mendips and south-west England, which supplied the site with a variety of raw materials, including tin, copper and lead. Hengistbury also received specialist-made pottery from Somerset and the south-west.

These patterns are quite well known, but it is important to realise how far they are rooted in earlier developments. It seems as if foreign traders were making use of well-established patterns of contact to link two economic systems, the British and the Roman, which had developed independently. One clue is provided by the coastal salt industry which was operating on an important scale long before 100 BC. This industry had already established a series of connections between coastal and inland areas, and it seems as if the existence of these links may account for the later spread of coins and amphorae (cf. Bradley 1975). Similarly, a number of the British resources which passed through Hengistbury Head were already being exploited before cross-Channel contacts were resumed. The rural industries of the Mendips and the Somerset Levels are a good example of this pattern (Cogbill, Bradley and Taylor, in prep.). It was only at a developed stage in the local sequence that close contacts were established with southern Wessex.

The Hengistbury crossing involved the introduction of coinage from Armorica, although this has been interpreted in purely economic terms. However, the earliest coins shared between south-east England and France have been viewed in a different light. Since some of these types are found in the area that Caesar called Belgium, they are taken to indicate a folk movement between the two regions (e.g. Rodwell 1976). Different writers have taken different approaches to the problem, some proposing several waves of settlers and others attempting to distinguish between those coins brought by colonists and others used mainly in trade. This has been achieved on an extremely subjective basis. The most striking links between the two areas postdate Caesar's account. Kent (1981) has even argued that coin types issued at different times in Gaul may have been introduced together as payment for mercenaries. On this basis four of the five early waves of coinage could be eliminated from this discussion.

Caesar came into contact only with the inhabitants of the south-east, although he did form treaties with other groups. It is interesting to see what light his experience sheds on the social organisation of the mid-first century BC. It is clear that this was a period of conflict. Local leaders were divided and were unable to sustain a united resistance to his advance. Cassivellaunus, the British war leader, owed his position to military ability rather than inherited office (Todd 1981: 22). This may reflect a more general contemporary practice. Opposition was also hampered by the small size of the different tribes. For instance, the area of modern Kent, which was occupied by one tribe at the Claudian invasion, was divided between four separate rulers (*ibid.*: 51). Caesar encountered the natives during a period of conflict, and took advantage of their internal divisions, as he had done in Gaul. The picture of small scale political units engaged in continual competition is much the same as that seen in the archaeology of Wessex.

It is worth considering these points in more detail, for one process which must have taken place during the ninety-seven years between Caesar's withdrawal and the Claudian conquest was the emergence of a small number of much larger territorial units. In some cases the coins themselves suggest that separate groups were incorporated together in a federal structure. For example, the Iceni may have developed from at least three 'sub-tribes' (Allen, 1970, 14–15). The explanation for this change may lie in the altered political relationship between Britain and Rome during this period. This has two distinct aspects: the impact of increased Roman trade in parts of southern England, and also the ever-present threat of another Roman invasion. Opinions differ concerning the extent of treaty obligations between the two areas, but it is known that Roman expeditions were being contemplated on a number of occasions between 34 and 16 BC (Todd 1981: 31).

We have seen that Cassivellaunus owed his position to his ability to create a temporary alliance against the Romans. It seems possible that the threat of another invasion precipitated the amalgamation of smaller groups into the great tribal kingdoms that we know from the Claudian conquest. It may also have led to the development of hereditary kingship. Morton Fried has argued that 'tribes' are formed in very much this way. They develop out of the impact of state societies on others with a more egalitarian structure (1967: 170). The presence of the state poses a threat to the existence of its neighbours who react by federating into larger political units for their own protection. Even after the Roman army had left, diplomatic efforts ensured that a balance of power existed. Under these circumstances, Fried's hypothesis seems to work rather well. The widening distribution of coins with tribal names indicates that some groups were expanding their influence over a wider area, whilst others mentioned in Caesar's narrative are never heard of again. As part of the same process we find evidence of individual rulers whose coins stress their royal lineage, suggesting that real or fictional descent was the basis of inherited power. The use of the term '*rex*' on some of these coins may imply that the Romans themselves regarded these individuals as client kings (Todd 1981: 47).

It seems that the orientation of trade altered after Caesar's expeditions, perhaps as a result of political directives (Peacock 1971). Contacts between Wessex and Armorica were more restricted, whilst those between Gaul and the south-east now increased. This change mirrors the balance of power within Britain. Caesar had concluded a treaty with the latter area, whilst the decline in trade with Armorica emphasises the reduced importance of the local tribes after their defeat in the Gallic Wars. This does not mean that contacts along this axis came to an end (Williams 1981; Cunliffe 1982), but it is true that the main social developments now occurred in eastern England.

This change had drastic effects on the archaeological evidence from southern Britain. By the end of the Iron Age it is possible to suggest that certain areas had been incorporated into a larger regional economy, more elaborate than that seen at the end of the Bronze Age. The first stage of this process has been described already and is evidenced by the extension of Gallic coinage into south-eastern England. Collis (1971) suggests that this may have taken place along already existing axes of contact. This process was under way by the time of Caesar, although the dating of individual coin issues is very difficult to achieve. The first coins were normally of gold and may have been used as bullion, or even as additional, if standardised prestige objects. The main focus of their distribution was close to London and seems to have been eclipsed after the time of Caesar (Kent 1978). Only in this area were gold coins matched by a lower value issue (*ibid.*: 56–7), but the two different types might have been used in entirely separate spheres of exchange (cf. Haselgrove 1979).

A second element in the assimilation of this region is the occurrence of pottery with close continental parallels. These vessels were wheel-made and some may have been imported. They are known on both sides of the Thames estuary and come mainly from distinctive cremation cemeteries similar to those of Collis's 'North Gallic Culture' (1977b). Together with their metal associations, these graves have been used to define the Aylesford Culture (Hodson 1964). For some time this unit seemed to be the archaeological counterpart of Caesar's Belgae, but it is now thought that the material could be too late in date for this to be correct (Stead 1976). Even so, we should not underestimate the importance of this link, whether it is seen as evidence of immigration or, more probably, as an indication of the willingness of local groups to emulate continental practices.

The third element in the transformation of south-east England is the increase in fine imports, which is seen most clearly in the rich burials of Welwyn type (Stead 1967). These may date from the period between 25 BC and the Claudian invasion. They are notable for the large number of exotic objects placed with the dead. It would be wrong to suppose that the appearance of these distinctive graves marks the first evidence of strong individual authority. It is better to follow the approach taken in Chapter 4 and to suggest that these deposits were made in order to reinforce the power structure. This may well have happened as the major dynasties became established. After all, it was from about the same time that the coins of this area refer to rulers by name.

Other developments over this period are equally important. Two questions have received particular attention: the economic function of Iron Age coinage and the role of the so-called *oppida*. As mentioned earlier, we do not know when the first coins were introduced to Britain. Similar difficulties attend their interpretation. The first coins were made of gold and could have served as valuable objects in themselves, in the same way as contemporary torcs. A major change seems to have happened when a dual currency was adopted. Collis (1971) suggests that this occurred because the gold coins were used to store wealth, mainly in the countryside, whilst the 'small change' was concentrated at sites where market transactions took place. We can check this idea by looking at the distribution of different types of coin. Those used in exchange transactions should have a clustered distribution, highlighting the locations of possible markets, whilst the gold coins should be distributed fairly evenly across the landscape. This does seem to be the case (Cunliffe (ed.) 1981). It may be unwise to suppose that coins could be used only in market exchange, or that their production necessarily took place under political control. It is possible that the major lines of exchange were still determined by social networks and not by the development of a market economy. One function of early coins may have been to allow conversions to be made between different spheres of exchange (Haselgrove 1979), for instance, the movement of subsistence goods and that of metalwork.

On the other hand, it is clear that gold coinage was initially the preroga- tive of the rich areas in the south-east and that it spread only gradually to tribes further north and west. Beyond Dorset and Lincolnshire it is hardly found at all (Cunliffe (ed.) 1981: 62–92). The later coins bear explicit state- ments of tribal affiliation, and for this reason their distributions have been used to chart the changing spheres of influence of different communities. It seems very likely that the development of this inscribed coinage belongs to the period of federation and was one attempt to foster a new unity. The development of formal temples may be another part of this process. A significant number of these sites are close to the edges of coin distributions (Stevens 1940; Hodder 1977: 336–8), or otherwise near to the coast. Usually this is explained by their use as peripheral markets, but in another sense religious practices may have been used to reinforce the tribal boundary. Most of the coins from these sites date from the period of the royal dynasties.

The second feature needing discussion is the development of '*oppida*' in south-east England. This term has given as much difficulty as the archae- ological evidence. There is no agreement on the sense in which it was used by Roman commentators, and it may not have indicated the existence of a tribal capital (Hawkes 1980). Suetonius used the term to describe a series of hill forts in his account of Vespasian's conquest of the south-west (Frere 1978: 89). As used by archaeologists the term has gathered more general connotations. For some writers it seems to denote a royal capital with a market, a mint and defences (*ibid.*: 38), whilst for others it is a descriptive term embracing some of the linear earthwork systems of the Late Iron Age (Cunliffe 1976b). Rodwell has applied it to almost any prosperous site of this period (1976). To avoid this confusion, it may be better to treat the main elements in turn and not to conflate them from the outset.

The first definition fails to account for some of the most important evidence. So long as it is assumed that all the major centres of Late Iron Age Britain served as political capitals, there will be a discrepancy between the number of suitable candidates and the number of tribes issuing coins. This suggests the existence of a more complex settlement hierarchy. Thus St Albans, the site of Verulamium, has a major system of linear earth- works, but both Baldock and Braughing are as important in terms of the artefacts found there (Rodwell 1976: 325–39). Indeed, all three of these sites have produced wealthy burials. There are rich open settlements like the recently excavated site at Skeleton Green (Partridge 1981), some of which contain rectangular timber buildings (Rodwell 1978). These may be derived from Roman, rather than 'Belgic', prototypes. Other important evidence is associated with Iron Age temples, notably the example at Harlow which has produced an outstanding number of coins (Selkirk 1968). We need to rank these sites according to the activities which took place there, rather than try to locate them in an over-schematic political geography. This is an unsatisfactory procedure, inspired by an inconclusive debate about their status as 'towns'. Too little is known of their functions for this discussion to serve much purpose.

The second element is the development of systems of linear earthworks, mainly in the first century AD. The principal examples were at Colchester (Hawkes and Hull 1947), St Albans (Wheeler and Wheeler 1936), Silchester (Boon 1969) and Chichester (Bradley 1971). For some authorities such dyke systems are the essential characteristic of an *oppidum,* but there is nothing particularly 'Belgic' about this concept, and the sites themselves bear little resemblance to the '*oppida*' of Iron Age Europe (cf. Collis 1975). They may have as much to do with the insular habit of building earthwork boundaries, which had lapsed at the end of the Bronze Age and been revived during the Middle Iron Age. Once the 'Belgic' connection is severed, it is easier to approach this evidence. We know very little about the internal organisation of any of these sites and only small elements have been sampled or investigated systematically from the air. Where any information is available, a range of different activities seems to be represented, dispersed over separate parts of the enclosed territory. For example, within the Colchester dykes, Gosbecks Farm includes a major series of fields and other enclosures, together with a ritual site (Crummy 1980). Sheepen, on the other hand, seems to have been used for industrial activity and the import of continental artefacts (*ibid.*). At St Albans, evidence of settlement has been located in several different places, including a large ditched enclosure and another area with a mint (Frere 1979). At Gorhambury a particularly elaborate settlement was established against one of the dykes (Grew 1981: 345), whilst another part of the system abutted a rich cremation cemetery (Stead 1969).

It may be necessary to distinguish between the role of these dyke systems and the broader pattern of settlement. The growth of larger occupation sites is really part of the process of nucleation which began in the third century BC. Some of the largest rural settlements in eastern England have produced a wealth of surface artefacts, including coins and fine metalwork (cf. May 1976). Their excavation is an urgent priority. Although these sites were undefended they may have been of at least equivalent status to the major hill forts in other areas. Linear earthworks are not the inseparable accompaniment of wealthy or extensive settlements. It is more likely that they define the land in use around major centres. They may even be the limits of royal estates. Todd has suggested that the development of Roman villas in south-east England could have occurred so rapidly because some land was privately owned by the time of the Roman conquest (1981: 132). A similar development is known in Gaul (*ibid.*). It is especially interesting that the earthwork boundaries around Chichester seem to have been respected in the post-Conquest period when a client king, Cogidubnus, was established in the area. Despite extensive fieldwork, it appears that the great site at Fishbourne was the only Roman building within the nucleus defined by these earthworks, whereas stone structures are fairly common outside this area.

So far this section has considered some of the changes which happened in southeast England after the time of Caesar. Now it is necessary to look at developments in Wessex. After the conquest of Gaul this region failed to keep pace with events further to the east. This is not to say that Wessex was cut off from continental contacts, but their major emphasis seems to have shifted. This is well illustrated by recent finds from the Hayling Island temple which is situated only 55 km east of Hengistbury Head. This site has produced a series of imported coins dating to the middle and late first century BC, but ten of these came from central Gaul and eight from Belgic Gaul, whilst only four originated in Armorica (Downey, King and Soffe 1980: 301).

Exotic material is not very often found in hill forts, and it is uncertain how fully their occupants participated in cross-Channel trade. Until parts of this region drew closer to eastern England, the only major change was in the further elaboration of these sites, in particular the building of additional ramparts (Cunliffe 1978a: 349–50). Although these changes have been seen as a response to Belgic invasion, it is more likely that they represent the logical culmination of the process of growth described earlier in this chapter. As Ian Hodder has noted, the late multivallate forts show signs of a complex internal hierarchy, whereas the univallate earthworks may not belong to a coherent system (1979b). Three of the largest sites, Maiden Castle, Hod Hill and Badbury Rings have produced quantities of coins (Collis 1971: Fig. 7). These multivallate hill forts were conceived on a larger scale than most of the other examples and may have enjoyed a higher status. Apart from a brief period of re-use at the Roman Conquest, the later history of Wessex hill forts reflects the changing orientations of different parts of this region. In those areas which show increased influence from the south-east, most of the defended sites were abandoned, but where communities remained aloof from these wider changes the hill forts continued to function (Cunliffe 1978a: 335).

The Durotrigian territory was one region which retained its distinctive identity. Like their neighbours, the Dobunni, the Durotriges failed to achieve much political cohesion, and at the Roman conquest it was necessary for Vespasian to capture over twenty separate hill forts before the resistance of these two tribes could be broken (Frere 1978: 89). It is clear that the Durotriges lacked a central political focus, and their coins were usually uninscribed.

To the east of the Durotrigian area, in Hampshire, there are signs that hill forts were being abandoned. It is not clear whether the main source of change was in the south-east, since the dominant tribe in Hampshire was led by a refugee from Gaul (Frere 1978: 56–7). There may have been direct links between his territory and the continent, in addition to those already recognised with other parts of Britain. One important coastal site was on Selsey Bill in West Sussex. Since Selsey seems to have been an island until the Saxon period, it is tempting to consider whether its isolated position could have encouraged its use for trade. Perhaps Selsey was the original port for a more protected settlement close to Chichester. Further light on this question may come from the Hayling Island temple, which is located within a sheltered harbour on the Hampshire-Sussex border. As mentioned earlier, the finds from this site include a significant number of imports, with an emphasis on coins from the middle Loire (Downey, King and Soffe 1980: 301).

The sequence in Wessex shows two important tendencies: there seems to have been a major expansion in the scale of different settlements, some of which were associated with linear boundary earthworks, and throughout this area there was a new peak of agricultural production. It is worth taking each point in turn before seeking a common explanation.

The developments in the settlement pattern are difficult to describe from the available evidence, but they seem to have two aspects. The first is the division of many existing settlements into a number of separate enclosures (A. Ritchie 1971). This pattern occurs quite widely and is certainly not confined to the chalkland. The scale of these sites varies from Gussage All Saints, where the new settlement was virtually the same size as its predecessor (Wainwright 1979b), to Casterley Camp in Wiltshire which covered 24 hectares (Cunnington and Cunnington 1913). The reason for this change remains unknown, although the detailed layout of a few examples may be connected with the management of livestock. In some cases these changes involved the abandonment of a defensible enclosure. This could be connected with the disuse of hill forts at about the same time.

The second feature was the development of more massive sites, which were partially defined by linear dykes. These have rarely been discussed and it is hard to resist the thought that in another area they would have been identified as 'oppida'. They include examples at Arundel in West Sussex (Curwen 1929: pl. 30) and others on the Grovely Ridge in Wiltshire (Cunliffe 1973b: 429–446). The two best known sites are at Gussage Hill in north Dorset and Minchinhampton Common in the Cotswolds (Royal Commission on Historical Monuments 1975: 24; 1976: 81–4). Gussage Hill is particularly informative since the linear earthworks associated with this site take in an area of fully 700 hectares. It has produced surface finds of Durotrigian coins, unlike the completely excavated settlement at Gussage All Saints three kilometres away (M. Green, pers. comm.) and may have been of higher status than the latter site. The appearance of these complexes could reflect the westward extension of a characteristically lowland pattern of settlement. This might also be represented by the far more massive dyke complexes at Bagendon in Gloucestershire (Royal Commission on Historical Monuments 1976: 6–9) and at Stanwick in north-east England (Wheeler 1954). Although the dating of both sites is rather controversial, they are very similar to the major earthworks of south-east England.

It is known that the final period of the Iron Age was another phase of agricultural growth. A particularly important development was the creation of numerous ditched fields and paddocks. Not only did these allow a more efficient use of resources, but in some cases they provided drainage on land which could not have been farmed otherwise. A study of the crop weeds of this period shows that agriculture was achieving even greater efficiency and that settlement was extending into new areas (M. Jones 1981). As a number of authorities have observed, such developments late in the Iron Age created the basic structure of the Roman landscape, and some of the innovations once attributed to the post-Conquest period really took place at this time (cf. Miles 1981).

Putting all this evidence together, one receives a clear impression that the economic system of eastern England was gradually extending its range into the edge of the hill fort-dominated zone. To trace this pattern in the archaeological record is not necessarily to explain it. At one level, these newer arrangements reveal another of those persistent changes of gravity between Wessex and the Thames estuary which we have seen in earlier phases and which were to continue into the Anglo-Saxon period. On this occasion they may mark the establishment of more complicated mechanisms of dominance and dependency.

These questions have been considered in an important paper by Haselgrove (1982) and in concluding this chapter we cannot do better than to follow his main arguments. He suggests that the influx of imported prestige goods in eastern Britain had similar effects to the long-distance trade in fine metalwork during the Bronze Age. Goods were accumulated by local elites and were distributed among their followers. Access to these objects may have been an element in the performance of essential social transactions. There could have been competition for such resources and this may account for some of the political changes of the later pre-Roman period, including the movement of the most elaborate sites from inland

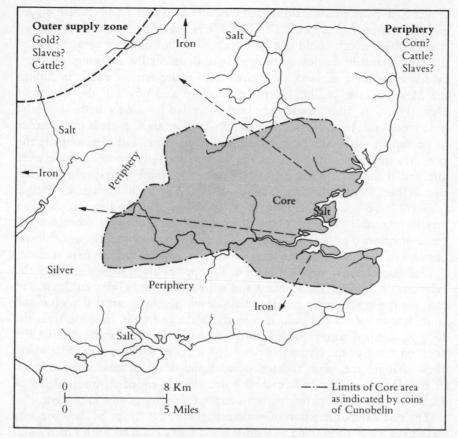

Fig. 6.5 The orientation of exchange during the Late Iron Age of south-east England (after Haselgrove 1982, with modifications).

areas to locations which had direct access to the sea. This might account for the progressive shift of power from St Albans to Colchester. It could also explain the placing of fortified sites along the major rivers.

Strabo tells us some of the imports which were entering the exchange network at this time: ivory necklaces, bracelets, amber and glass, and to these we can add metalwork, amphorae and fine pottery. Most of the items on this list are limited to a 'core area' which runs through Kent as far upstream as the Goring Gap and as far north as Suffolk (Fig. 6.5). It was within this core that the richest burials were deposited. So far this evidence suggests a purely local aggrandisement, resulting from the movement of trade into the core area after Caesar's two expeditions.

When we consider the other axis of exchange, the pattern is quite different. Strabo lists the chief British exports as slaves, cattle, gold, silver, iron, corn and hunting dogs. To these we might add those commodities which had been passing through Hengistbury Head at an earlier stage, including copper, lead and salt. The list is revealing for the number of commodities which could not be obtained within the core area. Some of the raw materials do not occur widely and, generally speaking, the best evidence for their exploitation comes from more remote areas, including the Mendips, the Weald, Northamptonshire and possibly the Forest of Dean (Fig. 6.5). Silver could have been extracted from Mendip lead, whilst gold would not be found nearer than Wales. The slave trade is even harder to document, although the maintenance of so many hill forts outside the core area might be a response to this threat. Certainly, some of these were attacked at this time. One area with evidence of quite widespread destruction is the Welsh Marches (Savory 1976). Although Roman or Belgic invaders have been blamed for these episodes, slave-raiding provides an equally plausible context. These areas may have been one source of the cattle mentioned by Strabo. It is also tempting to think that the agricultural changes of the Late Iron Age were directed partly towards an export trade.

Our discussion of Britain's place in Europe should consider not only the relationship between the Romans and native societies in the south-east, but also the more predatory relations that developed between that region and more fragmented societies further to the north and west. In some areas the long-established pattern of hill forts fell into abeyance, and communities took on some of the characteristics of societies in the core area. Elsewhere these changes met with resistance and social developments were arrested at the stage that they had reached when Britain ended its long period of isolation. These alternative patterns mark the poles of our argument.

The eastward orientation of societies around the fringe of the core area may have owed something to their less extensive contacts with Europe and its wealth. To that extent outside events may have made these areas more dependent on their powerful neighbours. At the same time, political developments in the core area itself could never be independent of Roman foreign policy or, indeed, of the shifting patterns of trade. These factors help to account for the dual structure which had emerged by the end of the Iron Age. Areas of south-east England were dependent on other parts of the country for the resources which they were trading to the Roman world. At the same time, the British Isles were on the extreme edge of a larger, imperial, system and the fortunes of her inhabitants were governed by much wider political considerations. It was only a matter of time before these links were strengthened by force. After seven centuries of continental drift, Britain and Europe came into collision.

7 Reasoning with the irrational
– *Summary and conclusions*

'Now is life solid or shifting? I am haunted by the two contradictions. This has
gone on for ever; will last for ever; goes down to the bottom of the world –
this moment I stand on. Also, it is transitory, flying, diaphanous. I shall pass
like a cloud on the waves. Perhaps it may be that though we change, one flying
after another, so quick, so quick, yet we are somehow successive and
continuous we human beings, and show the light through.'

Virginia Woolf, Diary 4 January 1929

'They will get it straight one day at the Sorbonne.
We shall return at twilight from the lecture
Pleased that the irrational is rational.'

Wallace Stevens, Notes Toward a Supreme Fiction

By this stage I would anticipate two very different reactions from readers:
either a basic agreement that social questions *can* be investigated by archaeological methods, or the conviction that this book, rather than Stevens'
poem, should be called 'Notes Toward a Supreme Fiction'. If the reader
feels entirely sceptical, it is unlikely that this closing summary will make
any difference. If more sympathetic readers also dissent, there is the
consolation of knowing that the matter can still be discussed. What is at
issue is the *possibility* of a more rounded approach to prehistory.

In some ways our problem is not the archaeological visibility of ancient
societies, even in their less mundane aspects; there is so much data that it
is hard to see the wood for the trees. M. A. Smith's comments on the
limits of inference in archaeology (1955) remind me of the debate between
the astronomer and the savants in Bertolt Brecht's play, *The Life of Galileo*.
The savants consider whether Galileo's observations of the heavenly bodies
can be philosophically sound – 'Can such planets exist?', they ask, 'Are
such stars necessary?' – and having rejected their existence on a purely
philosophical basis, they decline all invitations to view them through a
telescope. It is time that archaeologists accepted that they can recognise
patterns which they had not expected to see. Some of these have been

described in earlier chapters. I close my case by summarising their chief characteristics and a few of the links between them.

In Chapter 1 we argued that Smith had experienced so much difficulty in contemplating a 'social' archaeology because she misunderstood the objectives of this subject. Rather than confronting an ethnographic case study with the equally transient results of an excavation, she should have paid greater attention to archaeology's ability to trace long sequences of change. The two different time scales which so concerned Virginia Woolf are of crucial significance, and the longer perspective of prehistory has attracted the interest of scholars in other fields. Each chapter in this book has discussed a fairly clear-cut sequence, although its interpretation may be controversial. This section will review these characteristic sequences, for it is at this more abstract level that they could find an echo in other areas.

For this reason it is less helpful to offer a narrative account than to summarise the changing relationships between different parts of the archaeological record. Perhaps this approach is too empirical and by placing the emphasis so firmly on the field evidence we lose some theoretical elegance, but in doing so we bring the argument down to the one level at which these ideas can be tested. Six elements can be considered briefly: the character and layout of settlements; changing subsistence patterns; the provision of elaborate monuments or elaborate burials; the acquisition and consumption of exotic resources; the changing character of artefact distributions; and the changing scale of the system to which these elements belong.

In their papers on the limits of inference in archaeology, both Hawkes (1954) and M. A. Smith (1955) considered the difficulties of interpreting settlement plans. They were right to do so, but they did not comment on a more significant problem which can only be recognised in a lengthy *sequence*. It seems that settlement plans show the greatest variation during phases in which burials rites are fairly uniform. Conversely, when settlements are rather less complex, cemeteries show a more elaborate structure. The main phases in which the settlements show much variety, either in their form or their layout, are the Middle Neolithic, the Later Bronze Age and the Iron Age. All these periods have a rather uniform burial record. The elaborate Neolithic long barrows have an ostensibly 'communal' character, and there is fairly limited evidence for burial rites during the Later Bronze Age and much of the Iron Age. Outside a few restricted areas, there is little to suggest that significant social variations were being expressed through this medium. Even the Bronze Age cremation cemeteries may have suppressed actual distinctions among the living. By contrast, there is little sign of complex settlements during the Later Neolithic and the Earlier Bronze Age, when the burial record was much more elaborate. In these periods social position may have depended on access to exotic goods, rather than direct control of the food supply.

This contrast is not the only pattern shown by the settlements. The building of large monuments must also be considered, since these would have consumed an appreciable share of the energy budget. It seems likely that to some extent the construction and use of large monuments performed a communal function, although it probably concealed the power of a small elite. This may account for the alternation between consumption of energy on large corporate monuments, and consumption of wealth in elaborate funerals. At the same time, the energy devoted to building ceremonial centres may have been diverted from the domestic sphere. We can recognise three stages in this relationship. In the Earlier Neolithic period it is hard to distinguish between ceremonial sites and high status settlements since there may have been little separation of spheres; access to the supernatural could have been one road to political power. During the Later Neolithic and the Earlier Bronze Age phases, a far sharper division was made, and the gigantic ceremonial centres were built at times when domestic sites were at their least impressive. The use of these centres may have emphasised the separation of an elite and its rituals from the rest of the population. Lastly, in the late first millenium these priorities were reversed completely, and very complex domestic sites were constructed, whilst the formal shrines or temples of the Iron Age were remarkably unimpressive. By this stage greater energy was devoted to embellishing the *settlements* of an elite. Their massive defences seem to express the growing importance of military, rather than supernatural sanctions.

Also, it seems that settlements were more elaborate during periods in which the burial rite stressed the relationship of the community to the land. In the Later Bronze Age this is shown by the characteristic siting of cremation cemeteries, and even by their internal structure, with its emphasis on the 'family' group (Bradley 1981a). In the Iron Age the same relationship can be extended to the burials in corn storage pits (Whimster 1981: 5–15). It has been thought that such pits provided a convenient place to discard a body, but recent work has shown that other details of this practice show a striking formality (*ibid.*). Communities who were able to build immense hill forts could have dug proper graves had they wished to do so (*ibid.*: 16–25). It seems likely that this rite is connected with the function of these pits and their close association with the fertility of the land. If this is correct, we can suggest that social differences were expressed through settlements mainly in periods when position was linked directly to food production. When access to prestige goods was more important, rituals played a similar role.

This leads to the next topic. Subsistence has been studied intensively during the last ten years, and in Hawkes' scheme is one of the areas which raise fewest problems of interpretation. In fact the available evidence presents certain surprises. It might seem reasonable to look for a direct relationship between the periods of agricultural expansion and those with the greatest consumption of wealth and energy in other spheres. Indeed, it would be tempting to suggest that agricultural intensification was a precondition for such activities. The empirical evidence gives a rather different impression. Although some changes took place during the Later Neolithic, there may be less evidence of intensive agriculture in the period when the largest monuments were built than there is from the phases before and after this development. All too little is known about farming practices between about 2500 and 1200 bc, the period when large henges and rich burials were in use, and we have more evidence of agricultural growth from the Earlier Neolithic and the Later Bronze Age periods. This alternation ended by the Iron Age, when the larger monuments were closely integrated with local economic patterns. On a smaller scale, the colonisation of peripheral areas during the second millenium took place in between the two phases of complex burials.

Similarly, there may be more evidence for the consumption of prestige objects in between the periods of agricultural growth (cf. Bradley 1981b). In fact such reorganisation may be one consequence of the collapse of long distance exchange networks (*ibid.*). Despite local adjustments in the late third millenium, the phases of fairly rapid agricultural growth were during the Middle Bronze Age and the Iron Age, and in both cases they followed changes in the movement of fine metalwork. In the first case this happened with the re-routing of overseas exchange from Wessex to the Thames Valley, and in the second example it occurred as long distance trading lapsed because of the adoption of iron. The few recognisable changes in the Later Neolithic also followed the severance of links with Europe. All three examples suggest that agricultural growth is a feature of periods in which parts of Britain were cut off from a wider system. It is not linked directly with the development of large monuments or rich graves. As we shall see, this does not apply to the Late Iron Age.

In Chapter 4 we observed that monument building and the provision of elaborate burials are to some extent alternatives for one another, in the first case emphasising the cohesion of the social group and in the second stressing the role of the individual. The choice between these alternatives may be linked with the problems of creating an organised society. Generally speaking, the two proceed in sequence, although this is not inevitable, monument construction occurring before the provision of elaborate single graves. This can be seen in several phases. During the Neolithic period the development of individual burial took place at roughly the same time as the use of the last causewayed enclosures. Where long barrows were employed for this purpose the mounds were less impressive than earlier monuments. More often single burials were in less conspicuous round barrows or ring ditches. As we have seen, in the second millenium there was a fairly clear alternation between phases of monument building and periods with complex burials, and this continued after the collapse of the Wessex Culture when we find the development of defended enclosures. These hardly overlap the period of the furnished burials, and the main phase of hill fort building in the south came after formal cemeteries had gone out of use. Significantly, no Iron Age hill forts are known in the main area with Arras Culture graves.

Both types of evidence can be treated in combination in order to show still broader patterns. Several writers have stressed the way in which elaborate burials may have been deposited during periods of competition and culture contact (p. 75). Although the details are different, rather similar comments can be made concerning the provision of large monuments.

Individual burials are most elaborate after the Middle Neolithic 'standstill', during which there may have been some economic contraction, and in the period of culture contact which resulted from the renewal of relations with Europe early in the second millenium. The same pattern can be seen in the Iron Age, when the most elaborate burials are the cemeteries in Yorkshire, which show strong links with the Continent, and the Welwyn burials of the south-east, which date from a phase of rapid social change. Similarly, the largest monuments were built around the time of the Neolithic 'hiatus' and during the late third millenium when long-distance exchange developed. Two other phases of monument building took place, the first at the end of the Wessex Culture and the second in the period of contraction which marks the Bronze Age/Iron Age transition.

These observations are important because they bring together a series of monuments which served completely different functions. Some were ritual and ceremonial sites, but others were defended settlements. This distinction does not affect the usefulness of the broader scheme. In each case there was the same need to maintain a coherent organisation through the construction of large monuments.

We have seen that the importance of agricultural settlement varies according to the scale of the social system. It is most prominent during those periods in which long-distance contacts were uncommon and much less conspicuous once they had resumed – there may be exceptions to this generalisation in the Later Neolithic and the Late Iron Age. One of the key elements in this thinking is the exchange and consumption of prestige goods. This is found in four periods: the Later Neolithic, when the system was limited to Britain and Ireland; the Earlier Bronze Age, when the exchange network extended outwards into Europe; the Later Bronze Age, when this happened again; and the Late Iron Age. In most cases, the defining characteristic of these objects is their exclusion from the settlement record. For example, in the Bronze Age there is little chance of finding the more elaborate artefacts in deposits of domestic refuse (cf. Braun 1979). For the most part there is a direct relationship between the distances travelled by these objects and their chances of being found in specialised deposits. Thus Later Neolithic prestige objects are shared between different parts of Britain but are not distributed over a wider area. This contrasts with the far greater extent of second millenium exchange systems. It seems significant that the Neolithic material is sometimes found in settlements, but this is rarely the case after that time. Even in the Late Iron Age, when imported pottery was distributed quite widely, the types of object in the Welwyn graves are hardly known elsewhere.

The character of the more specialised deposits shows significant changes through time. Generally speaking, there is a division between grave goods and other deliberate deposits. In many cases these are not found in the same regions or in the same periods, and where this does occur the elaborate character of one type of deposit makes up for the simpler composition of the others. In the Later Neolithic period most of the deliberate deposits of elaborate or exotic artefacts were located close to large monuments – cursus monuments or henges – and were placed in graves in those areas where ceremonial centres played a less important role. For example, there are a number of Grooved Ware deposits on the Wessex chalkland, where elaborate burials are uncommon. Similarly, on the Yorkshire Wolds the most complex Late Neolithic deposits are near to the Rudston monolith, whilst the single burials of this date are some distance to the west. The same contrast carries over into the Earlier Bronze Age, when the distribution of metal hoards avoided the area with rich Wessex graves (S. Needham, pers. comm.). The relations between later grave offerings and river finds were considered in Chapter 5, and some of these characteristic patterns can be found on a smaller scale after the Bronze Age was over. For example, much of the elaborate metalwork produced during the Late Iron Age comes from hoards and rivers and avoids the distribution of the rich Welwyn graves. Different interpretations of deposition have been considered already.

The 'consumption' of prestige objects may have been combined with consumption of a more orthodox character. There are three or four phases in which there seem to be signs of large scale meat-eating. Apart from the earliest phase, this occurs in periods when fine artefacts were being deposited separately from burials. The evidence for large scale meat consumption starts in the Earlier Neolithic and is found on a series of long barrows and cairns, and also on causewayed enclosures. The contents of some of these sites already reveal the use of special types of artefact. This same principle may account for the almost ubiquitous association between Grooved Ware and pig bones, since pig is the only domestic animal which is not used for secondary products. The same sites contain an array of special artefacts and in some cases their status as settlements can be questioned. The association of pig bones with Grooved Ware contrasts with other assemblages of the same period.

The third period with evidence of large scale meat consumption is the Later Bronze Age, another phase in which the deposition of prestige objects assumed considerable importance. This evidence takes two forms. There are the distinctive 'burnt mounds' of this period, which have been interpreted as specialised facilities for cooking meat (M. O'Kelly 1954; Hedges 1975). Most of the associated radiocarbon dates cover the period of the main metal deposits – indeed, some of the contemporary bronze hoards themselves contain animal bones, and the bog and river finds can even include cauldrons. The other important evidence comes from the faunal remains at Egham and Thwing considered earlier (p. 119–20). Rather similar bone assemblages are known from Late Iron Age sites, in particular the unusually rich settlements of Old Sleaford (Higgs and White 1963: 282), Bagendon (Clifford 1961: 269) and Skeleton Green (Partridge 1981: 205). These sites also included quantities of coins and imported pottery. To sum up, despite the limited information available in print, there seems to be a direct relationship between the periods of highest meat consumption and those when fine artefacts were 'consumed'.

There are further links between the uses of such artefacts and their characteristic distributions. This question has been discussed in two recent papers (Bradley and Hodder 1979; Ellison 1981b). There are three types of distribution to consider: the existence of entirely discrete styles of artefacts and monuments; the presence of overlapping artefact distributions which mask a pattern of mutually exclusive associations; and a combination of both principles, in which ordinary 'domestic' artefacts have separate regional distributions, whilst the more elaborate forms cross-cut these divisions and are found over wider areas. We have seen how the existence of mutually exclusive distributions may relate to economic stress, for only periods of conflict or competition would communities symbolise their distinctive identity by this means (Hodder 1979a). Such patterns may be found in three periods: the Earlier Neolithic, where they are very weakly developed, the Middle Bronze Age and the Early Iron Age. In each case these patterns develop in phases of significant economic growth when the political structure was not very elaborate. The second type of distribution is more closely related to those periods in which special purpose artefacts were shared over larger areas, in particular the Later Neolithic and the Earlier Bronze Age. It seems that social tensions were directed beyond the local group and that competition was expressed through the formation of long-distance alliances. There is less evidence of a direct link between the local group and its territory. Lastly, in both the Late Bronze Age and the Late Iron Age there are signs that the two patterns operated together. We have already mentioned the existence of mutually exclusive distributions: again the finer objects cover very much larger areas. It seems likely that the contrast between these patterns may be essentially hierarchical; group identity is stressed at the lower level but long distance alliances are confined to an elite.

This scheme is matched by the changing sizes of the different distributions. As Ellison (1981b) has shown, artefact distributions cover much larger areas during the Later Neolithic and Earlier Bronze Age periods. Indeed, the scale of such patterns should provide an objective measure of the likely character of certain artefacts. Ideally, this should be combined with an estimate of their overall frequency, but the problems of deposition considered in Chapter 5 may limit the potential of this approach. Even so, there seems to be some relationship between the rarity of different objects, the effort involved in their production and the distance over which they travelled. As we have seen, the most widely travelled artefacts are found with elaborate monuments or burials.

The last element in this discussion is the changing scale of the system. In some ways this question has been implicit in virtually all the points made earlier, but it may be helpful to summarise them here. There seem to be two processes at work: an alternation between periods of relative isolation, in which social developments were essentially small scale; and periods in which parts of Britain were integrated with social and economic networks reaching into Europe. With the exceptions of the Earlier Neolithic and the Late Iron Age, the major periods of economic growth did not occur when the system was open to strong outside influence. Rather, the important developments of the Middle Bronze Age and the Middle Iron Age may have been stimulated by decreasing contacts with other areas. At the same time the character of these long distance links changed between the Neolithic period and the Iron Age.

Very little is known about connections with the Continent during the earlier third millenium, but the subsequent development of long-distance relationships within the British Isles is a very distinctive process. It has two main characteristics. The system was not connected with the movement of *economic* resources, except possibly axes. It was concerned with the sharing of special types of non-utilitarian artefact, of symbols and, probably, of ritual knowledge. This system connected a series of quite separate societies, all of which were fairly small. They seem to have lacked the economic reserves offered by a dependent periphery. The latter developed only during the Earlier Bronze Age, by which time some of these areas had lost their importance. The second period of long-distance exchange was during the Later Bronze Age and shows one significant development from the Neolithic system. This time it appears that the elite was still exchanging prestige items, but its own power base was secured by a supply of additional resources from the surrounding area. This may account for the different economic emphases of communities in Wessex and the Thames Valley. Whilst both groups engaged in the exchange of subsistence goods, only the high-ranking communities took part in the movement of fine metalwork. In the final phase of long-distance contact, we have moved still further from the exchange of ritual knowledge. In the Late Iron Age, there is more evidence that a rich core area in the south-east was able to exploit a dependent periphery in order to participate in long distance trade. In this case the relationship was rather one-sided, and the introduction of fine artefacts into parts of Britain was the result of a straightforward export trade, involving the movement of agricultural produce and natural resources. Whilst the introduction of luxury goods into south-east England can be described as 'prestige trade', the exports that Strabo lists have a purely economic character.

We have reached the end of the prehistoric period, having reviewed all six of these questions. Is it possible, using the long perspective of prehistory, to combine these different elements into one outline? The fact that these patterns are so repetitive suggests that *some* of the underlying processes may have been cyclical. If so, there seem to have been three, or possibly four, cycles of growth and decline in prehistoric Britain. The first of these took place in the Earlier Neolithic, in some areas giving way to a new sequence of changes, from the Later Neolithic to the Earlier Bronze Age. The second major cycle is found in the Later Bronze Age, while the last occurred in the Iron Age. Many of the reasons for these developments have been considered already. Now it is important to stress their links. Each sequence has some elements in common, but no two are the same.

Most often agricultural growth seems to precede the other developments, but in no sense does it *cause* them. In some areas changes in the economic system may have been supported by an ideology which emphasised the relationship of the community to its land. The next stage was the emergence of more powerful groups or individuals, revealed by evidence of feasting, the building of complex monuments and the production of special types of artefact. A number of these fine objects played no role in the domestic economy. Their circulation and consumption may have been carefully controlled, so that access to these objects could provide an alternative source of power by which people could distance themselves from the business of food production. At this stage they could also reinforce their local eminence by forming long-distance alliances. After a transitional phase in which the building of 'communal' monuments concealed the realities of power, sometimes we find the development of burial rites which stress the role of the individual and provide a permanent memorial to his or her achievement. The development of cemeteries or other monuments around such graves is a reference to the past as the source of legitimate authority. Once this stage is reached, the elite's position is harder to challenge without recourse to armed conflict.

Some aspects of this scheme come close to the model put forward by

Friedman (1979), which was summarised in Chapter 2, but by taking a more eclectic approach we have been able to discuss a wider range of information and ideas. There is a real danger in applying only one model to such a complex period, and it is crucially important to maintain a flexible approach. Above all this is shown by the divergences from this outline seen in each of the sequences. History does not repeat itself, and at either end of the period considered in this book it takes a very distinctive course. In the Earlier Neolithic period there are practical difficulties in recognising many patterns, partly because the chronology is poorly understood, but also because some of these processes may have been halted at an early stage. Similarly, the Iron Age poses very special problems. Events during this period took a different path from those in the other sequences, to some extent because warfare played a more decisive role than the types of social competition observed in other phases. Possibly this happened because there were greater pressures on land and other resources. More significant was the fact that native communities were trading with a much more complex society. This changed the course of events entirely.

Within the general framework suggested here there are numerous variants, many of which have been highlighted at appropriate points in the discussion. Three comments are of central importance. First, it must be understood that the actual processes of growth were never quite the same in different periods, or in different regions. Thus in the Later Neolithic the development of social ranking followed several alternative courses, even though elites formed alliances with one another at different stages of this process. Secondly, we must be aware of the important alternatives provided by competitive consumption and actual aggression. These may have been practised in different parts of Britain during the Later Bronze Age, although warfare became more important from the start of the Iron Age. Unless we realise the connection between these activities, an unnecessary contrast is created between different parts of the archaeological record. In the core areas of Later Bronze Age Britain conflicts could be transferred into competitive ritual, but in the more fragmented society of the Iron Age this was less likely to happen.

Lastly, prehistoric society grew steadily more complex and, despite the successive phases of devolution and decline, the rate of change increased. This can be seen if we consider the length of our sequences in calendar years. Thus the Earlier Neolithic sequence lasted over a millenium, and developments during the Later Neolithic and Earlier Bronze Age probably took even longer. By contrast, the Later Bronze Age sequence took about seven centuries, whilst Iron Age society had developed an equally complex structure in a shorter period.

This changing time scale emphasises that no two sequences could have been the same, whatever their common features. We have not been considering an exact cycle, and the end of every period of change was very different from its starting point. It is interesting to speculate that Iron Age society might have broken free of the constraints experienced in earlier periods, but we cannot be certain, since the entire process was curtailed by the Roman Conquest. Evidence from central Gaul, where similar developments reached a further stage, suggests that in time Iron Age Britain could have developed the political unity characteristic of early states.

We began by drawing a distinction between the fairly static picture provided by the ethnographic record and the longer perspectives of archaeology. It is this long time scale that allows us to discuss social change. The past is camouflaged and we recognise it when something moves. The emphasis on sequence means that our task is even more difficult than the writing of descriptive ethnography. I doubt whether this book has come to terms with the sheer complexity of the evidence. The immediacy of settlement excavation is lost in a growing abstraction. Archaeology has still to experience a hazardous rite of passage, but our confusion in the face of so many possibilities is not peculiar to our discipline. The point is made with more elegance in a novel which I quoted in Chapter 5. Our protagonists are so far away that they will always lack certain qualities. Let us leave the last word to Robert Musil:

There was a great deal going on and one was aware of it . . . Every school boy
understood the details of what was going on, but as regards the whole there
was nobody who quite knew what was really happening . . . Only a short time
later it might all just as well have happened in a different order or the other
way round, and everything would have looked pretty much as it always did,
and as indeed it always does except for certain changes that inexplicably
establish themselves in the course of time, forming the shiny track that is left by
the snail of history.

Abbreviations used in the bibliography

Amer. Anthrop.   American Anthropologist
Amer. Antiq.   American Antiquity
Antiq.   Antiquity
Antiq. Journ.   Antiquaries Journal
Arch.   Archaeologia
Arch. Cambrensis   Archaeologia Cambrensis
Arch. Cant.   Archaeologia Cantiana
Archaeol. Journ.   Archaeological Journal
Archaeol. Newsletter   Archaeological Newsletter
Atti 1 Congr Preist. e Proist. Mediter.   Atti del 1° Congresso Internazionale di Preistoria e Protistoria Mediterranea
B.A.R.   British Archaeological Reports
Beds. Archaeol. Journ.   Bedfordshire Archaeological Journal
Berks. Archaeol. Journ.   Berkshire Archaeological Journal
Bull. Inst. Archaeol. Univ. London   Bulletin of the London University Institute of Archaeology
Cambridge U.P.   Cambridge University Press
Current Archaeol.   Current Archaeology
East Anglian Archaeol.   East Anglian Archaeology
Edinburgh U.P.   Edinburgh University Press
H.M.S.O.   Her/His Majesty's Stationery Office
Int. Journ. Naut. Archaeol.   International Journal of Nautical Archaeology
Irish U.P.   Irish Universities Press

Journ. Archaeol. Science   Journal of Archaeological Science
Journ. Roy. Soc. Antiq. Ireland   Journal of the Royal Society of Antiquaries of Ireland
Leicester U.P.   Leicester University Press
Lincs. Hist. Archaeol.   Lincolnshire History and Archaeology
Liverpool U.P.   Liverpool University Press
Northants. Archaeol.   Northamptonshire Archaeology
Oxford Journ. Archaeol.   Oxford Journal of Archaeology
Oxford U.P.   Oxford University Press
Oxon.   Oxoniensia
Proc. Cambridge Antiq. Soc.   Proceedings of the Cambridge Antiquarian Society
Proc. Cotteswold Natur. Field Club   Proceedings of the Cotteswold Naturalists' Field Club
Proc. Devon Archaeol. Soc.   Proceedings of the Devon Archaeological Society
Proc. Devon Archaeol. Exploration Soc.   Proceedings of the Devon Archaeological Exploration Society
Proc. Dorset Natur. Hist. Archaeol. Soc.   Proceedings of the Dorset Natural History and Archaeological Society
Proc. Hants. Field Club and Archaeol. Soc.   Proceedings of the Hampshire Field Club and Archaeological Society
Proc. Prehist. Soc.   Proceedings of the Prehistoric Society
Proc. Roy. Irish Acad.   Proceedings of the Royal Irish Academy

Proc. Soc. Antiq. Scotland   *Proceedings of the Society of Antiquaries of Scotland*

Proc. Univ. Bristol Spelaeological Soc.   *Proceedings of the Bristol University Spelaeological Society*

Rec. Bucks.   *Records of Buckinghamshire*

Scottish Archaeol. Rev.   *Scottish Archaeological Review*

Surrey Archaeol. Soc.   *Surrey Archaeological Society*

Sussex Archaeol. Collect.   *Sussex Archaeological Collections*

Trans. Cumberland and Westmorland Antiq. Archaeol. Soc.   *Transactions of the Cumberland and Westmorland Antiquarian and Archaeological Society*

Trans. Essex Archaeol. Soc.   *Transactions of the Essex Archaeological Society*

Trans. Hunter Archaeol. Soc.   *Transactions of the Hunter Archaeological Society*

Trans. Leics. Archaeol. Hist. Soc.   *Transactions of the Leicestershire Archaeological and Historical Society*

Trans. London and Middlesex Archaeol. Soc.   *Transactions of the London and Middlesex Archaeological Society*

Ulster Journ. Archaeol.   *Ulster Journal of Archaeology*

Vale of Evesham Hist. Soc.   Vale of Evesham Historical Society

Warsaw U.P.   Warsaw University Press

Wilts. Archaeol. Mag.   *Wiltshire Archaeological Magazine*

World Archaeol.   *World Archaeology*

Yale U.P.   Yale University Press

Yorkshire Archaeol. Journ.   *Yorkshire Archaeological Journal*

Bibliography

Adkins, R. and Jackson, R. (1978) *Neolithic Stone and Flint Axes from the River Thames*, British Museum (Occasional Paper 1), London.

Agache, R. (1979) Informations archéologiques, circonscription de Picardie, *Gallia Préhistoire* **22**, 409–41.

Allen, D. (1967) Iron currency bars in Britain, *Proc. Prehist. Soc.*, **33**, 307–35.

Allen, D. (1970) The coins of the Iceni, *Britannia* **1**, 1–33.

Anon. (1926) Bronze Age hoard from Sussex, *Antiq. Journ.*, **6**, 444–6.

ApSimon, A. M., Musgrave, J. H., Sheldon, J., Tratman, E. K. and van Wijngaarden-Bakker, L. (1976) Gorsey Bigbury, Cheddar, Somerset: radiocarbon dating, human and animal bones, charcoals and archaeological reassessment, *Proc. Univ. Bristol Spelaeological Soc.*, **14**, 155–83.

Ashbee, P. (1966) The Fussell's Lodge long barrow excavations 1957, *Arch.*, **100**, 1–80.

Ashbee, P. (1970) *The Earthen Long Barrow in Britain*, Dent, London.

Ashbee, P. (1978) *The Ancient British*, Geo. Abstracts Ltd, Norwich.

Ashbee, P., Smith, I. S., Evans, J. G. (1979) Excavation of three long barrows near Avebury, Wiltshire, *Proc. Prehist. Soc.*, **45**, 207–300.

Ashmore, P. J. (1981) Callanish, *Discovery and Excavation in Scotland, 1981*, 49–50.

Atkinson, R. J. C. (1956) *Stonehenge*, Hamish Hamilton, London.

Atkinson, R. J. C. (1965) Wayland's Smithy, *Antiq.*, **39**, 126–33.

Atkinson, R. J. C. (1970) Silbury Hill, 1969–70, *Antiq.*, **44**, 313–14.

Atkinson, R. J. C. (1972) Burial and population in the British Bronze Age, pp. 107–16 in **Burgess**, C. and Lynch, F. (eds), *Early Man in Wales and the West*, Adams and Dart, Bath.

Atkinson, R. J. C., Piggott, C. M. and Sandars, N. K. (1951) *Excavations at Dorchester, Oxfordshire*, Ashmolean Museum, Oxford.

Avery, M. (1973) British La Tène decorated pottery: an outline, *Études Celtiques*, **13**, 522–51.

Avery, M. (1976) Hillforts of the British Isles: a student's introduction. pp. 1–58 in Harding, D. W. (ed.), *Hillforts: Later Prehistoric Earthworks in Britain and Ireland*, Academic Press, London and New York.

Bailey, C. J. (1980) Excavation of three round barrows in the parish of Kingston Russell, *Proc. Dorset Natur. Hist. Archaeol. Soc.*, **102**, 19–31.

Barclay, G. (1981) North Mains, Strathallan, *Current Archaeol.*, **78**, 218–21.

Barrett, J. C. (1976) Deverel-Rimbury: problems of chronology and interpretation, pp. 289–307, in Burgess. C. and Miket, R. (eds), *Settlement and*

Economy in the Third and Second Millenia BC, British Archaeological Reports (B.A.R. **33**), Oxford.

Barrett, J. C. (1980a) The evolution of later Bronze Age settlement, pp. 77–100, in Barrett, J. C. and Bradley, R. J. (ed), *Settlement and Society in the British Later Bronze Age*, British Archaeological Reports (B.A.R. **83**), Oxford.

Barrett, J. C. (1980b) The pottery of the later Bronze Age in lowland England, *Proc. Prehist. Soc.*, **46**, 297–319.

Barrett, J. C. and Bradley, R. J. (eds) (1980) *Settlement and Society in the British Later Bronze Age*, British Archaeological Reports (B.A.R. **83**), Oxford.

Barrett, J. C. and Bradley, R. J. (1980a) Later Bronze Age settlement in south Wessex and Cranborne Chase, pp. 181–208, in Barrett, J. C. and Bradley, R. J. (eds), *Settlement and Society in the British Later Bronze Age*, British Archaeological Reports (B.A.R. **83**), Oxford.

Barrett, J. C. and Bradley, R. J. (1980b) The later Bronze Age in the Thames valley, pp. 247–69, in Barrett, J. C. and Bradley, R. J. (eds), *Settlement and Society in the British Later Bronze Age*, British Archaeological Reports (B.A.R. **83**), Oxford.

Barrett, J. C., Bradley, R. J., Green, M. and Lewis, B. (1981) The earlier prehistoric settlement of Cranborne Chase, *Antiq. Journ.*, **61**, 203–37.

Benson, D. and Miles, D. (1974) *The Upper Thames Valley. An Archaeological Survey of the River Gravels*, Oxfordshire Archaeological Unit, Oxford.

Bersu, G. (1940) Excavations at Little Woodbury, Wiltshire, part 1: the settlement as revealed by excavation, *Proc. Prehist. Soc.*, **6**, 30–111.

Beswick, P. (1975) Report on the shale industry at Swine Sty, *Trans. Hunter Archaeol. Soc.*, **10**, 207–11.

Binford, L. (1971) Mortuary practises: their study and potential, pp. 6–29, in Brown, J. A. (ed.), *Approaches to the Social Dimensions of Mortuary Practises*, Memoirs of the Society for American Archaeology **25**.

Boon, G. (1969) Belgic and Roman Silchester: the excavations of 1954–8 with an excursus on the early history of Calleva, *Arch.*, **102**, 1–82.

Booth, A. St J. and Stone, J. F. S. (1952) A trial flint mine at Durrington, Wiltshire, *Wilts. Archaeol. Mag.*, **54**, 381–8.

Bowen, H. C. (1961) *Ancient Fields*, British Association for the Advancement of Science, London.

Bowen, H. C. (1978) 'Celtic' fields and 'ranch' boundaries in Wessex, pp. 115–23, in Limbrey, S. and Evans, J. G. (eds), *The Effect of Man on the Landscape: the Lowland Zone*, Council for British Archaeology (Research Report **21**), London.

Bradley, R. J. (1971) A field survey of the Chichester entrenchments, pp. 17–36, in Cunliffe, B. W., *Excavations at Fishbourne vol. 1*, Society of Antiquaries (Research Report **27**), London.

Bradley, R. J. (1975) Salt and settlement in the Hampshire-Sussex borderland, pp. 20–25, in de Brisay, K. and Evans, K. (eds), *Salt – the Study of an Ancient Industry*, Colchester Archaeological Group, Colchester.

Bradley, R. J. (1978a) *The Prehistoric Settlement of Britain*, Routledge and Kegan Paul, London and Boston.

Bradley, R. J. (1978b) Colonisation and land use in the Late Neolithic and Early Bronze Age, pp. 95–103, in Limbrey, S. and Evans, J. G. (eds), *The Effect of Man on the Landscape: The Lowland Zone*, Council for British Archaeology (Research Report **21**), London.

Bradley, R. J. (1979) The interpretation of later Bronze Age metalwork from British rivers, *Int. Journ. Naut. Archaeol.*, **8**, 3–6.

Bradley, R. J. (1980) Subsistence, exchange and technology: a social framework for the Bronze Age in southern England c. 1400–700 bc, pp. 57–75, in Barrett, J. C. and Bradley, R. J. (eds), *Settlement and Society in the British Later Bronze Age*, British Archaeological Reports (B.A.R. **83**), Oxford.

Bradley, R. J. (1981a) 'Various styles of urn': cemeteries and settlement in southern England c. 1400–1000 bc, pp. 93–104, in Chapman, R. W., Kinnes, I. and Randsborg, K. (eds), *The Archaeology of Death*, Cambridge U.P., Cambridge and New York.

Bradley, R. J. (1981b) Economic growth and social change: two examples from prehistoric Europe, pp. 231–7, in Sheridan, A. and Bailey, G. (eds), *Economic Archaeology*, British Archaeological Reports (B.A.R. International Series **96**), Oxford.

Bradley, R. J. (1981c) From ritual to romance: ceremonial enclosures and hill forts, pp. 20–27, in Guilbert, G. (ed.), *Hill-Fort Studies*, Leicester U.P., Leicester.

Bradley, R. J. (1982a) Position and possession: assemblage variation in the British Neolithic, *Oxford Journ. Archaeol.*, **1.1**, 27–38.

Bradley, R. J. (1982b) The destruction of wealth in later prehistory, *Man*, **17**, 108–22.

Bradley, R. J. (in press) The Bronze Age in the Oxford area: its local and regional significance, in Rowley, T. (ed.), *The Archaeology of Oxfordshire*.

Bradley, R. J. and Chapman, R. W. (in press) Passage graves in the European Neolithic: a theory of converging evolution, in Burrenhult, G. (ed.), *The Carrowmore Project – Final Report*, Institute of Archaeology, Stockholm.

Bradley, R. J. and Ellison, A. (1975) *Rams Hill: a Bronze Age Defended Enclosure and its Landscape*, British Archaeological Reports (B.A.R. **19**), Oxford.

Bradley, R. J. and Hodder, I. (1979) British prehistory: an integrated view, *Man*, **14**, 93–104.

Bradley, R. J., Lobb, S., Richards, J. and Robinson, M. (1980) Two Late Bronze Age settlements on the Kennet gravels; excavations at Aldermaston Wharf and Knight's Farm, Burghfield, Berkshire, *Proc. Prehist. Soc.*, **46**, 217–95.

Braun, D. (1979) Illinois Hopewell burial practices and social organisation: a reexamination of Klunk-Gibson mound group, pp. 66–79, in Brose, D. S. and Greber, N. (eds), *Hopewell Archaeology: The Chilliocothe Conference*, Kent State University Press, Kent, Ohio.

Briscoe, F. (1956) Swale's Tumulus: a combined Neolithic A and Bronze Age barrow at Worlington, Suffolk, *Proc. Cambridge Antiq. Soc.*, **50**, 101–12.

Britnell. W. (1975) An interim report upon excavations at Beckford, 1972–4, *Vale of Evesham Hist. Soc. Research Papers* **5**, 1–11.

Brogan, O. (1974) The coming of Rome and the establishment of Roman Gaul, pp. 192–219, in Piggott, S., Daniel, G. and McBurney, C. (eds), *France Before the Romans*, Thames and Hudson, London.

Brown, J. A. (1981) The search for rank in prehistoric burials, pp. 25–37, in Chapman, R. W., Kinnes, I. and Randsborg, K. (eds), *The Archaeology of Death*, Cambridge U.P., Cambridge and New York.

Burgess, C. (1968) The Later Bronze Age in the British Isles and north western France, *Archaeol. Journ.*, **125**, 1–45.

Burgess, C. (1974) The Bronze Age, pp. 165–232, in Renfrew, C. (ed.), *British Prehistory – A New Outline*, Duckworth, London.

Burgess, C. (1976a) Meldon Bridge: a Neolithic defended promontory complex near Peebles, pp. 151–79, in Burgess, C. and Miket, R. (eds), *Settlement and Economy in the Third and Second Millenia* BC, British Archaeological Reports (B.A.R. **33**), Oxford.

Burgess, C. (1976b) Burials with metalwork in the later Bronze Age in Wales and beyond, pp. 81–104, in Boon, G. and Lewis, J. (eds), *Welsh Antiquity*, National Museum of Wales, Cardiff.

Burgess, C. (1978) The background of early metalworking in Ireland and Britain, pp. 207–14, in Ryan, M. (ed.), *The Origins of Metallurgy in Atlantic Europe*, Stationery Office, Dublin.

Burgess, C. (1980a) *The Age of Stonehenge*, Dent, London and Toronto.

Burgess, C. (1980b) The Bronze Age in Wales, pp. 243–86, in Taylor, J. A. (ed.), *Culture and Environment in Prehistoric Wales*, British Archaeological Reports (B.A.R. **76**), Oxford.

Burgess, C. and Coombs, D. (1979) Preface, pp. i–vii, in Burgess, C. and Coombs, D. (eds), *Bronze Age hoards*, British Archaeological Reports (B.A.R. **67**), Oxford.

Burgess, C., Coombs, D. and Davies, G. (1972) The Broadward complex and barbed spearheads, pp. 211–83, in Burgess, C. and Lynch, F. (eds), *Early Man in Wales and the West*, Adams and Dart, Bath.

Burl, A. (1969) Henges: internal features and regional groups, *Archaeol. Journ.*, **126**, 1–28.

Burl, A. (1976) *The Stone Circles of the British Isles*, Yale U.P., New Haven.

Burl, A. (1981a) *Rites of the Gods*, Dent, London and Toronto.

Burl, A. (1981b) 'By the light of the cinerary moon'. Chambered tombs and the astronomy of death, pp. 243–74, in Ruggles, C. and Whittle, A. (eds), *Astronomy and Society during the period 4000–1500* BC, British Archaeological Reports (B.A.R. **88**), Oxford.

Burnham B. and Johnson, H. (eds) (1979) *Invasion and Response*, British Archaeological Reports (B.A.R. **73**), Oxford.

Burstow, G. P. (1958) A Late Bronze Age urnfield at Steyning Round Hill, Sussex, *Proc. Prehist. Soc.*, **24**, 158–64.

Callender, J. G. (1922) Three Bronze Age hoards recently added to the national collection, with notes on the hoard from Duddingston Loch, *Proc. Soc. Antiq. Scotland*, **56**, 351–65.

Care, V. (1979) The production and distribution of Mesolithic axes in southern England, *Proc. Prehist. Soc.*, **45**, 93–102.

Care, V. (1982) The collection and distribution of lithic raw materials during the Mesolithic and Neolithic periods in southern England, *Oxford Journ. Archaeol.*, **1.3**, 269–85.

Case, H. (1969) Neolithic explanations, *Antiq.*, **43**, 176–86.

Case, H. (1973) A ritual site in northeast Ireland, pp. 173–96, in Daniel, G. and Kjaerum, P. (eds), *Megalithic Graves and Ritual*, Jutland Archaeological Society, Moesgard.

Case, H. (1977) The Beaker Culture in Britain and Ireland, pp. 71–101, in Mercer, R. (ed.), *Beakers in Britain and Europe*, British Archaeological Reports (B.A.R. Supplementary Series **26**), Oxford.

Case, H. and Whittle, A. (eds) (1982) *Settlement Patterns in the Oxford Region*, Council for British Archaeology (Research Report **44**), London.

Catt, J. (1978) The contribution of loess to soils in lowland Britain, pp. 12–20, in Limbrey, S. and Evans, J. G. (eds), *The Effect of Man on the Landscape – The Lowland Zone*, Council for British Archaeology (Research Report **21**), London.

Challis, A. and Harding, D. (1975) *Later Prehistory from the Trent to the Tyne*, British Archaeological Reports (B.A.R. **20**), Oxford.

Chambers, R. and Bradley, R. (in prep.) Excavations at the Dorchester on Thames cursus.

Champion, S. (1971) The hillforts of the Cotswold scarp, *Proc. Cotteswold Natur. Field Club*, **36**, 18–23.

Champion, T. (1975) Britain in the European Iron Age, *Archaeologia Atlantica*, **1(2)**, 127–45.

Champion, T. (1980a) Settlement and environment in later Bronze Age Kent, pp. 223–46, in Barrett, J. C. and Bradley, R. J. (eds), *Settlement and Society in the British Later Bronze Age*, British Archaeological Reports (B.A.R. **83**), Oxford.

Champion, T. (1980b) Mass migration in later prehistoric Europe, pp. 31–42, in Sörbom, P. (ed.), *Transport Technology and Social Change*, Tekniska Museet, Stockholm.

Champion, T. (1980c) The early development of iron working, *Nature*, **284**, 513–14.

Chapman, R. W. (1981) The emergence of formal disposal areas and the 'problem' of megalithic tombs in prehistoric Europe, pp. 71–81, in Chapman, R. W., Kinnes, I. and Randsborg, K. (eds) *The Archaeology of Death*, Cambridge U.P., Cambridge and New York.

Chapman, R. W. (in prep.) Production, circulation and consumption.

Cherry, J. F. (1978) Generalisation and the archaeology of the state, pp. 411–37, in Green, D., Haselgrove, C. and Spriggs, M. (eds), *Social Organisation and Settlement*, British Archaeological Reports (B.A.R. International Series **47**), Oxford.

Cherry, J. F. (1981) Pattern and process in the earliest colonisation of the Mediterranean islands, *Proc. Prehist. Soc.*, **47**, 41–68.

Childe, V. G. (1940) *Prehistoric Communities of the British Isles*, Chambers, London.

Childe, V. G. (1942) *What Happened in History*, Penguin, London.

Childe, V. G. (1945) Directional changes in funerary practices during 50,000 years, *Man*, **45**, 13–19.

Childe, V. G. and Smith, I. F. (1954) The excavation of a Neolithic barrow on Whiteleaf Hill, Bucks., *Proc. Prehist. Soc.*, **20**, 212–30.

Chowne, P. (1980) Bronze Age settlement in south Lincolnshire, pp. 295–305, in Barrett, J. C. and Bradley, R. J. (eds), *Settlement and Society in the British Later Bronze Age*, British Archaeological Reports (B.A.R. **83**), Oxford.

Clark, J. D. G. (1952) *Prehistoric Europe: The Economic Basis*, Methuen, London.

Clark, J. D. G. (1966) The invasion hypothesis in British archaeology, *Antiq.*, **40**, 172–89.

Clark, J. D. G. and Fell, C. I. (1953) The Early Iron Age site at Micklemoor Hill, West Harling, Norfolk and its pottery, *Proc. Prehist. Soc.*, **19**, 1–40.

Clark, R. M. (1975) A calibration curve for radiocarbon dates, *Antiq.*, **49**, 251–66.

Clarke, D. L. (1972) A provisional model of an Iron Age society and its settlement system, pp. 801–69, in Clarke, D. L. (ed.) *Models in Archaeology*, Methuen, London.

Clarke, D. V. (1976a) Excavations at Skara Brae: a summary account, pp. 233–50, in Burgess, C. and Miket, R. (eds), *Settlement and Economy in the Third and Second Millenia* BC, British Archaeological Reports (B.A.R. **33**), Oxford.

Clarke, D. V. (1976b) *The Neolithic Village at Skara Brae, Orkney, 1972–73 Excavations: An Interim Report*, H.M.S.O., Edinburgh.

Clifford, E. (1961) *Bagendon: A Belgic Oppidum*, Heffer, Cambridge.

Clough, T. H. McK. and Cummins, W. A. (eds) (1979) *Stone Axe Studies*, Council for British Archaeology (Research Report **23**), London.

Cogbill, S., Bradley, R. J. and Taylor, A. (in prep.) Wookey Hole and the Iron Age occupation of the Mendips.

Coles, F. R. (1893) The motes, forts and doons in the east and west divisions of the Stewartry of Kircudbright, *Proc. Soc. Antiq. Scotland*, **27**, 92–182.

Coles, J. (1960) Scottish Late Bronze Age metalwork: typology, distribution and chronology, *Proc. Soc. Antiq. Scotland*, **93**, 16–134.

Coles, J. (1976) Forest farmers: some archaeological, historical and experimental evidence relating to the prehistory of Europe, pp. 59–66, in De Laet, S. (ed.), *Acculturation and Continuity in Atlantic Europe*, De Tempel, Bruges.

Coles, J., Orme, B., May, J. and Moore, C. N. (1979) Excavations of Late Bronze Age or Iron Age date at Washingborough Fen, *Lincs. Hist. Archaeol.*, **14**, 5–10.

Coles, J. and Taylor, J. (1971) The Wessex Culture: a minimal view, *Antiq.*, **45**, 6–14.

Collis, J. (1971) Functional and theoretical interpretations of British coinage, *World Archaeol.*, **3**, 71–84.

Collis, J. (1975) *Defended Sites of the Late La Tène*, British Archaeological Reports (B.A.R. Supplementary Series 2), Oxford.

Collis, J. (1977a) Iron Age henges? *Archaeologia Atlantica*, **2**, 55–63.

Collis, J. (1977b) Pre-Roman burial rites in north-western Europe, pp. 1–13, in Reece, R. (ed.), *Burial in the Roman World,* Council for British Archaeology (Research Report **22**), London.

Coombs, D. (1975) Bronze Age weapon hoards in Britain, *Archaeologia Atlantica*, **1**, 49–81.

Coombs, D. (1976) Beakers from Callis Wold, Barrow 275, Humberside (an interim report), pp. 144–50, in Burgess, C. and Miket, R. (eds), *Settlement and Economy in the Third and Second Millenia BC*, British Archaeological Reports (B.A.R. **33**), Oxford.

Cooney, G. (1979) Some aspects of the siting of megalithic tombs in County Leitrim, *Journ. Roy. Soc. Antiq. Ireland*, **109**, 74–91.

Corcoran, J. (1972) Multi-period construction and the origins of the chambered long cairn in western Britain and Ireland, pp. 31–63, in Burgess, C. and Lynch, F. (eds), *Early Man in Wales and the West*, Adams, and Dart, Bath.

Cotton, M. A. and Frere, S. S. (1968) Ivinghoe Beacon excavations 1963–65, *Rec. Bucks.*, **18**, 187–260.

Cowen, J. D. (1967) The Hallstatt sword of bronze: on the Continent and in Britain, *Proc. Prehist. Soc.*, **33**, 377–454.

Crummy, P. (1980) Camulodunum, *Current Archaeol.*, **72**, 6–10.

Cummins, W. A. (1979) Neolithic stone axes: distribution and trade in England and Wales, pp. 5–12, in Clough, T. H. McK. and Cummins, W. A. (eds), *Stone Axe Studies*, Council for British Archaeology (Research Report **23**), London.

Cummins, W. A. (1980) Stone axes as a guide to Neolithic communications and boundaries in England and Wales, *Proc. Prehist. Soc.*, **46**, 45–60.

Cunliffe, B. W. (1973a) Chalton, Hants.: the evolution of a landscape, *Antiq. Journ.*, **53**, 173–90.

Cunliffe, B. W. (1973b) The Late Pre-Roman Iron Age, pp. 426–38, in *Victoria County History of Wiltshire*, vol. 1.2.

Cunliffe, B. W. (1976a) Hillforts and oppida in Britain, pp. 343–58, in Sievking, G, Longworth, I. and Wilson, K. (eds), *Problems in Economic and Social Archaeology*, Duckworth, London.

Cunliffe, B. W. (1976b) The origins of urbanisation in Britain, pp. 135–161, in Cunliffe, B. W. and Rowley, T. (eds), *Oppida: The Beginnings of Urbanisation in Barbarian Europe*, British Archaeological Reports (B.A.R. Supplementary Series **11**), Oxford.

Cunliffe, B. W. (1978a) *Iron Age Communities in Britain* (second edition), Routledge and Kegan Paul, London.

Cunliffe, B. W. (1978b) Settlement and population in the British Iron Age: some facts, figures and fantasies, pp. 3–24, in Cunliffe, B. W. and Rowley, T. (eds), *Lowland Iron Age Communities in Europe*, British Archaeological Reports (B.A.R. Supplementary Series **48**), Oxford.

Cunliffe, B. W. (1978c) *Hengistbury Head*, Elek, London.

Cunliffe, B. W. (ed.) (1981) *Coinage and Society in Britain and Gaul*, Council for British Archaeology (Research Report **38**), London.

Cunliffe, B. W. (1982) Britain, the Veneti and beyond, *Oxford Journ. Archaeol.*, **1.1**, 39–68.

Cunnington, M. E. (1914) List of the long barrows of Wiltshire, *Wilts. Archaeol. Mag.*, **38**, 379–414.

Cunnington, M. E. (1923) *The Early Iron Age Inhabited Site at All Cannings Cross Farm, Wiltshire*, George Simpson, Devizes.

Cunnington, M. E. (1929) *Woodhenge*, George Simpson, Devizes.

Cunnington, M. E. (1931) The 'Sanctuary' on Overton Hill, near Avebury, *Wilts. Archaeol. Mag.*, **45**, 300–35.

Cunnington, M. E. and Cunnington, B. H. (1913) Casterley Camp excavations, *Wilts. Archaeol. Mag.*, **38**, 53–105.

Curwen, E. C. (1929) *Prehistoric Sussex*, The Homeland Association, London.

Darvill, T. (1979) Court cairns, passage graves and social change in Ireland, *Man*, **14**, 311–27.

Davies, J. and Spratling, M. (1976) The Seven Sisters hoard: a centenary study, pp. 121–47, in Boon, G. and Lewis, J. (eds), *Welsh Antiquity*, National Museum of Wales, Cardiff.

Dixon, P. (1981) Crickley Hill, *Current Archaeol.*, **76**, 145–7.

Douglas, M. and Isherwood, B. (1980) *The world of Goods – Towards an Anthropology of Consumption*, Penguin, London.

Downey, R., King, A. and Soffe, G. (1980) The Hayling Island temple and religious connections across the Channel, pp. 289–304, in Rodwell, W. (ed.), *Temples, Churches and Religion: Recent Research in Roman Britain*, British Archaeological Reports (B.A.R. **77**), Oxford.

Drewett, P. (1975) The excavation of an oval burial mound of the third millenium BC at Alfriston, East Sussex, 1974, *Proc. Prehist. Soc.*, **41**, 119–52.

Drewett, P. (1977) The excavation of a Neolithic causewayed enclosure on Offham Hill, East Sussex, 1976, *Proc. Prehist. Soc.*, **43**, 201–42.

Drewett, P. (1980) Black Patch and the later Bronze Age in Sussex, pp. 377–96, in Barrett, J. C. and Bradley, R. J. (eds), *Settlement and Society in the British Later Bronze Age*, British Archaeological Reports (B.A.R. **83**), Oxford.

Drury, P. (1978a) Little Waltham and pre-Belgic Iron Age settlement in Essex, pp. 43–76, in Cunliffe, B. W. and Rowley, T. (eds), *Lowland Iron Age Communities in Europe*, British Archaeological Reports (B.A.R. Supplementary Series **48**), Oxford.

Drury, P. (1978b) *Excavations at Little Waltham 1970–71*, Council for British Archaeology (Research Report **26**), London.

Dunning, G. (1976) Salmondsbury, Bourton-on-the-Water, Gloucestershire, pp. 76–118, in Harding, D. W. (ed.), *Hillforts: Later Prehistoric Earthworks in Britain and Ireland*, Academic Press, London and New York.

Earle, T. (1977a) A reappraisal of redistribution: complex Hawaiian chiefdoms, pp. 213–29, in Earle, T. and Ericson, J. (eds), *Exchange Systems in Prehistory*, Academic Press, London and New York.

Earle, T. (1977b) *Economic and Social Organisation of a complex Chiefdom: the Halelea District, Kaua'i, Hawaii*, University of Michigan (Museum of Anthropology Archaeological Papers **64**), Ann Arbor.

Edwards, D. (1978) The air photographs collection of the Norfolk Archaeological Unit: third report, *East Anglian Archaeol.*, **8**, 87–105.

Ehrenberg, M. (1977) *Bronze Age Spearheads from Berkshire, Buckinghamshire and Oxfordshire*, British Archaeological Reports (B.A.R. **34**), Oxford.

Ehrenberg, M. (1980) The occurrence of Bronze Age metalwork in the Thames: an investigation, *Trans. London and Middlesex Archaeol. Soc.*, **31**, 1–15.

Elliott, K., Ellman, D. and Hodder, I. (1978) The simulation of Neolithic axe dispersal in Britain, pp. 79–87, in Hodder, I. (ed.), *Simulation Studies in Archaeology*, Cambridge U.P., Cambridge and New York.

Ellison, A. (1980a) Deverel-Rimbury urn cemeteries: the evidence for social organisation, pp. 115–26, in Barrett, J. C. and Bradley, R. J. (eds), *Settlement and Society in the British Later Bronze Age*, British Archaeological Reports (B.A.R. **83**), Oxford.

Ellison, A. (1980b) Settlements and regional exchange: a case study, pp. 127–40, in Barrett, J. C. and Bradley, R. J. (eds), *Settlement and Society in the British Later Bronze Age*, British Archaeological Reports (B.A.R. **83**), Oxford.

Ellison, A. (1981a) Towards a socioeconomic model for the Middle Bronze Age in southern England, pp. 413–38, in Hodder, I., Isaac, G. and Hammond, N. (eds), *Pattern of the Past*, Cambridge U.P., Cambridge and New York.

Ellison, A. (1981b) Pottery and socio-economic change in British prehistory, pp. 45–55, in Howard, H. and Morris, E. (eds), *Production and Distribution: A Ceramic Viewpoint*, British Archaeological Reports (B.A.R. Supplementary Series **120**), Oxford.

Eogan, G. (1974) Regionale Gruppierungen in der Spätbronzezeit Irlands, *Archäologisches Korrespondenzblatt*, **4**, 319–27.

Eogan, G. (1976) Beaker material from Knowth, Co. Meath: preliminary note, pp. 251–66, in Burgess, C. and Miket, R. (eds) *Settlement and Economy in the Third and Second Millenia* BC, British Archaeological Reports (B.A.R. **33**), Oxford.

Evans, J. (1881) *The Ancient Bronze Implements of Great Britain and Ireland*, Longmans, Green and Co., London.

Field, N. H., Mathews, C. L. and Smith, I. F. (1964) New Neolithic sites in Dorset and Bedfordshire with a note on the distribution of Neolithic storage pits in Britain, *Proc. Prehist. Soc.*, **30**, 352–81.

Flannery. K. (1968) The Olmec and the valley of Oaxaca: a model for inter-regional interaction in Formative times, pp. 79–110, in Benson, E. P. (ed.) *Dumbarton Oaks Conference on the Olmec*, Dumbarton Oaks, Washington.

Fleming, A. (1971) Territorial patterns in Bronze Age Wessex, *Proc. Prehist. Soc.*, **37(i)**,138–66.

Fleming, A. (1972) Vision and design: approaches to ceremonial monument typology, *Man*, **7**, 57–73.

Fleming, A. (1973) Tombs for the living, *Man*, **8**, 177–93.

Fleming, A. (1978) The prehistoric landscape of Dartmoor: part 1, *Proc. Prehist. Soc.*, **44**, 97–123.

Fleming, A. (1982a) Review of *Farming Practice in British Prehistory* (ed. R. Mercer), *Scottish Archaeol. Rev.*, **1.2**, 127–32.

Fleming, A. (1982b) Social boundaries and land boundaries, pp. 52–55, in

Renfrew, C. and Shennan, S. (eds) *Ranking, Resource and Exchange*, Cambridge U.P., Cambridge and New York.

Ford, R. (1972) Barter, gift or violence: an analysis of Tewa inter-tribal exchange, pp. 21–45, in Wilmsen, E. (ed.), *Social Exchange and Interaction*, University of Michigan (Anthropological Papers of the Museum of Anthropology **46**), Ann Arbor.

Ford, S., Hawkes, J. and Bradley, R. (1983) Flint working in the Metal Age, paper given at the Fourth International Symposium on Flint. Publication forthcoming.

Foster, J. (1980) *The Iron Age Moulds from Gussage All Saints*, British Museum (Occasional Papers **12**), London.

Fowler, P. J. (1981) Wildscape to landscape, pp. 9–54, in Mercer, R. (ed.), *Farming Practice in British Prehistory*, Edinburgh U.P., Edinburgh.

Frankenstein, S. and Rowlands, M. (1978) The internal structure and regional context of Early Iron Age society in south-western Germany, *Bull. Inst. Archaeol. Univ. London*, **15**, 73–112.

Frere, S. S. (1978) *Britannia* (second edition), Routledge and Kegan Paul, London.

Frere, S. S. (1979) Verulamium: urban development and the local region, pp. 273–80, in Burnham, B. and Johnson, H. (eds), *Invasion and Response*, British Archaeological Reports (B.A.R. **73**), Oxford.

Fried, M. (1967) *The Evolution of Political Society*, Random House, New York.

Friedman, J. (1979) *System, Structure and Contradiction in the Evolution of 'Asiatic' Social Formations*, National Museum of Denmark (Social Studies in Oceania and South East Asia **2**), Copenhagen.

Friedman, J. and Rowlands, M. J. (eds) (1977) *The Evolution of Social Systems*, Duckworth, London.

Gamble, C. (1981) Social control and the economy, pp. 215–29, in Sheridan, A. and Bailey, G. (eds), *Economic Archaeology*, British Archaeological Reports (B.A.R. Supplementary Series **96**), Oxford.

Gardiner, J. P. (1980) Land and social status: a case study from eastern England, pp. 101–14, in Barrett, J. C. and Bradley, R. J. (eds), *Settlement and Society in the British Later Bronze Age*, British Archaeological Reports (B.A.R. **83**), Oxford.

Gelling, P. (1977) Excavations on Pilsdon Pen, Dorset, 1964–71, *Proc. Prehist. Soc.*, **43**, 263–86.

Gent, H. (1983) Centralised storage in later prehistoric Britain. Unpublished manuscript, Department of Archaeology, Reading University.

Gerloff, S. (1975) *The Early Bronze Age Daggers in Great Britain*, Prähistorische Bronzefunde **6**, **2**, Munich.

Gibson, A. (1982) *Beaker Domestic Sites*, British Archaeological Reports (B.A.R. **107**), Oxford.

Gingell, C. (1980) The Marlborough Downs in the Bronze Age: the first results of current research, pp. 209–22, in Barrett, J. C. and Bradley, R. J. (eds), *Settlement and Society in the British Later Bronze Age*, British Archaeological Reports (B.A.R. **83**), Oxford.

Gledhill, J. and Rowlands, M. J. (1982) Materialism and socio-economic process in multi-linear evolution, pp. 144–9, in Renfrew, C. and Shennan, S. (eds), *Ranking, Resource and Exchange*, Cambridge U.P., Cambridge and New York.

Godelier, M. (1977) *Perspectives in Marxist Anthropology*, Cambridge U.P., Cambridge and New York.

Goody, J. (1976) *Production and Reproduction*, Cambridge U.P., Cambridge and New York.

Gray, H. St. G. (1903) On the excavations at Arbor Low 1901–2, *Arch.*, **58**, 461–98.

Green, F. (1981) Iron Age, Roman and Saxon crops: the archaeological evidence from Wessex, pp. 129–153, in Jones, M. and Dimbleby, C. (eds), *The Environment of Man: The Iron Age to the Anglo-Saxon Period*, British Archaeological Reports (B.A.R. **87**), Oxford.

Green, H. S. (1974) Early Bronze Age territory and population in Milton Keynes, Buckinghamshire, and the Great Ouse Valley, *Archaeol. Journ.*, **131**, 75–139.

Green, H. S. (1980) *The Flint Arrowheads of the British Isles*, British Archaeological Reports (B.A.R. **75**), Oxford.

Gregory, C. A. (1980) Gifts to men and gifts to god: gift exchange and capital accumulation in contemporary Papua, *Man*, **15**, 628–52.

Grew, F. (1981) Roman Britain in 1980: 1. Sites explored, *Britannia*, **12**, 314–68.

Grimes, W. F. (1960) *Excavations on Defence Sites 1939–45*, H.M.S.O., London.

Guido, C. M. (1978) *Prehistoric and Roman Glass Beads in Britain and Ireland*, Society of Antiquaries (Research Report **35**), London.

Guilbert, G. (1975) Planned hillfort interiors, *Proc. Prehist. Soc.*, **41**, 203–21.

Haggett, P. (1965) *Location Analysis in Human Geography*, Edward Arnold, London.

Hall, D. N. and Hutchings, J. B. (1972) The distribution of archaelogical sites between the Nene and the Ouse valleys, *Archaeol. Journ.*, **7**, 1–16.

Harbison, P. and Laing, L. (1974) *Some Iron Age Mediterranean Imports in England*, British Archaeological Reports (B.A.R. **5**), Oxford.

Harden, D. (1950) Italic and Etruscan finds from Britain, *Atti 1 Congr. Preist. e Proist. Mediterr.*, 315–24.

Harding, A. (ed.) (1982) *Climatic Change in Later Prehistory*, Edinburgh U.P., Edinburgh.

Harding, D. W. (1972) *The Iron Age in the Upper Thames Basin*, Oxford U.P., Oxford.

Harding, D. W. (1974) *The Iron Age in Lowland Britain*, Routledge and Kegan Paul, London.

Hart, C. (1981) *The North Derbyshire Archaeological Survey*, North Derbyshire Archaeological Trust, Chesterfield.

Haselgrove, C. (1979) The significance of coinage in pre-Conquest Britain, pp. 197–209, in Burnham, B. and Johnson, H. (eds), *Invasion and Response*, British Archaeological Reports (B.A.R. **75**), Oxford.

Haselgrove, C. (1982) Wealth, prestige and power: the dynamics of Late Iron Age political centralisation in south-east England, pp. 79–88, in Renfrew, C. and Shennan, S. (eds) *Ranking, Resource and Exchange*, Cambridge U.P., Cambridge and New York.

Hawke-Smith, C. F. (1981) Land use, burial practice and territories in the Peak District c. 2000–1000 BC, pp. 57–72, in Barker, G. (ed.), *Prehistoric Communities in Northern England*, Sheffield University Department of Prehistory and Archaeology, Sheffield.

Hawkes, C. F. C. (1940) The excavations at Quarley Hill, 1938, *Proc. Hants. Field Club and Archaeol. Soc.*, **14**, 136–94.

Hawkes, C. F. C. (1954) Archaeological theory and method: some suggestions from the Old World, *Amer. Anthrop.*, **56**, 155–68.

Hawkes, C. F. C. (1972) Europe and England, fact and fog, *Helinium*, **12**, 105–16.

180   *Bibliography*

Hawkes, C. F. C. (1975) *Pytheas: Europe and the Greek Explorers*, J. L. Myres Memorial Lecture, Oxford.

Hawkes, C. F. C. (1980) Caesar's Britain: an oppidum for Cassivellaunus, *Antiq.*, **54**, 138–9.

Hawkes, C. F. C. and Hull, M. R. (1947) *Camulodunum*, Society of Antiquaries (Research Report 14), London.

Healy, F. (1981) Lithics in a landscape: the Neolithic and Bronze Age in the ploughsoil of Norfolk, *Lithics* **2**, 12–19.

Healy, F. (1982) A round barrow at Trowse: Early Bronze Age burials and medieval occupation, *East Anglian Archaeol.*, **14**. 1–27.

Hedges, J. (1975) Excavation of two Orcadian burnt mounds at Liddle and Beaquoy, *Proc. Soc. Antiq. Scotland*, **106**, 39–98.

Hedges, J. and Buckley, D. (1978) Excavations at a causewayed enclosure, Orsett, Essex, 1975, *Proc. Prehist. Soc.*, **44**, 219–308.

Hedges, J. and Buckley, D. (1981) *Springfield Cursus and the Cursus Problem*, Essex County Council (Occasional Paper 1), Chelmsford.

Heggie, D. (1981) *Megalithic Science*, Thames and Hudson, London.

Henshall, A. S. (1963) *The Chambered Tombs of Scotland, vol. 1*, Edinburgh U.P., Edinburgh.

Henshall, A. S. (1972) *The Chambered Tombs of Scotland, vol. 2*, Edinburgh U.P., Edinburgh.

Herity, M. (1974) *Irish Passage Graves*, Irish U.P., Dublin.

Hicks, S. (1972) The impact of man on the East Moor of Derbyshire from Mesolithic times, *Archaeol. Journ.*, **129**, 1–21.

Higgs, E. S. and White, J. P. (1963) Autumn Killing, *Antiq.*, **37**, 282–9.

Hodder, I. (1977) Some new directions in the spatial analysis of archaeological data at the regional scale, pp. 223–351, in Clarke, D. L. (ed.), *Spatial Archaeology*, Academic Press, London.

Hodder, I. (1979a) Social and economic stress and material culture patterning, *Amer. Antiq.*, **44**, 446–54.

Hodder, I. (1979b) Simulating the growth of hierarchies, pp. 117–44, in Renfrew, C. and Cook, K. (eds), *Transformations: Mathematical Approaches to Culture Change*, Academic Press, London and New York.

Hodges, R. (1982) *Dark Age Economics*, Duckworth, London.

Hodson, F. R. (1964) Cultural groupings within the British pre-Roman Iron Age, *Proc. Prehist. Soc.*, **30**, 99–110.

Hogg, A. H. A. (1981) The plan of Woodhenge, *Science and Archaeology* **23**, 3–14.

Holden, E. W. (1972) A Bronze Age cemetery-barrow on Itford Hill, Beddingham, *Sussex Archaeol. Collect.*, **110**, 70–117.

Holden, E. W. and Bradley, R. J. (1975) A Late Neolithic site at Rackham, *Sussex Archaeol. Collect.*, **113**, 85–103.

Holgate, R. (1981) The Medway megaliths and Neolithic Kent, *Arch. Cant.* **97**, 221–34.

Horsey, I. and Shackley, M. (1980) The excavation of a Bronze Age round barrow on Canford Heath, Poole, Dorset, *Proc. Dorset, Natur. Hist. Archaeol. Soc.*, **102**, 33–42.

Houlder, C. (1961) The excavation of a Neolithic stone implement factory on Mynydd Rhiw in Caernarvonshire, *Proc. Prehist. Soc.*, **27**, 108–43.

Houlder, C. (1968) The henge monuments at Llandegai. *Antiq.*, **42**, 216–21.

Houlder, C. (1976) Stone axes and henge monuments, pp. 55–62, in Boon, G. and Lewis, J. M. (eds), *Welsh Antiquity*, National Museum of Wales, Cardiff.

Howard, H. (1981) In the wake of distribution: towards an integrated approach to ceramic studies in prehistoric Britain, pp. 1–30, in Howard, H. and Morris, E. (eds). *Production and Distribution: A Ceramic Viewpoint*, British Archaeological Reports (B.A.R. Supplementary Series **120**), Oxford.

Huntingdon, R. and Metcalf, P. (1979) *Celebrations of Death*, Cambridge U.P., Cambridge and New York.

Ingold, T. (1980) *Hunters, Pastoralists and Ranchers*, Cambridge U.P., Cambridge and New York.

Jackson, D. (1975) An Iron Age site at Twywell, Northamptonshire, *Northants. Archaeol.*, **10**, 31–93.

Jackson, D. (1976) The excavation of Neolithic and Bronze Age sites at Aldwincle, Northants, 1967–71, *Northants. Archaeol.*, **11**, 12–70.

Jacobi, R. (1973) Aspects of the 'Mesolithic Age' in Britain, pp. 237–65, in Kozlowski, S. K. (ed.), *The Mesolithic in Europe*, Warsaw U.P., Warsaw.

Jacobi, R. (1979) Early Flandrian hunters in the south west, *Proc. Devon Archaeol. Soc.*, **37**, 48–93.

Johnson, N. (1980) Later Bronze Age settlement in the south west, pp. 141–80, in Barrett, J. C. and Bradley, R. J. (eds), *Settlement and Society in the British Later Bronze Age*, British Archaeological Reports (B.A.R. **83**), Oxford.

Jones, G. D. and Kautz, R. R. (1981) Issues in the study of New World state formation, pp. 3–34, in Jones, G. D. and Kautz, R. R. (eds), *The Transition to Statehood in the New World*, Cambridge U.P., Cambridge and New York.

Jones, M. (1981) The development of crop husbandry, pp. 95–127, in Jones, M. and Dimbleby, G. (eds), *The Environment of Man: The Iron Age to the Anglo-Saxon Period*, British Archaeological Reports (B.A.R. **87**), Oxford.

Jones, M. U. (1974) Excavations at Mucking, Essex: a second interim report, *Antiq. Journ.*, **54**, 183–99.

Jones, M. U. and Bond, D. (1980) Later Bronze Age settlement at Mucking, Essex, pp. 471–82, in Barrett, J. C. and Bradley, R. J. (eds), *Settlement and Society in the British Later Bronze Age*, British Archaeological Reports (B.A.R. **83**), Oxford.

Jope, E. M. (1952) The porcellanite axes of the north of Ireland: Tievebulliagh and Rathlin, *Ulster Journ. Archaeol.*, **15**, 31–60.

Jope, E. M. (1961) Daggers of the Early Iron Age in Britain, *Proc. Prehist. Soc.*, **27**, 307–43.

Keiller, A. and Piggott, S. (1938) Excavation of an untouched chamber in Lanhill long barrow, *Proc. Prehist. Soc.*, **4**, 122–50.

Kendall, D. G. (1974) Hunting quanta, pp. 231–66, in Hodson, F. R. (ed.), *The Place of Astronomy in the Ancient World*, British Academy, London.

Kent, J. (1978) The London area in the Late Iron Age: an interpretation of the earliest coins, pp. 53–8, in Bird, J., Chapman, H. and Clark, J. (eds), *Collectanea Londinensia: Studies Presented to Ralph Merrifield*, London and Middlesex Archaeological Society, London.

Kent, J. (1981) The origins of coinage in Britain, pp. 40–42, in Cunliffe, B. (ed.), *Coinage and Society in Britain and Gaul*, Council for British Archaeology (Research Report **38**), London.

Kinnes, I. (1975) Monumental function in British Neolithic burial practices, *World Archaeol.*, **7**, 16–29.

Kinnes, I. (1978) A Bronze Age bone dagger from Bawburgh, Norfolk, *Antiq. Journ.*, **58**, 367–8.

Kinnes, I. (1979) *Round Barrows and Ring–ditches in the British Neolithic*, British Museum (Occasional Paper 7), London.

Kossak, G. (1974) Prunkgräber. Bemerkungen zu Eigenschaften and Aussagewert, pp. 3–33, in Kossak, G. and Ulbert, G. (eds), *Studien zur Vor- und Frühesgeschichtlicken Archäologie*, Beck, Munich.

Kristiansen, K. (1978a) Periodevergange i bronzealderen, *Hikuin* **4**, 77–88.

Kristiansen, K. (1978b) The consumption of wealth in Bronze Age Denmark, pp. 158–90, in Kristiansen, K. and Paludan–Müller, C. (eds), *New Directions in Scandinavian Archaeology, vol. 1*, National Museum of Denmark, Copenhagen.

Lambrick, G. and Robinson, M. (1979) *Iron Age and Roman Riverside Settlements at Farmoor, Oxfordshire*, Council for British Archaeology (Research Report **32**), London.

Langmaid, N. (1971) Norton Fitzwarren, *Current Archaeol.*, **28**, 116–20.

Lanting, J. N. and van der Waals, J. D. (1972) British beakers as seen from the Continent, *Helinium* **12**, 20–46.

Lawson, A. J., Martin, E. A. and Priddy, D. (1981) The Barrows of East Anglia, *East Anglian Archaeol.*, **12**.

Leach, G. (1976) *Energy and Food Production*, International Institute for Environment and Development, London.

Legge, A. (1981) Aspects of cattle husbandry, pp. 169–81, in Mercer, R. (ed.) *Farming Practice in British Prehistory*, Edinburgh U.P., Edinburgh.

Levy, J. (1982) *Social and Religious Organisation in Bronze Age Denmark*, British Archaeological Reports (B.A.R. Supplementary Series **124**), Oxford.

Liddell, D. (1935) Report on the excavations at Hembury Fort, *Proc. Devon Archaeol. Exploration Soc.*, **2**, 134–75.

Liversage, G. D. (1968) Excavations at Dalkey Island, Co. Dublin, 1956–1959, *Proc. Roy. Irish Acad.*, **66**, 53–231.

Longley, D. (1980) *Runnymede Bridge 1976: Excavations on the Site of a Late Bronze Age Settlement*, Surrey Archaeol. Soc. (Research Volume **6**), Guildford.

Loughlin, N. and Miller, K. (1979) *A Survey of Archaeological Sites in Humberside*, Humberside Joint Archaeological Committee, Hull.

Loveday, R. (1980) The first Leicestershire long barrow? *Trans. Leics. Archaeol. Hist. Soc.*, **55**, 86–7.

Lynch, A. (1981) *Man and Environment in South West Ireland*, British Archaeological Reports (B.A.R. **85**), Oxford.

Lynn, C. (1977) Trial excavations at the King's Stables, Tray townland, County Armagh, *Ulster Journ. Archaeol.*, **40**, 42–62.

MacCormack, C. (1981) Exchange and hierarchy, pp. 159–66, in Sheridan, A. and Bailey, G. (eds), *Economic Archaeology*, British Archaeological Reports (B.A.R. Supplementary Series **96**), Oxford.

Macfarlane, A. (1978) Modes of reproduction, *Man* **13**, 67–8.

McKie, E. (1975) The brochs of Scotland, pp. 72–92, in Fowler, P. (ed.), *Recent Work in Rural Archaeology*, Moonraker Press, Bradford-on-Avon.

McKie, E. (1976) The vitrified forts of Scotland, pp. 205–35, in Harding, D. W. (ed.), *Hillforts: Later Prehistoric Earthworks in Britain and Ireland*, Academic Press, London and New York.

McKie, E. W. (1977) *Science and Society in Prehistoric Britain*, Elek. London.

Manby, T. (1965) The distribution of roughout 'Cumbrian' and related axes of Lake District origin in northern England, *Trans. Cumberland and Westmorland Antiq. Archaeol. Soc.* **65**, 1–37.

Manby, T. G. (1970) Long barrows of northern England: structural and dating evidence, *Scottish Archaeological Forum* **2**, 1–27.

Manby, T. G. (1974) *Grooved Ware Sites in Yorkshire and the North of England*, British Archaeological Reports (B.A.R. **9**), Oxford.

Manby, T. G. (1975) Neolithic occupation sites on the Yorkshire Wolds, *Yorkshire Archaeol. Journ.*, **47**, 23–59.

Manby, T. G. (1979) Typology, materials and distribution of flint and stone axes in Yorkshire, pp. 65–81, in Clough, T. H. McK. and Cummins, W. A. (eds), *Stone Axe Studies*, Council for British Archaeology (Research Report **23**), London.

Manby, T. G. (1980a) Excavation of barrows at Grindale and Boynton, East Yorkshire, 1972, *Yorkshire Archaeol. Journ.*, **52**, 19–47.

Manby, T. G. (1980b) Bronze Age settlement in eastern Yorkshire, pp. 307–70, in Barrett, J. C. and Bradley, R. J. (eds), *Settlement and Society in the British Later Bronze Age*, British Archaeological Reports (B.A.R. **83**), London.

Mannion, J. (1974) *Irish Settlements in East Canada: a Study of Cultural Transfer and Adaptation*, University of Toronto Press, Toronto.

Marsden, B. (1977) *The Burial Mounds of Derbyshire*, privately printed.

May, J. (1970) Dragonby: an interim report on excavations on an Iron Age and Romano-British site near Scunthorpe, Lincolnshire, 1964–9, *Antiq. Journ.*, **50**, 222–45.

May, J. (1976) The growth of settlements in the later Iron Age in Lincolnshire, pp. 163–80, in Cunliffe, B. W. and Rowley, T. (eds), *Oppida: The Beginnings of Urbanisation in Barbarian Europe*, British Archaeological Reports (B.A.R. Supplementary Series **11**), Oxford.

Megaw, V. and Simpson, D. (1979) *Introduction to British Prehistory*, Leicester U.P., Leicester.

Meillassoux, C. (1968) Ostentation, destruction, reproduction, *Economie et Societé* **2**, 760–72.

Meillassoux, C. (1972) From reproduction to production, *Economy and Society* **1**, 93–105.

Meillassoux, C. (1981) *Maidens, Meal and Money. Capitalism and the Domestic Economy*, Cambridge U.P., Cambridge and New York.

Mellars, P. (1976) Fire ecology, animal populations and man: a study of some ecological relationships in prehistory, *Proc. Prehist. Soc.*, **42**, 15–45.

Mercer, R. (1974) Carn Brea, *Current Archaeol.*, **47**, 360–5.

Mercer, R. (1980) *Hambledon Hill – a Neolithic Landscape*, Edinburgh U.P., Edinburgh.

Mercer, R. (1981) *Grimes Graves, Norfolk. Excavations 1971–2, Vol. 1*, H.M.S.O. (Department of the Environment Archaeological Reports **11**), London.

Miket, R. (1981) Pit alignments in the Milfield basin, and the excavation of Ewart 1, *Proc. Prehist. Soc.*, **47**, 137–46.

Miles, D. (1981) Social landscapes: pattern and purpose? pp. 9–18, in Jones, M. and Dimbleby, G. (eds) *The Environment of Man: The Iron Age to the Anglo-Saxon Period*, British Archaeological Reports (B.A.R. **87**), Oxford.

Milisauskas, S. (1978) *European Prehistory*, Academic Press, London and New York.

Miller, D. (1982) Structures and strategies: an aspect of the relationship between social hierarchy and cultural change, pp. 89–98, in Hodder, I. (ed.), *Symbolic and Structural Archaeology*, Cambridge U.P., Cambridge and New York.

Ministry of Public Building and Works (1964) *Excavations Annual Report 1963*, H.M.S.O., London.

Money, J. (1978) Aspects of the Iron Age in the Weald, pp. 38–40, in Drewett, P. (ed.), *Archaeology in Sussex to AD 1500*, Council for British Archaeology (Research Report **29**), London.

Morgan, F. de M. (1959) The excavation of a long barrow at Nutbane, Hants., *Proc. Prehist. Soc.*, **25**, 15–51.

Morris, E. (1981) Ceramic exchange in western Britain: a preliminary view, pp. 67–81, in Howard, H. and Morris, E. (eds), *Production and Distribution: a Ceramic Viewpoint*, British Archaeological Reports (B.A.R. Supplementary Series **120**), Oxford.

Morris, S. and Buckley, D. (1978) Excavations at Danbury Camp, Essex, 1974 and 1977, *Trans. Essex Archaeol. Soc.*, **10**, 1–28.

Morrison, A. (1980) *Early Man in Britain and Ireland*, Croom Helm, London.

Mortimer, J. R. (1905) *Forty Years' Researches in British and Saxon Burial Mounds of East Yorkshire*, A. Brown and Sons, London.

Mounteney, G. (1981) Faunal attrition and subsistence reconstruction at Thwing, pp. 73–86, in Barker, G. (ed.), *Prehistoric Communities in the North of England*, University of Sheffield Department of Prehistory and Archaeology, Sheffield.

Muckleroy, K. (1981) Middle Bronze Age trade between Britain and Europe; a maritime perspective, *Proc. Prehist. Soc.*, **47**, 275–97.

Nash, D. (1978) Territory and state formation in central Gaul, pp. 455–75, in Green, D., Haselgrove, C. and Spriggs, M. (eds), *Social Organisation and Settlement*, British Archaeological Reports (B.A.R. Supplementary Series **47**), Oxford.

Needham, S. (1980) An assemblage of Late Bronze Age metalworking debris from Dainton, Devon, *Proc. Prehist. Soc.*, **46**, 177–215.

Needham, S. and Burgess, C. (1980) The later Bronze Age in the lower Thames valley: the metalwork evidence, pp. 437–70, in Barrett, J. C. and Bradley, R. J. (eds), *Settlement and Society in the British Later Bronze Age*, British Archaeological Reports (B.A.R. **83**), Oxford.

Needham, S. and Longley, D. (1980) Runnymede Bridge, Egham: a Late Bronze Age riverside settlement, pp. 397–436, in Barrett, J. C. and Bradley, R. J. (eds), *Settlement and Society in the British Later Bronze Age*, British Archaeological Reports (B.A.R. **83**), Oxford.

Newton, R. G. and Renfrew, C. (1970) British faience beads reconsidered, *Antiq.*, **44**, 199–204.

Northover, P. (1982) The metallurgy of the Wilburton hoards, *Oxford Journ. Archaeol.*, **1.1**, 69–109.

Nylen, E. (1974) Bronze, Eisen und Gesellschaft. Eine soziale Umwalzung mit Wirtschaftlichem Hintergrund zwischen Bronze – und Eisenzeit im nordischen Raum? *Die Kunde* **25**, 103–10.

O'Connor, B. (1980) *Cross Channel Relations in the Later Bronze Age*, British Archaeological Reports (B.A.R. Supplementary Series **91**), Oxford.

O'Kelly, C. (1969) Bryn Celli Ddu, Anglesey: a reinterpretation, *Arch. Cambrensis* **118**, 17–48.

O'Kelly, M. (1954) Excavations and experiments in ancient Irish cooking-places, *Journ. Roy, Soc. Antiq. Ireland*, **84**, 105–55.

O'Kelly, M. (1982) *Newgrange: Archaeology, Art and Legend*, Thames and Hudson, London.

Orme, B., Coles, J., Caseldine, A. and Bailey, G. (1981) Meare Village West 1979, *Somerset Levels Papers* **7**, 12–69.

O'Shea, J. (1981a) Social configurations and the archaeological study of mortuary practices: a case study, pp. 39–52, in Chapman, R., Kinnes, I. and Randsborg, K. (eds) *The Archaeology of Death*, Cambridge U.P., Cambridge and New York.

O'Shea, J. (1981b) Coping with scarcity: exchange and social storage, pp. 167–83, in Sheridan, A. and Bailey, G. (eds), *Economic Archaeology*, British Archaeological Reports (B.A.R. Supplementary Series **96**), Oxford.

Ottaway, B. (1974) Cluster analysis of impurity patterns in Armorico-British daggers, *Archaeometry* **16**, 221–31.

Ozanne, P. (1972) The excavation of a round barrow on Rollestone Down, Winterbourne Stoke, Wiltshire, *Wilts. Archaeol. Mag.*, **67**, 43–60.

Palmer, R. (1976) Interrupted ditch enclosures in Britain: the use of aerial photography for comparative studies, *Proc. Prehist. Soc.*, **52**, 161–86.

Parker-Pearson, M. (1982) Mortuary practices, society and ideology: an ethnoarchaeological study, pp. 99–113, in Hodder, I. (ed.), *Symbolic and Structural Archaeology*, Cambridge U.P., Cambridge and New York.

Parrington, M. (1978) *The Excavation of an Iron Age Settlement, Bronze Age Ring–Ditches and Roman Features at Ashville Trading Estate, Abingdon (Oxfordshire) 1974–76*, Council for British Archaeology (Research Report **28**), London.

Partridge, C. (1981) *Skeleton Green: A Late Iron Age and Romano-British Site*, Society for the Promotion of Roman Studies (Britannia Monograph **2**), London.

Patrick, J. (1974) Mid-winter sunrise at New Grange, *Nature* **249**, 517–9.

Peacock, D. (1971) Roman amphorae in pre-Roman Britain, pp. 161–88, in Hill, D. and Jesson, M. (eds), *The Iron Age and its Hill-forts*, Southampton University Archaeological Society, Southampton.

Pearson, G. W. (1979) Belfast radiocarbon dates IX, *Radiocarbon* **21.2**, 274–90.

Peebles, C. and Kus, S. (1977) Some archaeological correlates of ranked societies, *Amer. Antiq.*, **42**, 421–48.

Perry, B. (1972) Excavations at Bramdean, Hampshire, 1965 and 1966, and a discussion of similar sites in southern England, *Proc. Hants. Field Club Archaeol. Soc.*, **29**, 41–77.

Petersen, F. (1972) Traditions of multiple burial in later Neolithic and Early Bronze Age England, *Archaeol. Journ.*, **129**, 22–55.

Petersen, F. (1981) *The Excavation of a Bronze Age Cemetery on Knighton Heath, Dorset*, British Archaeological Reports (B.A.R. **98**), Oxford.

Phillips, C. W. (1935) The excavation of Giants' Hill long barrow, Skendleby, Lincolnshire, *Arch.*, **85**, 37–106.

Pierpoint, S. (1980) *Social Patterns in Yorkshire Prehistory*, British Archaeological Reports (B.A.R. **74**), Oxford.

Piggott, C. M. (1938) A Middle Bronze Age barrow and Deverel Rimbury urnfield at Latch Farm, Christchurch, Hampshire, *Proc. Prehist. Soc.*, **4**, 69–87.

Piggott, S. (1938) The Early Bronze Age in Wessex, *Proc. Prehist. Soc.*, **4**, 52–106.

Piggott, S. (1950) Swords and scabbards of the British Early Iron Age, *Proc. Prehist. Soc.*, **16**, 1–28.

Piggott, S. (1954) *Neolithic Cultures of the British Isles*, Cambridge U.P., Cambridge.

Piggott, S. (1962) *The West Kennett Long Barrow Excavations 1955–6*, H.M.S.O. (Ministry of Works Archaeological Report **4**), London.

Piggott, S. (1972) Excavation of the Dalladies long barrow, Fettercairn, Kincardinshire, *Proc. Soc. Antiq. Scotland* **104**, 23–47.

Piggott, S. (1979) South west England – north west Europe: contrasts and contacts in prehistory, *Proc. Devon Archaeol. Soc.*, **37**, 10–20.

Pitt-Rivers, A. (1898) *Excavations in Cranborne Chase vol. 4*, privately printed.

Pitts, M. (1980) *Later Stone Implements*, Shire Publications, Princes Risborough.

Pryor, F. (1978) *Excavation at Fengate, Peterborough, England: the Second Report*, Royal Ontario Museum (Archaeology Monograph **5**), Toronto.

Pryor, F. (1980) *Excavations at Fengate, Peterborough: The Third Report*, Royal Ontario Museum (Archaeology Monograph **6**), Toronto.

Pryor, F. and Cranstone, D. (1978) An interim report on excavations at Fengate, Peterborough 1975–77, *Northants. Archaeol.*, **13**, 9–27.

Radley, J. (1967) The York hoard of flint tools, *Yorkshire Archaeol. Journ.*, **42**, 131–2.

Raftery, B. (1976) Rathgall and Irish hillfort problems, pp. 339–57, in Harding, D. W. (ed.), *Hillforts – Later Prehistoric Earthworks in Britain and Ireland*, Academic Press, London and New York.

Rathje, W. (1975) The last tango in Mayapan: a tentative trajectory of production-distribution systems, pp. 409–48, in Sabloff, J. and Lamberg–Karlovsky, C. (eds), *Ancient Civilisation and Trade*, University of New Mexico Press, Albuquerque.

Redman, C. L., Berman, M. J., Curtin, E. V., Langhorne, W. T., Versaggi, N. M. and Wanser, J. C. (eds) (1978) *Social Archaeology*, Academic Press, London and New York.

Reed, R. C. (1974) Earthen long barrows: a new perspective, *Archaeol. Journ.*, **131**, 33–57.

Renfrew, C. (1968) Wessex without Mycenae, *Annual of the British School at Athens* **63**, 277–85.

Renfrew, C. (1973) Monuments, mobilisation and social organisation in Neolithic Wessex, pp. 539–58, in Renfrew, C. (ed.), *The Explanation of Culture Change*, Duckworth, London.

Renfrew, C. (1976) Megaliths, territories and populations, pp. 198–220, in De Laet, S. (ed.), *Acculturation and Continuity in Atlantic Europe*, de Tempel, Bruges.

Renfrew, C. (1977) Alternative models for exchange and spatial distribution, pp. 71–90, in Earle, T. and Ericson, J. (eds), *Exchange Systems in Prehistory*, Academic Press, London and New York.

Renfrew, C. (1979) *Investigations in Orkney*, Society of Antiquaries (Research Report **38**), London.

Renfrew, C. (1981) Polity and power: interaction, intensification and exploitation, pp. 264–90, in Renfrew, C. and Wagstaff, J. M. (eds), *An Island Polity: The Archaeology of Exploitation in Melos*, Cambridge U.P., Cambridge and New York.

Renfrew, C. and Shennan, S. (eds) (1982) *Ranking, Resource and Exchange*, Cambridge U.P., Cambridge and New York.

Richards, J. (1978) *The Archaeology of the Berkshire Downs: An Introductory Survey*, Berkshire Archaeological Committee, Reading.

Richmond, I. A. (1968) *Hod Hill vol. 2*, British Museum, London.

Riley, D. N. (1980) Recent air photographs of Duggleby Howe and the Ferrybridge henge, *Yorkshire Archaeol. Journ.*, **52**, 174–8.

Ritchie, A. (1971) Settlement archaeology – methods and problems, pp. 91–5, in Hill, D. and Jesson, M. (eds), *The Iron Age and its Hill-forts*, Southampton University Archaeological Society, Southampton.

Ritchie, J. N. G. (1976) The Stones of Stenness, Orkney, *Proc. Soc. Antiq. Scotland*, **107**, 1–60.

Robertson–Mackay, R. (1962) The excavation of the causewayed camp at Staines, Middlesex. *Archaeol. Newsletter* **7.6**, 131–4.

Rodwell, W. (1976) Coinage, oppida and the rise of Belgic power in south-eastern Britain, pp. 181–366, in Cunliffe, B. W. and Rowley, R. T. (eds), *Oppida in Barbarian Europe*, British Archaeological Reports (B.A.R. Supplementary Series **11**), Oxford.

Rodwell, W. (1978) Buildings and settlements in south-east Britain in the late Iron Age, pp. 25–41, in Cunliffe, B. and Rowley, T. (eds), *Lowland Iron Age Communities in Europe*, British Archaeological Reports (B.A.R. Supplementary Series **48**), Oxford.

Roe, F. (1979) Typology of stone implements with shaftholes, pp. 23–48, in Clough, T. H. McK. and Cummins, W. A. (eds) *Stone Axe Studies*, Council for British Archaeology (Research Report **23**), London.

Rosman, A. and Rubel, P. (1971) *Feasting With Mine Enemy*, Columbia U.P., Columbia.

Rowlands, M. J. (1976) *The Production and Distribution of Metalwork in the Middle Bronze Age in Southern Britain*, British Archaeological Reports (B.A.R. **32**), Oxford.

Rowlands, M. J. (1980) Kinship, alliance and exchange in the European Bronze Age, pp. 15–55, in Barrett, J. C. and Bradley, R. J. (eds), *Settlement and Society in the British Later Bronze Age*, British Archaeological Reports (B.A.R. **83**), Oxford.

Royal Commission on Ancient Monuments in Wales and Monmouthshire (1956) *Caernarvonshire vol. 1*, H.M.S.O., London.

Royal Commission on Historical Monuments (1970) *County of Dorset vol. 2, part 3*, H.M.S.O., London.

Royal Commission on Historical Monuments (England) (1975) *Dorset vol. 5*, H.M.S.O., London.

Royal Commission on Historical Monuments (1976) *County of Gloucester vol. 1*, H.M.S.O., London.

Royal Commission on Historical Monuments (1979) *Stonehenge and its Environs*, Edinburgh U.P., Edinburgh.

Sahlins, M. (1961) The segmentary lineage: an organisation of predatory expansion, *Amer. Anthrop.*, **63**, 322–43.

Savory, H. (1976) Welsh hillforts: a reappraisal of recent research, pp. 237–91, in Harding, D. W. (ed.), *Hillforts: Later Prehistoric Earthworks in Britain and Ireland*, Academic Press, London and New York.

St. Joseph, J. K. (1965) Air reconaissance: recent results, 3, *Antiq.* **39**, 60–64.

Schmidt, P. K. (1979) Beile als Ritualobjekte in der Altbronzezeit der Britischen Iseln, pp. 311–20, *Jahresbericht des Instituts für Vorgeschichte der Universität Frankfurt (1979)*.

Scott, J. (1969) The Clyde Cairns of Scotland, pp. 175–222, in Powell, T. G. E. (ed.), *Megalithic Enquiries*, Liverpool U.P., Liverpool.

Scott, J. (1970) A note on Neolithic settlement in the Clyde region of Scotland, *Proc. Prehist. Soc.*, **36**, 116–24.

Seaby, W. A. (1932) Some pre-Roman remains from south Reading, *Berks. Archaeol. Journ.*, **36**, 121–5.

Selkirk, A. (1968) Harlow Roman temple, *Current Archaeol.*, **11**, 287–90.

Selkirk, A. (1970) Navan Fort, *Current Archaeol.*, **22**, 304–8.

Selkirk, A. (1977) Stone axes: the second revolution, *Current Archaeol.*, **57**, 294–302.

Service, E. (1971) *Primitive Social Organisation* (second edition), Random House, New York.

Shanks, M. and Tilley, C. (1982) Ideology, symbolic power and ritual communication: a reinterpretation of Neolithic mortuary practices, pp. 129–54, in Hodder, I. (ed.), *Symbolic and Structural Archaeology*, Cambridge U.P., Cambridge and New York.

Shee Twohig, E. (1981) *The Megalithic Art of Western Europe*, Clarendon Press, Oxford.

Shennan, S. (1982a) Ideology, change and the European Bronze Age, pp. 155–61, in Hodder, I. (ed.), *Symbolic and Structural Archaeology*, Cambridge U.P., Cambridge and New York.

Shennan, S. (1982b) Exchange and ranking: the role of amber in the earlier Bronze Age of Europe, pp. 33–45, in Renfrew, C. and Shennan, S. (eds), *Ranking, Resource and Exchange*, Cambridge U.P., Cambridge and New York.

Shepherd, I. (1981) Bronze Age jet working in north Britain, *Scottish Archaeological Forum* 11, 43–51.

Shortt, H. de S. (1949) A hoard of bangles from Ebbesborne Wake, Wilts, *Wilts. Archaeol. Mag.*, 53, 104–12.

Simpson, D. and Thawley, J. (1973) Single grave art in Britain, *Scottish Archaeological Forum* 4, 81–104.

Smith, A. G. (1975) Neolithic and Bronze Age landscape changes in Northern Ireland, pp. 64–73, in Evans, J. G., Limbrey, S. and Cleere, H. (eds). *The Effect of Man on the Landscape: The Highland Zone*, Council for British Archaeology (Research Report 11), London.

Smith, I. F. (1965) *Windmill Hill and Avebury*, Oxford U.P., Oxford.

Smith, I. F. (1966) Windmill Hill and its implications, *Palaeohistoria* 12, 469–81.

Smith, I. F. (1971) Causewayed enclosures, pp. 89–112, in Simpson, D. (ed.), *Economy and Settlement in Neolithic and Early Bronze Age Britain and Europe*, Leicester U.P., Leicester.

Smith, I. F. (1974) The Neolithic, pp. 100–36, in Renfrew, C. (ed.), *British Prehistory – A New Outline*, Duckworth, London.

Smith, I. F. (1979) The chronology of British stone implements, pp. 13–22, in Clough, T. H. McK. and Cummins, W. A. (eds), *Stone Axe Studies*, Council for British Archaeology (Research Report 23), London.

Smith, K., Coppen, J., Wainwright, G. and Beckett, S. (1981) The Shaugh Moor project: third report – settlement and environmental investigations, *Proc. Prehist. Soc.*, 47, 205–73.

Smith, M. A. (1955) The limitations of inference in archaeology, *Archaeol. Newsletter* 6.1, 3–7.

Snodgrass, A. (1980) *Archaic Greece: The Age of Experiment*, Dent, London.

Spratt, D. and Simmons, I. (1976) Prehistoric activity and environment on the North York Moors, *Journ. Archaeol. Science* 3, 193–210.

Stanford, S. (1972) The function and population of hill forts in the Central Marches, pp. 307–20, in Burgess, C. and Lynch, F. (eds), *Early Man in Wales and the West*, Adams and Dart, Bath.

Startin, W. and Bradley, R. J. (1981) Some notes on work organisation and society in prehistoric Wessex, pp. 289–96, in Ruggles, C. and Whittle, A. (eds), *Astronomy and Society During the Period 4000–1500 BC*, British Archaeological Reports (B.A.R. 88), Oxford.

Stead, I. (1967) A La Tène III burial at Welwyn Garden City, *Arch.*, 101, 1–62.

Stead, I. (1969) Verulamium 1966–8, *Antiq.*, 43, 45–52.

Stead, I. (1976) The earliest burials of the Aylesford Culture, pp. 401–16, in Sieveking, G., Longworth, I. and Wilson, K. (eds), *Problems in Economic and Social Archaeology*, Duckworth, London.

Stead, I. (1979) *The Arras Culture*, Yorkshire Philosophical Society, York.

Steponaitis, V. (1978) Location theory and complex chiefdoms: a Mississippian example, pp. 417–53, in Smith, B. D. (ed.), *Mississippian Settlement Patterns*, Academic Press, London and New York.

Stevens, C. E. (1940) The Frilford site – a postscript, *Oxon.*, 5, 166–7.

Stone, J. F. S. (1932) Easton Down, Winterslow, S. Wilts., flint mine excavation 1930, *Wilts. Archaeol. Mag.*, 45, 350–65.

Stone, J. F. S. (1936) An enclosure on Boscombe Down East, *Wilts. Archaeol. Mag.* **47**, 468–89.

Stone, J. F. S. and Young, W. E. V. (1948) Two pits of Grooved Ware date near Woodhenge, *Wilts. Archaeol. Mag.*, **52**, 287–306.

Strathern, A. (1971) *The Rope of Moka*, Cambridge U.P., Cambridge and New York.

Sweetman, P. D. (1976) An earthen enclosure at Monknewtown, Slane, Co. Meath, *Proc. Roy. Irish Acad.* section C. **76**, 25–72.

Switsur, V. R. and Jacobi, R. (1979) A radiocarbon chronology for the earliest postglacial stone industries of England and Wales, pp. 41–68, in Berger, R. and Suess, H. (eds), *Radiocarbon Dating*, University of California Press, Berkeley.

Tainter, J. (1978) Mortuary practices and the study of prehistoric social systems, pp. 106–41, in Schiffer, M. (ed.), *Advances in Archaeological Method and Theory vol. 1*, Academic Press, London and New York.

Taylor, J. (1980) *Bronze Age Goldwork of the British Isles*, Cambridge U.P., Cambridge and New York.

Taylor, R. (1980) An Armorican socketed axe from the sea off Chesil Beach, Dorset, *Archaeologia Atlantica* **3**, 133–7.

Thom, A. (1967) *Megalithic Sites in Britain*, Oxford U.P., Oxford.

Thom, A. (1971) *Megalithic Lunar Observatories*, Clarendon Press, Oxford.

Thom, A. and Thom, A. S. (1978) *Megalithic Remains in Britain and Brittany*, Clarendon Press, Oxford.

Thorpe, I. J. (1981) Ethnoastronomy: its patterns and archaeological implications, pp. 275–88, in Ruggles, C. and Whittle, A. (eds), *Astronomy and Society During the Period 4000–1500* BC, British Archaeological Reports (B.A.R. **88**), Oxford.

Tinsley, H. M. and Grigson, C. (1981) The Bronze Age, pp. 210–49, in Simmons, I. G. and Tooley, M. J. (eds), *The Environment in British Prehistory*, Duckworth, London.

Todd, M. (1981) *Roman Britain*, Harvester Press, Brighton.

Toll, H. W. (1981) Ceramic comparisons concerning redistribution in Chaco Canyon, New Mexico, pp. 83–121, in Howard, H. and Morris, E. (eds), *Production and Distribution: a Ceramic Viewpoint*, British Archaeological Reports (B.A.R. Supplementary Series **120**), Oxford.

Trigger, B. (1981) Archaeology and the ethnographic present, *Anthropologica* new series **23**, 3–17.

Wainwright, G. (1969) A review of henge monuments in the light of recent research, *Proc. Prehist. Soc.*, **35**, 112–33.

Wainwright, G. (1971) The excavation of a late Neolithic enclosure at Marden, Wiltshire, *Antiq. Journ.*, **51**, 177–239.

Wainwright, G. (1972) The excavation of a Neolithic settlement on Broome Heath, Ditchingham, Norfolk, *Proc. Prehist. Soc.*, **38**, 1–97.

Wainwright, G. (1979a) *Mount Pleasant, Dorset: Excavations 1970–1971* Society of Antiquaries (Research Report **37**), London.

Wainwright, G. (1979b) *Gussage All Saints – An Iron Age Settlement in Dorset*, H.M.S.O., London.

Wainwright, G. and Longworth, I. (1971) *Durrington Walls: Excavations 1966–1968*, Society of Antiquaries, London.

Wainwright, G. and Smith, K. (1980) The Shaugh Moor project: second report – the enclosure, *Proc. Prehist. Soc.*, **46**, 65–122.

Ward Perkins, J. P. (1939) Iron Age metal horse bits of the British Isles, *Proc. Prehist. Soc.*, **5**, 173–92.

Warren, H. (1922) The Neolithic stone axes of Graig Lwyd, Penmaenmawr, *Arch. Carnbrensis*, **77**, 1–36.

Webster, D. (1976) On theocracies, *Amer. Anthrop.*, **78**, 812–28.

Wheeler, R. E. M. (1943) *Maiden Castle, Dorset*, Society of Antiquaries (Research Report **12**), London.

Wheeler, R. E. M. (1954) *The Stanwick Fortifications*, Society of Antiquaries (Research Report **17**), London.

Wheeler, R. E. M. and Wheeler, T. V. (1936) *Verulamium: a Belgic and Two Roman Cities*, Society of Antiquaries (Research Report **11**), London.

Whimster, R. (1981) *Burial Practices in Iron Age Britain*, British Archaeological Reports (B.A.R. **90**), Oxford.

White, D. A. (1982) *The Bronze Age Cremation Cemeteries at Simons Ground, Dorset*; Dorset Natural History and Archaeological Society: (Monograph **3**), Dorchester.

Whittle, A. (1977) *The Earlier Neolithic of Southern England and its Continental Background*. British Archaeological Reports (B.A.R. Supplementary Series **35**), Oxford.

Whittle, A. (1978) Resources and population in the British Neolithic, *Antiq.*, **52**, 34–42.

Whittle, A. (1981) Later Neolithic Society in Britain: a realignment, pp. 297–342, in Ruggles, C. and Whittle, A. (eds), *Astronomy and Society During the Period 4000–1500* BC, British Archaeological Reports (B.A.R. **88**), Oxford.

Williams, D. (1981) The Roman amphora trade with Late Iron Age Britain, pp. 123–32, in Howard, H., and Morris, E. (eds), *Production and Distribution: A Ceramic Viewpoint*, British Archaeological Reports (B.A.R. Supplementary Series **120**), Oxford.

Wilson, A. E. (1940) Report on the excavations at Highdown Hill, Sussex, August 1939, *Sussex Archaeol. Collect.*, **81**, 173–204.

Wilson, A. E. (1950) Excavations on Highdown Hill, 1947, *Sussex Archaeol. Collect.*, **89**, 163–78.

Wilson, C. (1981) Burials within settlements in southern Britain during the pre-Roman Iron Age, *Bull. Inst. Archaeol. Univ. London.*, **18**, 127–69.

Woodman, P. C. (1976) The Irish Mesolithic/Neolithic transition, pp. 296–307, in de Laet, S. (ed.) *Acculturation and Continuity in Atlantic Europe*, De Tempel, Bruges.

Woodman, P. C. (1978) *The Mesolithic in Ireland*, British Archaeological Reports (B.A.R. **58**), Oxford.

Index

Note: Numerals in italic type refer to the figures. Numerals in brackets refer to the pages on which figures are positioned.